Crowley

D0758458

# STRANGER TO HISTORY

# STRANGER TO HISTORY

A Son's Journey Through Islamic Lands

## Aatish Taseer

McCLELLAND & STEWART

Published in Canada in 2009 by McClelland & Stewart Ltd.
Published in Great Britain in 2009 by Canongate Books Ltd.

Library and Archives Canada Cataloguing in Publication
Stranger to history : a son's journey through Islamic lands / Aatish
Taseer.
ISBN 978-0-7710-8425-6
1. Taseer, Aatish–Travel–Islamic countries. 2. Taseer, Aatish–Family.
3. Islamic countries–Description and travel. I. Title.
DS35.57.T33 2009          910'.91767          C2008-904241-7

We acknowledge the financial support of the Government of Canada
through the Book Publishing Industry Development Program and that of
the Government of Ontario through the Ontario Media Development
Corporation's Ontario Book Initiative. We further acknowledge the
support of the Canada Council for the Arts and the
Ontario Arts Council for our publishing program.

Printed and bound in the United States of America

This book was produced using paper with a minimum of 17% recycled
content (10% post-consumer waste).

McClelland & Stewart Ltd.
75 Sherbourne Street
Toronto, Ontario
M5A 2P9
www.mcclelland.com

1   2   3   4   5      13   12   11   10   09

*For Ma*

# Contents

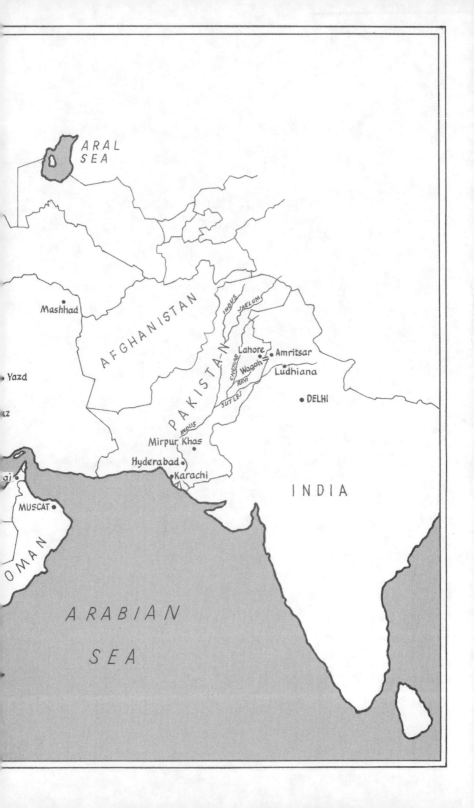

## A Pilgrim's Prelude

Once the car had driven away, and we were half-naked specks on the marble plaza, Hani said, 'I'll read and you repeat after me.' His dark, strong face concentrated on the page and the Arabic words flowed out.

Kareem, pale with light eyes, and handsome, also muttered the words. We stood close to each other in our pilgrims' clothes – two white towels, one round the waist, the other across the torso, leaving the right shoulder bare.

'I seek refuge in Allah the Great, in His Honourable Face and His Ancient Authority from the accursed Satan. Allah, open for me the doors of Your Mercy.'

It was a clear, mild night and we were standing outside the Grand Mosque in Mecca. The plaza was vast, open and powerfully floodlit. The pilgrims were piebald dots, gliding across its marble surface. The congested city, the Mecca of hotels and dormitories, lay behind us.

The mosque's slim-pillared entrance, with frilled arches and two great minarets, lay ahead. It was made of an ashen stone with streaks of white; its balustrades, its minarets and its lights were white. A layer of white light hung over the entire complex. Towers, some unfinished with overhanging cranes, vanished into an inky night sky.

We paused, taking in the plaza's scale.

\*

I was mid-point in a much longer journey. I had set out six months earlier in the hope of understanding my deep estrangement from my father: what had seemed personal at first had since shown itself to contain deeper religious and historical currents. And it was to discover their meaning that I travelled from Istanbul, on one edge of the Islamic world, through Syria, to Mecca at the centre and the Grand Mosque itself. The remaining half of my journey was to take me through Iran and, finally, into Pakistan, my father's country.

We walked on like tiny figures in an architect's drawing towards the mosque. The plaza's white dazzle and my awe at its scale had made me lose the prayer's thread. Hani now repeated it for me slowly, and I returned the unfamiliar words one by one. My two Saudi companions, experienced in the rituals we were to perform, took seriously their role as guides. They seemed to become solemn and protective as we neared the mosque's entrance. Hani took charge, briefing me on the rites and leading the way. Kareem would sometimes further clarify the meaning of an Arabic word, sometimes slip in a joke. 'Now, no flat-screen TVs and electronics,' he warned, of the prayer we would say inside the sanctum.

We were channelled into a steady stream near the entrance. The pilgrims, who had been sparse on the plaza, gathered close together as we entered. The women were not in the seamless clothes required of the men, but fully covered in white and black robes. Inside, the mosque felt like a stadium. There were metal detectors, signs in foreign languages, others with letters and numbers on them. Large, low lanterns hung from the ceilings, casting a bright, artificial light over the passage. On our left and right, there were row after row of colonnades, a warren of wraparound prayer galleries. The mosque was not filled to even a fraction of its capacity, and its scale and emptiness made it feel deserted. Then, Hani whispered to me the prayer that was to be said around the Kaba. The Kaba! I had forgotten about it. It hovered now, black and cuboid, at the end of the passage. And once again, confronted with an arresting vision, Hani's whispered prayer was lost on me.

The Kaba's black stone was concave, set in what looked like a silver casque, and embedded in one corner of the building. It had been given by the angel Gabriel to Ishmael, the progenitor of the Arab race, when he was building the Kaba with his father, Abraham. Many queued to touch it and kiss its smooth dark surface. We saluted it and began the first of seven circumambulations. Hani read as we walked and I repeated after him. After every cycle, we saluted the stone, and said, 'God is Great.'

The pilgrims immediately in front of us were three young men in a mild ecstasy. They had their arms round each other and skipped through their circuits. The language they spoke gave them away as south Indians. They overlapped us many times and their joy at being in Mecca was infectious. Behind us, a man who seemed Pakistani moved at a much slower pace, pushing his old mother in a wheelchair round the Kaba. She was frail and listless, her eyes vacant: she had saved their fading light for the sacred house in Mecca. Then another overlapper hurried past in an effeminate manner, flashed us a bitter smile, and hastened on.

The vast array of humanity at the mosque, their long journeys encoded in the languages they spoke and the races they represented, brought a domiciliary aspect to the mosque's courtyard. People napped, sat in groups with their families, prayed and read the Book. The hour was late, but no one seemed to notice; this, after all, was the destination of destinations.

When we had circled the Kaba seven times, we moved out of the path of orbiting pilgrims and prayed together. Behind the double-storey colonnades and their many domes, there were brightly lit minarets and skyscrapers. I felt as if I was in a park in the middle of a heaving modern city.

We had rushed things. We sat next to each other, a little sweaty now, at one end of the courtyard. Kareem, prolonging the prayer, sat on his shins. His handsome face, normally bright with an ironic smile, was quiet and closed. Hani's eyes were closed too, his dark lips moving silently. A moment later we rose for the last rite: Hagar's search for water.

There are many versions of the story, but the key facts are that Hagar, Abraham's wife, is stranded with the infant Ishmael in the vicinity of Mecca. She runs seven times between Mounts Safa and Marwa until an angel appears to her. He stamps on the ground and water springs up – where the ZamZam well is – to quench the thirst of mother and child. It was Hagar's steps, her fear and deliverance, a sign of God watching over Muslims, that we were to retrace.

Hani led us out of the courtyard and into a separate part of the mosque. On the way, we stopped at Abraham's feet, gold-plated and in a case. We gazed at them; Hani murmured the prayer that is said at the station of Abraham. We continued towards a long, enclosed walkway. Rectangular pillars at even intervals seemed to make an infinite reflection, like two mirrors facing each other, down the corridor's length. A metal railing ran down the centre, separating those who were going from Mt. Marwa to Mt. Safa, re-created in brown paint and concrete at either end of the walkway, from those who were returning. There was a stretch in the middle, marked out by two green lights, where Hagar's distress had been at its highest. We were obliged to cover this distance at a run. It made the pilgrims sweaty and the air was heavy. On one side of the corridor, there were grilles that let in the cooler night air and on the other it was possible to see the vastness of the mosque, its many floors, with escalators running between them, and black men in blue clothes cleaning the building.

At one point on the run, which was long and exhausting, I caught sight of the Kaba in its courtyard. It possessed the place. Thousands stood in tight circles around it, but they seemed hardly to fill the giant courtyard. I tried to gauge the building's size, but it defied assessment. And this was part of its mystery, like the near invisible, black-on-black calligraphy, woven into the silk covering its solid masonry.

The Kaba could not disappoint because it was nothing. Its utter poverty expressed cosmic contempt for the things of the world. It was solid, mute, no triumph of architecture and virtually impenetrable, more like a rent in the sky than a monument. So silent and unrevealing a sanctum was this, that it implied faith, rewarding the believer with nothing, as if faith itself was the reward, and mosaic ceilings and tiled domes, mere trifles.

This thought of faith seemed to lead into what happened next. A fellow pilgrim approached us at the end of our run. He was dark, with a pointed face and a curt manner. He addressed me in Arabic. I didn't understand so he turned to Hani and Kareem. They nodded and walked on without a word.

'What did he say?'

'He said, "This is the House of God. You will receive divine merit if you make him take those off,"' Hani explained, pointing to the religious strings round my neck and wrists.

I couldn't even remember where the strings were from. Some were from temples, others from Muslim shrines. 'Tell him they're from a Sufi shrine,' I said defensively.

'Don't say that.' Hani smiled. 'That's even worse. The Wahhabis hate Sufis.'

Faith was the reward at the sacred house, and faith would have answered the objection the pilgrim had raised, but I had come faithless to Mecca. And justly, I was found out.

# PART I

# The Licence-plate Game

My earliest sense of being Muslim was bound to my earliest perception of my father's absence; it could almost be said that it was a twin birth in which one superseded the other.

It was midsummer at my aunt's house, a Lutyens Delhi bungalow, on a wide road lined with *neem* trees. Their fruit, fat green berries, fell everywhere. They lay on the large lawn in front of the house and on the long shallow steps leading up to the pillared veranda; they even made their way into the house on the backs of huge black colonial ants.

I was five, maybe six. My mother was a journalist and used to go away on assignments. When she did, I was sent to spend afternoons and sometimes nights at my cousins' house. My aunt had married the heir of a rich Sikh family and the house was always full of his nephews and nieces, who also lived in big houses on similar wide roads with *neem* berries and fat ants. I lived with my mother, another aunt and my grandparents in a small house past several roundabouts and a flyover that separated the Delhi of white bungalows and *neem* trees from the post-independence Delhi of colonies.

My mother thought that as I had no brothers and sisters it was better for me to be with other children rather than inactive grandparents. But I dreaded the house and if the decision had been left to me, I would not have gone at all. To come from my small uneventful house to the bigger house full of children was to come with nothing to share. Unlike my cousins, I rarely had any opportunity to devise games, especially not for the numbers that came. So on the occasions I was sent, I seemed always to arrive late, or mid-game, with no hope of catching up.

One morning I arrived to find that the cousins, and the cousins' cousins, had all been given notebooks and pens by their fathers and put to the task of recording the licence-plate numbers of passing cars. A special prize awaited whoever at the end of the day had jotted down the most. The game was already underway when I arrived. Main roads surrounded the five-acre property and the cousins were scattered to perches on its periphery from where they could see passing cars. I couldn't find anyone to ask for a notebook, but was quite happy not to play and relieved that my absence would not be felt. I was settling into a planter chair under the portico of the house when my aunt, who had just finished doing the household accounts, found me.

She was furious to discover her only nephew, son of the sister she loved, excluded from the game. I tried to explain that it wasn't anyone's fault, that I had arrived late, but here, she thought she recognised her own family's good manners and it angered her further. She called two servants and sent them to round up all the cousins from the different corners of the property. I withered at hearing these orders and pleaded again to be allowed to join the game on my own terms, but the servants had gone and my aunt, too, in search of a notebook for me.

In a short time, nearly a dozen coloured turbans had assembled at the front veranda, looking at me for an explanation. I muttered something and tried, turbanless, to blend into the

crowd by engaging my immediate cousins, but they were irritated by the mid-morning interruption and could speak only of
the game.

Minutes later my aunt returned with a notebook, which she
handed to me. She explained that she hadn't been able to find
one like my cousins had been given, but that this would do just
as well. It was much longer and narrower than theirs, and when
I opened it, I saw it was the accounts book from which she
had torn out the used pages.

She called aside her children, my first cousins, and within
earshot of everyone, yelled at them for leaving me out. Then
she came up to the other cousins and said that since I had
arrived late I couldn't be expected to catch up. In the interests
of bridging the gap, I would be given a handicap: they were all
to give me twenty licence-plate numbers from their lists before
they resumed the game. Muffled groans and cries of 'Unfair!'
rose, as they submitted to the slow, arduous process of selecting
twenty unique licence-plate numbers to give me. Like an
unwilling tax collector, I sat on the shallow steps as my cousins,
all older, taller and turbaned, came up to me. My mortification
must have appeared as ingratitude, which further annoyed them.
When nearly three of my book's long, narrow pages were filled,
my cousins vanished. Careful not to be caught alone by my
aunt again, I ran after them to find a spot from which to watch
the road.

And it was like this that I, who from an early age possessed
a horror of competitive games, passed the longest day of my
life. Fiats and Ambassadors ambled down the wide boulevards,
and wobbly heat strands rising off the tar, nearly concealed
their black-and-white number plates. From the roof of the
house, it was possible to see the palms around the Imperial
Hotel's swimming-pool. The hint of moisture accentuated the
dryness of the land. Fumes, dust and temperature came

together to form a parched feeling of nausea. The day grew into an impossible fever, rich with boredom and hallucination. If any of my cousins registered the game's monotony, they didn't let on. They ran from perch to perch, sometimes shrieking with excitement at spotting a blue-and-white diplomatic plate, which, like the newly introduced Suzukis, were higher in points.

The game broke for lunch, but its inferences dominated the conversation. Diplomatic cars were easier to spot than Suzukis, but harder than white VIP number plates. Of course an ambassador's car was the hardest to spot and so should be awarded higher points. One cousin claimed to have spotted 15 CD 1, the British High Commissioner's car, but was suspected of lying. Overhearing the conversation, I could tell that the handicap had been unfairly given. I was well ahead, despite being the slowest at spotting cars. The others seemed to register this and left me out of the conversation.

When they returned to their posts, I was determined to spot even fewer cars. I knew the day's humiliations would only increase if I were to end up winning the prize. As the afternoon wore on, I added barely a single entry. The cousins, despite the scorching white heat, remained fanatical. In the worst hours, I had none of the excitement of the competition, just fear of victory. It wasn't till evening when traffic filled the streets, like rising water behind a lock that I could tell I was no longer ahead. With the falling temperature, the sky regained its colour, and birds and insects, also paralysed by the heat, returned to their movements. The vast white torment of the day sank to a compact stratum just above the earth, drawing pinks and blues out of the areas that it surrendered.

At close to six, nearly the time when my mother was meant to pick me up, the nannies came running to call everyone in for milk. Drinking milk was viewed in my aunt's house as the secret to growing tall. Committed to this goal, my cousins drank great quantities of it at competitive speeds. Everyone's nanny brought their child's special milk mug to the house as if it were a piece of professional sporting equipment.

I didn't mind drinking milk, but I wasn't used to the amount drunk at my aunt's house. I hadn't brought a mug, and hoped that if I delayed the process I might be able to slip away with my mother before the points from the licence-plate game were counted. So, as the others ran back to the house, I clambered over a small mound and went to the boundary wall. I unzipped my trousers and started to pee. I was concentrating on the small frothy puddle forming before me when I looked up and saw my first cousin similarly relieving himself. He saw me too, and after staring intently in my direction, his face turned to horror. I looked round to see what had alarmed him and began to say something, but he turned his head away, muttering to himself. Then, squeezing out a few last drops, he pulled up his zip and fled. He ran up the mound and down into the garden, screaming, 'Aatish ka susu nanga hai!'

He had chosen his words well. I felt their embarrassment even before I understood their meaning. '*Nanga*' meant naked; it was a nanny's word used to instil in children the shame of running around with no clothes on. It was used in little ditties to make the point clearer and its resonance was deep. *Susu* was a little boy's penis. And though I knew each word my cousin had spoken, I couldn't piece together the meaning of the sentence. Why had he said that my penis was naked?

I zipped up my trousers and ran down the hill after him in the hope of figuring out what he meant before the others did. I reached the lawn as the news was being broken to the rest of the cousins, who collapsed, coughing and spluttering, when they heard. They were not quite sure what it meant, but the nannies screeched with laughter.

13

The commotion was so great that the adults were drawn out on to the veranda. Again, my cousin yelled, 'Aatish ka susu nanga hai!' This time, seeing all the adults, including my aunt, laughing, I laughed too, louder than anyone else. The cousins, who earlier had been perturbed rather than amused, were now also laughing. The time for explanations had passed and I decided to ask my mother in private about what the nannies had dubbed my hatless willie. Fortunately, amid the disruption the licence-plate game had also been forgotten and when my mother turned up, she found me agitating to leave before the others remembered.

In the car, as my mother drove from roundabout to roundabout, like in a game of joining the dots, I agonised over the day's discovery. I could now tell the difference between my *susu* and my cousin's, but its implication was impossible to guess.

The truth turned out to be more implausible than anything I could have invented. If there was a link between the missing foreskin and my missing father, it was too difficult to grasp. My mother had always explained my father's absence by saying that he was in jail for fighting General Zia's military dictatorship in Pakistan, but she had never mentioned the missing foreskin until now. My idea of my father was too small and the trauma of the day too great to take in the information that he came from a country where everyone had skin missing from their penises.

It was a loose, but not disturbing, addition to my life. I felt oddly in on the joke and laughed again. The sun slipping behind Safdarjung's tomb, the little car climbing up the dividing flyover with my mother at the wheel; it was too familiar a view of the world to change over a *susu* without a hat.

\*

I grew up with a sense of being Muslim, but it was a very small sense: no more than an early awareness that I had a

Muslim-sounding name, of not being Hindu or Sikh and of the circumcision. In Delhi, my mother had many Muslim friends; we saw them often, and especially for the important Muslim festivals. On these occasions – in them teaching me the Muslim customs and greetings for instance – I felt somehow that they saw me as one of their own. But in Delhi, steeped in Muslim culture, it was hard to pry apart this sense, here related to food, there to poetry, from the shared sensibilities of so many in the city, Muslim and non-Muslim alike.

On the sub-continent religion is patrilineal so it was inevitable that my awareness of religious identity and my father's absence would arise together. At times, over the years, when the twin birth of that day surfaced again, it was always as a Siamese tangle rather than as distinct questions. My mother didn't raise me with religion, but my grandmother, though Sikh herself, told me stories from the different faiths that had taken root in India. As a child I made my way through all the sub-continent's major religions. When I was five or six, I was a devout Hindu, lighting incense, chanting prayers and offering marigolds to the gods; Shiva remained the focus of my devotion until I discovered He-Man. Then, aged seven or eight, I threatened to grow my hair and become a Sikh, but was dissuaded by my mother and my cousins, who had fought their parents for the right to cut their hair. Through all this, I retained my small sense, gained on that hot day, of being Muslim.

When I was ten a Kuwaiti family, escaping the Gulf War, moved into our building and their three sons became my best friends. One night, sitting on their father's bed, the subject of religion came up. Either from some buried conviction or just the wish to be included, I told them I was Muslim. Their father seemed surprised and asked whether I had been circumcised, making a whistling sound and a snip of his fingers that reduced us to cackles. And just as it began, the question of the circumcision, and the patrilineal connection to Islam that it stood for, was obscured in confusion and laughter.

It was only a few years later, when Hindu–Muslim riots erupted across India and Hindu nationalist groups drove through Delhi pulling down men's trousers to see if they were circumcised, that my early memory of the link between my circumcision and my father's religion acquired an adult aspect. But by then, my desire to know whose son I was had consumed any interest I might have had in knowing which religion I belonged to. I was also on my way to a Christian boarding-school in south India, adding the final coat of paint to a happy confusion that was as much India's as my own. And it wasn't until I was in my mid-twenties, far away from my childhood world in India, that religion surfaced again.

# The Beeston Mail

The colourful Virgin train that took me north on a low, grey morning in 2005 was heading for Leeds. I was twenty-four and had been living in London for a year. A few days before, a group of British Pakistanis had bombed London buses and trains; most had been from Beeston, a small Leeds suburb.

Beeston that morning, with its rows of dark brick, semi-detached houses, could hardly cope with the attention that had come to it. The world's press filled its quiet residential streets with TV cameras and outside-broadcast vans. The police were also there in large numbers and the residents, caught between camera flashes, yellow tape and controlled explosions, either hid in their houses or developed a taste for talking to the press. The majority were Punjabis, Muslims and Sikhs, Pakistanis and Indians, re-creating pre-Partition mixtures – especially evocative for me – of an undivided India that no longer existed.

Walking around Beeston, interviewing its residents, I became aware of a generational divide among its Muslims that I hadn't noticed in previous trips round England. The older generation could have come straight from a bazaar in Lahore. They wore the long-tailed *kameez* and baggy *salwar* of Punjab, their best language was Punjabi, and although they were opposed to

Britain's involvement in the Iraq war and hated America, they were too balanced to be extremists, too aware of their hard-earned economic migration from Pakistan.

Their children were unrecognisable to them and to me. Some were dressed in long Arab robes with beards cut to Islamic specifications. They lacked their parents' instinctive humour and openness; their hatred of the West was immense and amorphous. One appeared next to his father, carrying a crate into their corner shop. He had small, hard eyes, a full black beard, and wore a grey robe with a little white cap. He seemed almost to be in a kind of fancy dress. I asked him why he was dressed that way.

'It is my traditional dress,' he answered coldly, in English.

'Isn't your father in traditional dress?' I asked.

'Yes, but this is Islamic dress.'

His father looked embarrassed.

An older man standing next to me chuckled. 'I was complaining to my neighbour that my son never did any work and the neighbour said, "You think that's bad, mine's grown a beard and become a *maulvi* [priest]."' The joke was intended for me especially because the *maulvi* on the sub-continent is a figure of fun and some contempt.

Walking around Beeston, it was possible to feel, as I had for most of that year, meeting second-generation British Pakistanis in England, that an entire generation of *maulvi*s had grown up in northern Britain. The short exchange with the men at the corner shop was a view in miniature of the differences between the two generations. Though neither felt British in any real sense, the older generation had preserved their regional identity and an idea of economic purpose and achievement. The younger generation was adrift: neither British nor Pakistani, removed from their parents' economic motives and charged with an extra-national Islamic identity, which came with a sense of grievance.

A large, solemn man, the owner of a convenience store, who knew the bombers, said, 'They were born and raised here. We did the work and these kids grew up and they haven't had a day's worry. They're bored. They don't do any work. They have no sense of honour or belonging.'

Later that week, on the train home, I considered their story. It began in rootlessness, not unlike my own, and led to the discovery of radical Islam, which was largely unknown to me. I had encountered it for the first time the year before when I had met Hassan Butt, a young British Pakistani who had been a spokesman for the extremist group Al-Muhajiroun and active in recruiting people to fight in Afghanistan. Butt later recanted these views, although in 2008, he was arrested while boarding a flight to Lahore. We had sat in an Indian restaurant on Manchester's Curry Mile. Butt was short and muscular, with a warm but intense manner. He was exactly my age, and took me into his confidence at least in part because he saw me, on account of my having a Muslim father, as Muslim.

His ambition for the faith was limitless. 'Fourteen hundred years ago,' he told me, 'you had a small city state in Medina and within ten years of the Prophet it had spread to Egypt and all the way into Persia. I don't see why the rest of the world, the White House, Ten Downing Street, shouldn't come under the banner of Islam.' It was Butt's nearness to me in some ways – in age, in the split worlds he had known, in the warmth he showed me – that drew me to him, and the faith he had found that created distance between us. At last, I said, 'So what now? You're as old as I am, where do you go from here?'

'First things first,' he replied. 'Fight to the utmost to get my passport back [the British authorities had impounded it]. The quicker I get it, the faster I get my plan of action together that I have with a group of guys who ... Since leaving Muhajiroun I'm focusing on them. There are about nine of us now and we're not willing to accept anybody else because we have the same ideas, same thoughts. Each one of us will maybe play a different role from the other, but all collectively to gain a wider picture. Once I get my passport back, I definitely see myself, *inshallah*, not out of pride, not out of arrogance, not out of ambition, but rather because I believe I have the ability – I pray to Allah to give me more ability – to become a face for Islam in the future, something Muslims have been lacking for a very long time.'

His answer put still greater distance between us. My small sense of being Muslim, gained so haphazardly over the years, was not enough to enter into the faith that Butt had found.

Now, travelling back from Leeds to London, I realised how short I was on Islam. I knew that the young men I had met in Beeston, and Butt, felt neither British nor Pakistani, that they had rejected the migration of their parents, that as Muslims they felt free of these things. But for me, with my small cultural idea of what it meant to be Muslim and no notion of the Book and the Traditions, the completeness of Islam, it was impossible to understand the extra-national identity that Beeston's youth and Butt had adopted. I wouldn't have been able to see how it might take the place of nationality. My personal relationship with the faith was a great negative space. And despite this, I was also somehow still Muslim.

So, with only an intimation of their aggression; their detachment and disturbance; and some sense that Islam had filled the vacuum that other failed identities had left, I came back to London and wrote my article. It was an accumulation of my experience with radical Islam in Britain. I wrote that the British second-generation Pakistani, because of his particular estrangement, the failure of identity on so many fronts, had become the genus of Islamic extremism in Britain. The article appeared on the cover of a British political magazine alongside my interview with Hassan Butt and, proud to have written my first cover story, I sent it to my father.

I received a letter in response, the first he'd ever written to me. But as I read it, my excitement turned quickly to hurt and defensiveness. He accused me of prejudice, of lacking even 'superficial knowledge of the Pakistani ethos', and blackening his name:

> Islamic extremism is poisonous, as is that of the IRA and the RSS [a Hindu nationalist party]. The reason why it is on the rise is because of Palestine and Iraq. If Hindus were bombed, occupied and humiliated you may find the same reaction . . . By projecting yourself as an 'Indian Pakistani' you are giving this insulting propaganda credibility as if it is from one who knows it all.

Cricket, that old dress rehearsal for war on the sub-continent, came up: 'Look at the way the Lahore crowd behaved after losing a Test match and compare that to the "Lala crowds" in Delhi. It seems the Hindu inferiority complex is visceral.' A *lala* was a merchant, and here my father articulated prejudices of his own, textbook prejudices in Pakistan, of Hindus as sly shop-owners, smaller, weaker, darker and more cowardly than Muslims. 'Oh, I'm so glad you weren't a little black Hindu,' my half-sister would laugh, or 'I hate fucking Hindus, man,' my half-brother once said. Pakistanis, for the most part converts from Hinduism to Islam, lived with a historical fiction that they were descendants of people from Persia, Afghanistan and elsewhere, who once ruled Hindu India.

I wasn't sure which side my father placed me on when he wrote his letter, whether he thought of me as one of them or, worse, as a traitor he had spawned. He did say, 'Do you really think you're doing the Taseer name a service by spreading this kind of invidious anti-Muslim propaganda?' To me, that was the most interesting aspect of the letter: my father, who drank Scotch every evening, never fasted or prayed, even ate pork, and once said, 'It was only when I was in jail and all they gave me to read was the Koran – and I read it back to front several times – that I realised there was nothing in it for me,' was offended as a Muslim by what I had written. The hold of the religion, deeper than its commandments, of religion as nationality, was something that I, with my small sense of being Muslim, had never known.

When I came to the end of my father's letter, I felt he was right: I couldn't have even 'a superficial knowledge' of the Pakistani, but more importantly Islamic, ethos. I had misunderstood what he had meant when he described himself as a cultural Muslim. I took it to mean no more than a version of what I grew up with in Delhi – some feeling for customs, dress, food, festivals and language – but it had shown a reach deeper than I knew. And the question I kept asking myself was how my father, a professed disbeliever in Islam's founding tenets, was even a Muslim. What made him Muslim despite his lack of faith?

For some weeks, during a still, dry summer in London, the letter percolated. It prompted a defence on my part in which my back was up. My father responded with silence that turned colder as the weeks went by. His wife and daughter tried to intervene, but I wasn't willing to apologise for something I'd written. And although I minded the personal attack, I didn't mind the letter: it aroused my curiosity. Caught between feeling provoked and needing to act, I thought of making an Islamic journey.

My aim was to tie together the two threads of experience from that summer: the new, energised Islamic identity working on young Muslims and my own late discovery of my father's religion. My father's letter presented me with the double challenge to gain a better understanding of Islam and Pakistan.

But I wanted a canvas wider than Pakistan. Something deeper

than national identity acted on my father, something related to Islam, and to understand this, I felt travelling in Pakistan alone would not be enough. Pakistan, carved out of India in 1947, was a country founded for the faith. But it was also a lot like India, and I felt that unless I travelled in other Muslim countries I would not be able to separate what might be common Islamic experience from what might feel like an unexplained variation of India. I also wanted to take advantage of the fact that the whole Islamic world stretched between my father and the place where I read his letter. A strange arc of countries lay on my route: fiercely secular Turkey, where Islam had been banished from the public sphere since the 1920s; Arab-nationalist Syria, which had recently become the most important destination for those seeking radical Islam; and Iran, which in 1979 had experienced Islamic revolution.

In a classical sense, except for Turkey, the lands that lay between my father and me were also part of the original Arab expansion when the religion spread in the seventh and eighth centuries from Spain to India. I decided on a trip from one edge of the Islamic world, in Istanbul, to a classical centre, Mecca, and on through Iran to Pakistan. The first part of the trip would be an old Islamic journey, almost a pilgrimage, from its once greatest city to its holiest. The trip away, through Iran and Pakistan, was a journey home, to my father's country, where my link to Islam began, and, finally, to his doorstep.

## 'Homo Islamicos'

It was November. The sky was damp and heavy. I waited for Eyup outside a Starbucks on Istiklal. It was an old-fashioned European shopping street, with a tram, in central Istanbul. The road was being resurfaced and rain from the night before spread a muddy layer of water over the newly paved white stone. The youth that filled the street, sidestepping wide, wet patches of sludge and splashing brown sprinklings on the ends of jeans, were of remarkable beauty.

Here, it seemed, was a confluence of racial attributes that produced tall men with high central-Asian cheekbones, light European eyes and the olive colouring of the Mediterranean. They were narrow-waisted and muscular, in close-fitting jeans, small T-shirts and dark jackets. The haircuts were short with cleanly shaved edges and sloping, bristly backs. They walked with a strut, looking ahead, seeming a little vain. The women's painted faces and peroxided hair took away from their looks. Still, the abundance of idle, well-dressed youth gave the street a heady, sexual character.

Istiklal, like its youth, was a hybrid: European archways, fashionable shops and stone apartment buildings, with little balconies and pilasters, ran down its length, while its side-streets led into Eastern bazaars, selling fish and vegetables. It had seen better days, then worse days, and now again its fortunes were turning. There were pick-up bars, cafés, bookshops, an Adidas store, nightclubs, gay saunas, health clubs, embassies and offices. Varied music poured into the street from all sides, not just popular music but Sanskrit chanting with hidden techno undertones.

*

I had arrived a few days before by train, dropping south from Budapest to Sofia and then to Istanbul, a slow movement through the ghostlands of the old Ottoman Empire. Very little remained of its once deep European reach: in Budapest, a reconstructed, tiled shrine, Europe's northernmost Muslim monument, dedicated to a Turkish dervish; and in Sofia, the last of its sixty-nine mosques: small and slightly run-down, it sat at an angle to a busy main road with one stone pillar stepping gingerly into the pavement.

In Istanbul, I was staying in a squat, modern hotel on a central square with a view of the Bosphorus. On the morning after I arrived, I witnessed an amazing scene on the strait's leaden waters. I had come down to the shore, and next to me a few soldiers and old men sipped coffee at a kiosk doing steady business. Then everyone stopped what they were doing and looked at the water. The man at the kiosk turned off his stove and looked too. The soldiers jittered.

The first horn that sounded over the now quiet Bosphorus was like the moan of a great mammal, an elephant or a whale, in lament of a fallen leader. The soldiers stood to attention and their arms snapped into salute. Then other horns, with the eagerness of the young in a tribe, responded. The traffic behind me stopped. Some pedestrians, new on the scene, froze in mid-step. The city ground to a silence. The minute stretched and the city waited. White gulls circled overhead as if fastened by cords to the ships. The horns faded gradually, and after a few stray sounds lost over the water, the Bosphorus came to life again and, with it, the roar of the traffic behind me.

It was 9.06 a.m. on 10 November and the man being honoured in the minute-long silence was Mustafa Kemal Atatürk, the founder of the modern republic of Turkey and the man who had given the state its fiercely secular identity. When Atatürk had founded the modern state in the 1920s, fighting off foreign incursions on all sides, he had shut down the traditional Sufistic centres, thrown out fez and veil, cleansed the language of its Persian and Arabic borrowings, changed the script to roman and abolished the office of caliph. He brought to an end the idea of a sanctifying political authority that had existed in Islam since its founding. It was as if he wanted to break the new state's cultural links to the larger Islamic world, rendering unto Turkey what was Turkey's and throwing out the rest.

My father had mentioned the caliphate in his letter: 'European countries occupied by Muslims for hundred of years, like Greece and Spain, did not enforce conversion. In fact, throughout history the Jews were protected by the Muslim caliphates and Christians were allowed to flourish.' The caliphate was part of my father's idea of a collective Muslim history, which he could possess without faith. It was one of the things – the idea of the great Islamic past – that my small sense of being Muslim didn't cover. And yet my father also admired Atatürk for his strength and modernising mission despite Atatürk's break with the collective Islamic past and his creation of a state that was, in its approach to religion, the exact opposite of Pakistan. So, at the very beginning of my journey, with six weeks set aside for Turkey, and with the words of men like Butt on one side and my father on the other – both, in their way, speaking of the great Islamic past – I wished to see how the faith had fared in the state that had broken with Islam.

\*

The man I waited for outside Starbucks on Istiklal was a young Marxist student who, when he heard of my interest, offered to show me a fuller Istanbul. He appeared a few minutes later with his hands in his pockets. He was short and wide, with dark, greasy hair, intense blue eyes and an erratic, jarring laugh. With Eyup, there were no pleasantries. A quick smile, a hello and immediately down to business. 'Should we go to this very religious neighbourhood?' he said, as if it were one of many possible plans. He hailed a taxi on Taksim Square, close to where I was staying, and asked the driver to take us to Fatih Carsamba.

'They are very religious there, and they want to be like Arab countries and Iran,' he explained. 'It's a kind of sub-culture.' Istanbul was protean. It became another city on the way to Fatih Carsamba. Within an intersection, peroxide Turkish blondes, with lithe bodies, vanished, and stout women, in long, dark coats and beige headscarves, moved down a busy street, selling domestic wares and cheap synthetic fashions. It was difficult to connect the gaudy advertising, the cars and house-hold goods with the city we had left behind near Istiklal. The buildings were different, newer, but plainer, more rundown. There seemed even to be racial differences; the features here were coarser, less mixed, more Arab somehow. But this area was not a preparation for the religious neighbourhood: it was not a sub-culture.

We paid the taxi driver and started to walk. And now Eyup and I, in jeans and winter jackets, looked out of place. Fatih Carsamba had made Eyup uncomfortable when he visited it as a teenager, and I soon began to see why. It came on with sinister suddenness. After a gentle bend in an inclining road, we seemed to come under a new law by which all women wore black and, but for a triangular opening for their noses and eyes, were covered completely. The men were in long robes with shaven upper lips and fistfuls of beard. There were bookshops with names like Dua, or Prayer, more bookshops than anywhere else so far, but they all carried the same green and red leatherbound religious books, Korans of all shapes and sizes and defensive pamphlets – *Jesus and Islam, Modern Science and Islam, Status of Women and Islam* – forestalling the questions people ask. Other shops delivered a steady drone of Koranic readings. Their racks of religious CDs were on display in polished glass windows, just like on Istiklal. Dull-coloured robes with machine embroidery, black on black, navy blue on navy blue, hung on wire coat-hangers in the doors of clothes shops. All varieties of Arab clothing from slinky latex under-veil garments to white skullcaps were available. It was an Islamic facsimile of a modern high street.

'Sub-culture', I thought, was a good word. It implied an aberration not just from urban Istanbul culture, but also from the traditional Islam of Turkey; it brought out the radical aspect of the new faith. For me, the word suggested punks and hippies, even neo-Nazis. It was a word I would have liked to have been able to use, when I first saw young radicalised British Pakistanis in northern England. There again, people were not simply religious in a traditional way; they were religious in a new way. The religion they embraced constituted an abrupt break from what had come before.

We were attracting hostile attention and Eyup was trying already to edge me out of the area. I suggested we turn into a teashop and reassess the situation.

Eyup seemed nervous. 'Something might happen,' he said ominously, as we entered.

A young man with a light brown Islamic beard and a matching robe worked behind the counter. His eyes fixed on us as we came in. He seemed weary and irritated when Eyup ordered tea, as if he had been denied the opportunity to tell us we were in the wrong place. His gaze remained on us as we drank our tea and he went about his chores, wiping the counter and working the till. The hot sugary liquid and the smells from the stove were just beginning to act against the odourless cold of the street, when my question to the man gave him his chance. I asked him about his dress. Eyup looked nervous, but then translated.

The man stopped what he was doing and his face darkened. When he had finished speaking to Eyup, I could see that the exchange had not gone well.

'He suggests,' Eyup began, looking for solace in the change of language, 'that we don't try to ask any questions around here as there may be a violent reaction.'

The words landed cold and hard on me, more menacing for issuing from Eyup's disinterested lips. The man spoke again and Eyup translated: 'He says, "Our way of life is personal so it's not right for others to ask about it. The Prophet Muhammad wore these clothes and that is why we wear them."'

There was more conversation between Eyup and the man, but when it was over, Eyup did not translate. I heard Pakistan mentioned.

'We should go,' he said. 'Something might happen.' Eyup's natural calm was disturbed. He was not easily excitable and I was keen to follow his judgement. We said goodbye and the man walked us to the door of his shop.

'What else did he say?' I asked Eyup.

'I'll tell you later,' he said. 'We should go.'

It was early in the day and the street was still waking up. Shops were opening and the women who hovered down the street in their long robes turned their triangular faces to us in puzzlement. I asked Eyup if I could find a place like this in small towns or in the countryside.

'No,' he said, 'this is not how they dress.'

The hidden world of Fatih Carsamba fell away as the road sloped downhill. The rest of the city returned and the sub-culture vanished as suddenly as it had appeared. It was only a hilltop of radicalism, but before it was gone, we were met with a haunting scene. In this environment of segregation and austerity, on a cemented quadrangle surrounded by a high chain-link fence, a school was breaking between classes. The screams and laughter from dozens of uniformed young boys and girls disturbed the morning pall.

After the muffled threats from the man in the teashop, the sight of children playing was an unexpected comfort. They were occupied in some variation of catch and mixed teams of boys and girls swept from side to side of the playground. The girls were in skirts and the boys in trousers; they seemed entirely at ease with each other, entirely without inhibition.

Outside their chain-link world, the last shrouded figure vanished over the crest of the hill. I was struck by the thought that these were the children of this neighbourhood. The shrouded figure might have been one of their mothers or elder sisters. Would she have gone to the school too? And, if so, what a strange passage it must have been from this freedom to the violent purity of her dress and the segregation it stood for.

Then, as we turned the corner, we saw a self-standing struc-ture whose presence here was at once fierce and absurd. About three feet from the ground, placed dead centre on the extremity of the playground, and lost in children's games was the unlikely, the implausible, the almost chimeric object: a head-and-shoul-ders bust of Atatürk in smooth black stone, watching over the cemented playground.

In the taxi, Eyup recounted the rest of what the man in the teashop had said to him. Speaking of Fatih Carsamba, he had said, 'This is the only place we can live like Muslims so we have to protect that. If someone comes from outside, like a journalist or writer, he can cause problems for us. The police could come and break up the neighbourhood.' Of his dress, he added, 'I am dressed like this because the Prophet Muhammad dressed this way. None of our other leaders dressed like that, not Atatürk, not anyone else.'

At the time, I didn't appreciate how daring a remark this was. The cult of Atatürk was sacrosanct in Turkey and his forceful brand of secularism, backed by the army, could silence the boldest Islamists. For the man in the teashop to discuss him in disparaging tones, and to a fellow Turk, was a jailable gesture of defiance. It was an introduction to how important physical appearance would become over the course of my journey, especially in regard to Islam's relationship with the modern world; it was part of the completeness of the challenge the faith presented. It had been a battleground for Atatürk and it was a battleground for the man in the teashop.

The man had asked Eyup if I was Muslim. Eyup knew only the facts of my parentage and, though he was not a believer himself, he made a leap of reason that others around me would make for the next eight months: if your father's Muslim, you're Muslim. He might only have been trying to cool the situation, but he knew that the man in the teashop was forced to accept this information. This level of being Muslim was more important than anything that came afterwards, such as the actual components of your faith. It was primary, built into one's birth and recognised by all Muslims, religious or not. 'He is from Pakistan and is a Muslim,' Eyup had said. The man, obligated by his religion to accept this, replied, 'If you're a Muslim, you know that this is how real Muslims dress.'

Muslims living in a Muslim country with a sense of persecution. The link to the great Islamic past, and the cultural threads to the larger Muslim world, proscribed and broken. The modern republic of Turkey aspired to be part of the European Union. Turkey had been among the most open Muslim countries, but its secularism was dogmatic, almost like a separate religion. The state didn't stay out of religion, it co-opted religion: it wrote Friday sermons, appointed priests and hounded people it thought to be religious out of the establishment. Why did it have to be so extreme? What threat to his modern, secular republic had Atatürk perceived in the Islamic identity?

It was the army, along with Istanbul's educated élite, who had enforced his aggressive secularism since the founding of the republic in the 1920s. At first people had obeyed, but in recent years, as migration from more religiously conservative Anatolia to Istanbul increased, people became emboldened, more sure of who and what they were. The radical hilltop, with its high street refashioned along Islamic lines, was the response of a few, but many more wanted to know why they couldn't wear their headscarves. They set up centres of business and capital, 'green capital', to counter the power of Istanbul's secular rich. The prime minister, Recep Tayyip Erdoğan, was of their ilk. The city was full of women wrapped in Versace headscarves driving SUVs. Islam was coming in through the back door. The army and the bourgeois Kemalists eyed them with deep suspicion.

But what was really meant by this reassertion of Islamic identity? What cultural wholeness had been lost and what would it take for the world to be whole again?

*

I don't know what my time in Turkey would have been like had I not met Abdullah. Months later, when I recalled his agony,

so difficult to match with his plump face and soft manner – I
never forgot that before he gave himself to the faith, before
he was penalised for being from a religious school, he was
almost a business student. And though he studied Arabic and
religion, unlike Beeston's Islamists and religious students in other
Muslim countries, he studied them as part of a larger, secular
curriculum, and in the way someone in Britain might study
divinity. He had not come off a radical hilltop, and though he
might always have been a believer, his degree of self-realisa-
tion was new. He was like a symbol of the enforced absence
of religion in Turkey and of what a conspicuous absence it was.

I had been a few times to the Islamic Cultural Centre on the
Asian side of the Bosphorus. Eyup had taken me once to hear
a visiting Saudi diplomat speak and then, in his irreligious way
and with his Turkish disdain for Arabs, laughed out loud when
the man appeared in traditional Arab dress. After the lecture,
I had begun a conversation with a student of religion, and it
was him who first told us about Abdullah. We tried on many
occasions to arrange a meeting with him, but it was only days
before I was due to leave Istanbul, when the December rain
and wind were at their fiercest and traffic clogged Istanbul's
major arteries, that we managed to arrange a time. We took a
small, shared bus along the Bosphorus' steely waters and a taxi
over a giant, slab-like bridge, entering Asia with an ease that
never ceased to delight me.

At the Islamic Cultural Centre, the rain drove us out of the
open courtyards into covered walkways that led to the cafeteria. It was a bare white room, with one corner churning out
cups of tea. We sat round a Formica table which was too low
for me to write on. Eyup went to get us tea and I started to
test the language abilities of the two students who had just
walked in. Abdullah was heavy-set, with a round face, thick

lips, and an auburn Islamic beard. He had a friendly, docile manner and spoke English slowly but precisely. Oskan was clean-shaven with an angular face and close-set eyes. He spoke little English and next to Abdullah's smiles and gentle voice, there seemed something hard about his manner. Eyup returned with a round of plain tea, the sugar cubes crumbling at the bottom of the glasses.

'This is something very hard to explain,' Abdullah began, in response to my question about why he had entered the theology faculty. I thought he meant that language would pose a problem, but this was not the case; he was thinking of the actual complication of his decision. 'The simple and basic reason for it is that I want to learn about my religion. I'm studying Arabic language actually, not theology, but as a general education I have studied the Islamic sciences such as *hadis* [the sayings of the Prophet], and *fiqh* [jurisprudence].' I was still under the impression that Eyup would have to translate from here on when Abdullah surprised me with his fluency.

'You have to be a well-qualified and educated person,' he said, picking his words carefully, 'to represent your religion, culture and point of view in the world.'

'Do you feel you have to do it some service?' I asked, surprised at the new firmness of his tone.

'Yes, of course.'

'What do you have in mind?'

'There is a conflict between the world and our ideas, our beliefs, our culture . . .' Suddenly he was embarrassed at his exclusive conversation with me in English and asked if Oskan could participate. I was happy for him to do so, but wanted Abdullah to continue in English. Oskan seemed to understand better than he could speak, and Eyup agreed to translate where necessary. Abdullah returned to the question: 'We have to understand the conditions we are living in today. This world is a very different world from that of our religion, our history and our background. The first thing we have to do is grasp that, to take the point of what is going on in the world and to understand the political, philosophical and historical root of this system. Of course, we also have to study and practise our own beliefs and culture. It is not easy to take in the culture as a whole because it is a huge culture of more than a thousand years.'

I was forced to stop him; he was losing me in his separations. 'Do you mean Turkish culture or Islamic culture?'

'Islamic,' he replied, 'because we are part of that big culture. For example, Arabic language, there are lots of people who have studied it, Arabs, Turks, Persians. It is a big tradition, hard to grasp as a whole, but we have to do what we can. Then we need to create a response, an answer to this world, and try to solve the problem between the reality around us and our own beliefs and ideals.' It was at this point that I realised that when Abdullah spoke of the 'world', he didn't mean the rest of the world or his world, but something alien, which he later described as a 'world system', shorthand for the modern world.

'What is this conflict?'

Oskan, who had been listening watchfully until now, said, 'The conflict starts with information. All knowledge orders and determines things. It makes the systems of the world. For example, Western civilisation, which is at the centre of the system, is trying to control others. It is getting the knowledge in its hand and trying to control others with it. Once it has, we find that in our practice we no longer think as the early Muslims thought.'

I sensed that I would have to be vigilant about abstraction and the traps of philosophy and theology. 'Do you find that this is something that Western civilisation is trying to do or has successfully done? Do you consider yourself out of the "world system"?'

'I don't mean we are out of the system,' Abdullah answered. 'We are living in it. We are just thinking about what is going on, trying to understand what is being done to us. We are becoming more and more a part of this system, but if you ask me, "Is that OK?" of course the answer is no. For example, Islam says you should live in a particular way, but in today's world system, if you try to follow the orders of your religion, it is really hard to stand up in a capitalist economy.'

'How do you mean?'

'Interest, for example, is such a big problem. This is one of the ingredients of conflict.' I must have looked a little baffled at how the Islamic injunction against usury could make so much difference to Abdullah's life because he added, 'Another example is of some American people I know. One of them said to me last month that he has a son. He is trying to make him fulfil his religious obligations, but is finding it really hard.'

'They're American Muslims?'

'Yes, and his father is trying to make him do his obligations, but the system is working against him. It is stealing your child from you.'

His description of the system as something encircling him, and yet alien, puzzled me. I was part of the system he described, but couldn't think of myself in any other way, couldn't peel away the system. I was curious as to how the other system, the Islamic system, could even remain active within him as something distinct. 'I can see why you describe the system as founded on Western values. I also see why you feel the need for your own system, but why do you think Islam, founded so long ago, would have answers for today?'

'To be a person,' Abdullah answered, 'to be a human being, is one thing, but I have a mode of being. It is to be a Muslim.

It is a unique mode of being because it does not change in any time or in any place. Islam is not something man-made. It was given to us. That means it is above history, above man and above culture, but we are only now beginning to get relevant to it, trying to practise it.'

Abdullah's tone had changed and become tighter. I was worried that the curtain of faith had come down early on our conversation. The certainties of faith had obstructed other discussions I had had, but I was sure that I could find common vocabulary with Abdullah. After all, it was him who brought up this term, the 'world system', which, even though he had never left Turkey, was common to us both. It could mean anything from mobile phones, to air travel, to modern education, but perhaps its most significant component was the exposure to the culture and values of Europe and America that ran like a live wire through Istiklal.

'What is it about the modern experience that is problematic?'

'It is that today's system is putting man at the centre. It is anthrocentric. Our system is theocentric. Western civilisation says we are able to do what we want, that we don't need a God to make a cultural or religious system. That is the difference and it is a big one. This modern system is different from all other traditional systems, not just Islamic but Christian and Judaic systems too.' Man instead of God, progress instead of the afterlife, reason instead of faith: these were the transfers Abdullah felt he was being forced to make, and yet my own feeling was that his regret came not from the prospect of having to make them but from already having done so.

'The modern system has a great power,' Oskan started, 'which is not just against Islam but against Chinese culture too, and other traditional cultures. It's just that any response from another culture may be used by the modern system and made into an empty box, a consumer product. It can't do that to Islam because

Islam is a religion that is interested in this world and the other world.'

'What is the difference in the way Islam treats the physical world?'

'Islam has many rules about this world,' Abdullah said. 'We believe that for a person who is a Muslim the religion will have something to say to him in every second of his life. This is what we try to do in *fiqh*. We try to place value on what a man does. We have a scale and whatever you do must be within that scale. You cannot go out of it. It begins with *farz*, obligation, and ends with *haram*, what is forbidden. There are many levels between these two parameters, but there is no way out of the scale. Other religions don't have these kinds of orders and permissions, but Islam has this unity. It is a whole system for this world and the other world.' Islam offered an enclosed world of prescriptive and forbidden action, which was more detailed than most other religions, but in the end could only cover those things that were common to the world of today and the Prophet's world in Arabia. Within decades of the thousand-year history that Abdullah had spoken of earlier, the Prophet's example was abandoned for the ways of the new worlds of Persia, Syria and Egypt that the early Muslims had gained. But now, in Turkey, that great Islamic past, which had absorbed so much, could not be seen to continue and, with Abdullah, I felt both the nearness and sadness of its end; just the other day, it seemed.

'You think the West is trying to impose its way of life on the rest of the world,' I said. 'Have you ever thought that in the seventh century when Islam was a conquering religion, the Arabs imposed their way of life on the people they conquered?'

Both Oskan and Abdullah choked with laughter and, I thought, some degree of amazement. 'No one has ever asked me that before,' Abdullah said good-humouredly. 'Good question, good question.'

And, although it was as blasphemous a thing as I could have said – that history was a golden history; those Arabs were the bringers of the faith – Oskan fielded it: 'Islam is an organising religion, but these others are destroying . . .'

Abdullah, recovering from his shock, said, 'For example, the Europeans went to America. They found many people living there, but today we don't find many of its original inhabitants living there. But the Ottoman state controlled the Balkans for many hundreds of years, and if you go there, you still find churches.'

The conversation was heading in a dangerous direction: churches destroyed or not in lands Muslims conquered versus mosques destroyed or not in retaliation. I wanted to avoid it, hoping to reach beyond the sanctity with which Muslims viewed their past, a historical perfection held up in contrast to the errors of others.

'If what you're saying,' I said, 'is that there is something in Islam that orders and preserves while there is something in the West that destroys, I want to know what that ordering is.'

Abdullah returned to mosque, temple and church destruction. 'I may say,' he began, 'that if a Muslim has destroyed temples in India, acting as a Muslim, then we can say that that is not OK.'

'Not OK?'

'Yes, definitely without any doubt.'

'Even if he was destroying idols?'

Abdullah smiled. A discussion began between him and Oskan. Arabic verses were traded back forth. At last Abdullah, as if reading the jury's verdict said, 'Our Prophet destroyed idols by his own hand so of course worshipping idols is not OK.' Still smiling, he made a smooth transition to People of the Book. 'But we call all Christians and Jews People of the Book and respect them. If someone who is a Person of the Book cuts an animal, a Muslim may eat it.'

'Tell me one thing: is it possible for someone who is a Person of the Book to follow his own religion, not accepting Islam and Muhammad, and still go to heaven?'

They began to laugh again and traded more verses. 'There are different points of view on that,' Abdullah said, 'but the major and central opinion is that, no, it's impossible.'

My thoughts were on neither theology nor the afterlife. What interested me was Abdullah's mention of an almost biological sense of being Muslim. Perhaps that was why Muslims always wanted to establish – and it had started as soon as I arrived in Turkey – whether or not I was Muslim, and it didn't seem to matter what kind of Muslim I was.

'You have a pan-Islamic idea of the world, yet the Muslim world has been so divided.'

'Sunni and Shia?'

'Yes, but also within countries. Turkey has its eyes one way, Iran another. What gives you hope that Muslims will overcome their differences?'

'Maybe political views will not come together,' Abdullah said, 'but the people . . . You may say there are two levels. The ones at the top care about the political system, but there is something under that. And so if you look at those people in Muslim countries, they are not very different from each other. There might be differences in political structures – and even these are related to the West – but not in people's lives.'

Abdullah had never been to a Muslim country other than Turkey, but he was sure of his brotherhood with Muslims beyond any national or political difference. This was also an aspect of the faith: looking upon governments and political classes as corrupt, in foreign hands, and the average Muslim as inherently good and of one mind. My father later spoke to me of this brotherhood, and what I wondered again and again was what his admission into this brotherhood was based on.

And why was I so definitely shut out of it where he was concerned?

'When you go to a country and you see two groups of people,' Abdullah said, 'you can easily tell who is a Muslim and who is not because to be a Muslim requires many things. For example when the time for prayer is called, he goes to prayer. Another example, a Muslim doesn't lie—'

'Oh, come on, that's nonsense. You might be talking about good Muslims, but good Christians don't lie either. Half the Islamic world is filled with bad Muslims.'

Abdullah laughed. I had heard this talk a lot already. Muslims couldn't kill other Muslims. So what was happening in Iraq? Israelis. Muslims would never have dropped the atomic bomb, and so on.

'You mentioned the conflict between Islamic countries,' Abdullah said, his face growing serious, 'but I'm trying to say that to be a Muslim is a very different experience from any other, no matter where you are. To be a Muslim is to be above history. It is a mode of being, an ideal, but the closer you get to that ideal, the better a Muslim you are.'

To be a Muslim is to be above history. That formulation, like an echo of Gletkin in Arthur Koestler's *Darkness at Noon*, saying 'Truth is what is useful to humanity,' explained so much about the faith's intolerance of history that didn't serve its needs.

Familiar with Islamic logic, Abdullah explained, 'Therefore Islamic countries have an advantage, and that advantage will not go. You say there are differences between them, we accept there are, but these are temporary differences. We can overlook them because we have something that never changes.'

'What do you think the West wants from the Muslim world?'

'That's a big question,' Abdullah said, leaning back a little.

It was nearly dark outside and more glasses of tea arrived.

'I think they realise,' Abdullah said, 'that Islam has an ideal system with the power to make their political and cultural system as a whole go back. Islam has that advantage. It is the unique system with that power. Other systems, Buddhism or Taoism, they don't have that power because the world system can easily turn them into empty boxes. But Islam still has that power because you cannot change it. For example, if you want moderate Islam, you just make yourself far from Islam, but Islam is still there. You cannot do anything to it. If you obey its orders, you're a good Muslim. If you leave it, it's your choice, but you cannot change it.'

For a moment I wondered if the unchanging aspect of Islam that Abdullah seemed so proud of was also the source of his frustrations. After all, it meant living in another still more complete system, the 'world system', that reached into so many aspects of his life and with which he could never be at ease as long as he believed in Islam the way he did. I was grateful for his formulation, 'the world system'. It was like shared experience between us; Islam was his response.

'Fine,' I said. 'This "world system" that you and I are part of, many things come from it, your phone, for instance . . .'

I was looking round the room for other things to mention when he stopped me. 'Everything,' he said, with fresh pain in his voice. 'Everything.'

'Right. Everything,' I repeated, my eyes fixed on him. I felt I had to tread gently now. 'Has anything of value come out of it?'

They talked among themselves. I sensed they understood the question well, but were now picking their way through the rubble of our conversation.

'Marlboro cigarettes,' Oskan laughed, 'and technology are OK.'

Abdullah had thought harder about it. 'No, actually,' he said, 'this is a big issue among Muslim intellectuals. There are many discussions on the subject and, no, it is not so easy to say that technology is OK. For example, let's talk about cinema. The Persians have made many good films. Now, maybe that's OK. By doing that we may stand up against the system by representing our ideals.'

I was about to interrupt him, to say that most of the Iranian films he had spoken about actually stood *against* the Islamic regime, when he introduced a more interesting idea.

'But some other people say we have to discuss the camera itself, not the films. Before making good films, we have to discuss the camera itself. Good or bad? We are not interested in the product, we are interested in the camera.'

'What's the problem with the camera?'

'It's something Western civilisation made. We have to discuss that camera. What does it represent?'

His words chilled me. I thought I heard in them a desire to take the world apart, to have it sanctified in some way by the faith. At the same time, I admired his consistency, the way in which he felt it was wrong to profit from the 'world system' while guarding yourself against its values. Few thought so hard about the issue or cared so much about falling into hypocrisy as Abdullah did, but I couldn't imagine any closed completeness pure enough for him. The world couldn't be put through an Islamic filter: that kind of recasting, like with Fatih Carsamba, could only ever be cosmetic.

He must have seen my discomfort because he tried immediately to console me, supplanting the hate that had risen in him moments ago with reason. 'There was a time in Turkey,' he said, 'when people could not wear turbans and fezes. They had to wear hats. At that time, we discussed whether it was OK to wear turbans or not. It's a very important discussion. There are things that are a symbol of a culture, and if you partake in them, you give a picture of your cultural side.'

'Why is this ownership so important? The West has borrowed from the East, things have gone back and forth. Why must you reinvent everything yourself?'

The irony in what he had said was that for centuries Islam absorbed a great deal that was outside the faith, from Greek medicine and philosophy to Persian architecture, but only at the end of our conversation did Abdullah explain why the faith today was saturated, its cultural circle closed, almost as if American culture, having taken in yoga and Italian food, was to say, 'No more.'

'Of course,' he said. 'Yes, definitely. I don't know what to do. OK? I don't mean that we're going to leave everything that comes from the West. That would be ridiculous. I don't mean that. I'm saying that we have to think and discuss everything that we believe and have today because . . .' The words failed him, '. . . because we didn't do that till today,' he finished a moment later, in a voice that almost broke.

A long, silent moment passed between us. Then, recovering himself, he spoke again: 'We need to discuss everything and maybe we're going to create a new structure. I don't know if we will, but what we need to do is to discuss everything from the beginning, from start to finish. We need to do that.'

Histories swept away, hidden under laminates like Turkey's dogmatic secularism, produced men like Abdullah, who were not content to be told to conceal their religion and wear European clothes. He was studying the past, 'the big Islamic culture' that Atatürk rejected, learning the languages that Atatürk sought to cleanse modern Turkish of, wearing the clothes Atatürk banned; and he had had to pay a price.

'Growing up, what did you and the people around you think of Atatürk?' I asked.

I received the standard embarrassed smile that this question produced in religious people. I pressed Abdullah for an honest answer and assured him that it was not for a newspaper article. 'Of course it wasn't so good,' he said at last. 'We weren't talking so much about the man . . . In my family, you mean?'

'Yes. Just growing up, in school, at home.'

'I would go to school, and Atatürk was in school, just in school. Outside there was no Atatürk. It's difficult to describe. There are some things you don't say but you understand.' Abdullah grew up in a conservative neighbourhood and, briefly, I imagined him in a playground like the one I had seen, a cemented patch of secular life surrounded by men and women of faith.

He complained about secularism: 'It is being used to create a new population, to push Muslims out of the system, and I think they have succeeded on a certain level. For example, if today a religious man, the prime minister, for instance, reaches a high position, it is something we must focus on, something bad. Muslims in Turkey are still out of the system and trying to get in. All the changes in Turkey are coming from the top. They don't ask people if they want these changes.'

Abdullah had suffered at the hands of the system. He came, like Erdoğan, the prime minister, from the religious Imam Hatip schools. He was penalised for this in his college entrance exams; his marks had been docked. It hadn't occurred to me until now to ask him whether he had even wanted to study religion and Arabic.

'There is an ironic story about that,' he said, 'We were meant to write fifteen choices of faculties we wanted to join. Theology was thirteenth on my list. The first was commerce. I was nineteen at the time, not an age when you evaluate things properly, but after entering the theology faculty, I realised that it was the best faculty for me.'

Commerce! I balked. Abdullah, so full of rage against the system, might have been climbing its rungs, drawn in by its rewards. Cast out from that system, he now wanted to be a researcher in the Islamic studies department.

It was late and I rose to leave, but was detained by one last question. It had arisen because I felt at odds with someone I liked. 'You say Muslims have to develop their own system,' I asked, 'separate from the "world system". Why is it not possible for there to be a "world system" that Muslims could be part of?'

'Let me tell you a story,' Abdullah said in reply. 'If a Muslim girl marries someone who is not Muslim, we say that's not OK. She cannot do this. But if a Muslim man marries a girl who is a Person of the Book, that's OK. Jewish people criticise us for allowing our men to marry Jewish and Christian girls, but not allowing our women to marry Jewish and Christian men. You know what the reason for this is? We accept all their prophets, all their books, we don't say anything bad about Christ, but they don't accept our Prophet. They don't accept our Book, they don't accept our religion, they don't accept *our* system. That's the difference. I think that Muslims have to be at the top, at the centre of the system. We have to determine all the things in the world, otherwise we won't be free ourselves. That doesn't mean we will destroy other cultures. No. We want to be at the top so that we can realise what has been ordered by Allah, to make it real in this world by our own hand. We believe that that is the right thing to be done in the world.'

He stopped, and I thought he felt bad that the goodwill between us had evaporated again, but he went on anyway: 'For instance, a Christian may live here with us but not like a Muslim. He may live here, but we have to be dominant.'

I left Abdullah and Oskan on that cold, wet afternoon, in

the cafeteria on the Asian side of the Bosphorus. I was taking the train to Damascus the next morning and had to pick up my tickets.

Abdullah was also planning a trip to Syria the following summer. I wanted him to go; he had asked about Pakistan and the level of freedom its people enjoyed; I wanted him to go there too. Turkey and Pakistan had had similar histories: strong, politically involved armies, a coup every decade and the execution of a sitting prime minister, but Turkey had gone one way and Pakistan another. I felt that travelling in the Muslim world might produce new respect in Abdullah for what his country, outside its Islamic commonality, had achieved.

Pakistan shared an important link with Turkey. When it gained its independence in 1947, carved out of a diverse, pluralistic society, it became, as Turkey had, what it had never been before: an almost pure Muslim state with fixed borders. But while Pakistan, intended as a secular homeland for Indian Muslims, re-asserted its connection to the great Islamic past – even importing Urdu as a suitably Islamic national language – Turkey, founded as a secular state for Turks, broke its links to that past.

I had started out wanting to see how men of faith had fared in the state that had broken with Islam. What I hadn't expected to find was the extent to which Abdullah's faith, in its sense of politics and history, spoke directly to the alien and hostile 'world system' that sought to turn Islam into an 'empty box'. For this aspect of his faith, faith didn't even seem necessary: the same feeling of affront could have come to a people occupied by a foreign power.

The Islamic world also meant something distinct to him: not just a world, but a world order, 'a big culture', to which Arabs, Persians and Turks had contributed. He had never been to any other Muslim country, but he was certain its people would be of the same mind as him, almost in the way that someone in America who'd never left his country might feel about Europe. I didn't ask him about Muslim India, but I'm sure he would have included it as part of what a man in Karachi was later to describe to me as the 'Civilisation of Faith'. To listen to him was almost to feel that a world as complete, as connected, as difficult to contain as the modern world, or the 'world system' that we knew today, had existed, with its origins in faith, in the Muslim world.

The date Abdullah put to its demise, though he would have agreed that its decline was many hundreds of years in the making, was 1924, when Atatürk abolished the office of the caliph in Istanbul. The date chosen was important because it suggested a notion of sanctifying political authority, rule in the name of Islam, that accompanied the millennia-long history that had ended. Its end meant that Islam, at least in the world post-Islamic history, was not as effortlessly complete as Abdullah made out: its completeness had to be asserted. There were constant incursions – technological, moral and political – from the 'world system'. And to realise the Islamic completeness, as Abdullah had spoken of it, the world would have to be recast, passed through an Islamic filter, and the 'world system' kept out. For this reason it was both possible to see why Atatürk had wanted the modern, Turkish state to break its connection with the 'Civilisation of Faith' and how the Turkish approach had been perhaps too extreme, needlessly alienating men like Abdullah.

*

On my last night in Istanbul, a gay couple I had been staying with took me to a club called Love. We entered a dark room where a show was about to begin. I couldn't make out the people around me, but the room smelt of a mixture of sweat and cologne. A dim purple light came on over the stage. My eyes adjusted to the darkness and I saw rowdy transvestites covered with jewellery, a few plain, dumpy girls and, interspersed among the crowd, tall, fine-looking men in their twenties wearing dark trousers and collared shirts. One was telling me about biotechnology when the show began.

In the purple shade, I could make out four men in white underwear. Their bodies were smooth and taut. It made the mind reach for its gym Latin: quadriceps, erector spinae, pectoral major and anterior all toned to the point of plasticity. Their faces showed the best of the region's warm colouring, dark features and high cheekbones. Their hair was shiny and short, and they smirked and joked among themselves as if bound by soldierly comradeship. It was unclear what they intended to do with the green and orange paint in their hands, which glowed luridly in the purple gloom.

Then the music started and the men stopped chatting. Their faces poised and pouting, they broke off in pairs and started to dance. The light dimmed and only their white underwear and the glowing paint were visible. They danced closer together, quadriceps brushed against quadriceps; the crowd let out a scream. Then a diagonal gash of phosphorescent green, from gluteus maximus to shoulder-blade, made it clear what the paint was for, and sent the crowd to frenzy. The two pairs of white underwear moved closer together, the paint changed hands, partners were exchanged and the music picked up. The men rubbed the glowing paint on to each other's bodies in time to the music and as part of a dance. At last so much green and orange paint had been spilt that the figures of the men reappeared like a scene from *The Invisible Man*. The crowd was cheering in rhythm and the men were laughing, half in embarrassment, it seemed, and half in vanity.

This was the Turkey the visitor could never discount, the Turkey of freedoms such as these, of the Istanbul biennale, of the first Picasso exhibition in the Muslim world, the country a professor living in Istanbul described to me as 'the only livable place from here to Singapore – no offence'. It was this same country that was anathema to men like Abdullah, where freedom meant licence, where secularism was a tool of oppression and foreign values prevailed in place of the rule of God. In secular Turkey, it was impossible to see what his vision of the world was. The Islamic completeness he had spoken of, though touched with a sense of loss and attack, was hard to visualise. It was only in Syria, and later, to a greater extent, in Iran and Pakistan, that Abdullah's words gained physical reality.

The show ended and the activity at Love resumed. My Turkish friend had caught my eye from time to time. And now turning to me, he said, in a sibilant whisper, 'This is why we'll never be Iran.'

# Recompense

'**A** human being,' my grandfather always asserted, when people asked whether I was being brought up as a Sikh or a Muslim. 'He's being brought up to be a human being.'

Perhaps all children feel that their grandparents were born for the job. In the case of my grandparents, it was as if their years as very young army parents, distant and old-fashioned, had been a preparation for their true calling as devoted, dependable grandparents. And, as a child, I depended on them a great deal. I lived with them, travelled with them; they were my guardians when my mother was on assignment in Punjab and Kashmir; I was in their care when mobs roamed the streets in 1984, very nearly attacking our house, killing Sikhs in revenge for Mrs Gandhi's assassination at the hands of her Sikh bodyguard.

The religious violence that followed Mrs Gandhi's assassination was a painful reminder of the main historical drama of my grandparents' lives. They had become engaged a few months before the 1947 partition of India. They were married at the end of that year when my grandfather, made homeless by the partition, arrived as a refugee bridegroom in Delhi. And as much as my grandmother rejoiced in the plurality of religion in India, my grandfather kept his distance. Because, if not for religion, he would also have been Pakistani. It could be said, growing up with them in Delhi, that my grandparents were a living historical record of the event whose shadow fell on me four decades later.

In 1947, as landowning people in what was to become Pakistani Punjab, when the time came to divide India, my grandfather's family opted for Pakistan. It was not just a question of land: my grandfather's regiment, Probyn's Horse, just back from fighting the Japanese in Burma and temporarily stationed in southern India, was going to Pakistan. 'We thought,' my great-grandmother once said, 'that first it had been the rule of the Muslims, then it was the rule of the English, and now again if it was to be the rule of the Muslims, what difference would it make?'

She discovered the difference in a painful and abrupt way at Lahore railway station in August 1947. In the weeks before, she had been part of an August insouciance that had prevailed on both sides of the border, a feeling that the partition was nominal and that there would be no transfer of populations. So, when India was being divided, my Sikh great-grandmother, a young widow, spent the summer with her younger son in the hill station of Mussoorie on what was to be the Indian side. When doctors suggested that my great-uncle, suffering from tuberculosis, go up to Kashmir for a change of air, she thought she would stop at their house on the plains before heading north again.

By then the carnage in Punjab, which was to take a million lives, had begun. A Muslim police superintendent recognised their party at Lahore station; my great-grandmother recalled fires swelling on all sides. The policeman told them, with sorrow and disbelief, that there was now no place for them there.

'Where will we go?' my great-grandmother asked.

The policeman put them on a train to Amritsar, the first town on the new Indian side, but the train didn't leave. They waited all day in the monsoon heat and humidity. At last, the policeman took them off the train and put them on another that left soon after, and in this way saved their lives. The train they had been on was a death train, attacked soon after it left the platform. They heard in Amritsar that it had pulled into the station with everyone aboard dead.

My great-grandmother never recovered from Partition. After Amritsar, she and my great-uncle moved to Karnal, a rural town near Delhi, where she lived in a gloomy house till her death in 1989. She never discussed Partition, until five decades afterwards, when my mother interviewed her on the fiftieth anniversary. Then she spoke about what had been lost. She mentioned land and silver, but her mind fastened on one genteel image that appalled her especially. 'I can't believe the tenants' wives are wearing my shawls,' she said. 'I used to have the most beautiful shawls.' When I was born and my mother took me to her, she said bitterly, 'Yes, he is lovely, but Muslim nonetheless.'

The resentment my great-grandmother felt for Muslims became, in my grandfather – younger and spared Partition scenes – a general suspicion of religious politics and an unlikely love for Muslims, feeling they were also the victims of the futile wrong committed in the partition of Punjab. What my great-grandmother dealt with by forgetting, my grandfather dealt with by remembering, and remembering well. With age, even as his present perceptions became dull, his memory of the Punjab where he had grown up became sharper. He recalled certain shops, gentlemen's clubs, society beauties, and missed old friends. He thirsted for his Punjab. Cobwebs dropping over his eyes, heavy on the Scotch and prone to tears, his longing for the country he would never see again was touched with the special irony of finding that, after all these years, he had a half-Pakistani grandson.

His face came alive as he'd tell me the story of how he had called my father from London to inform him of my birth. When the operator on the Pakistani side spoke, and my grandfather heard the music in his accent, he gasped, 'He spoke my Punjabi!' It might have been the first time since 1947 that he had heard a voice from the Punjab he had left behind. It was his nostalgia for undivided India, as well as the knowledge that I was twice connected to the land that was Pakistan, that my grandfather transmitted to me as I grew up with him in Delhi.

This feeling for the land and its common culture, deeper than the present boundaries that divided it, might have been a way for him to put to rest some of the absurdities he faced in his lifetime, such as the 1965 war against Pakistan when he fought against the men in his old regiment. Partition was then still a recent event; the men knew each other, and at the end of the day when the fighting stopped, they would call to one other. He was proud of the Pakistani prisoner-of-war from his old regiment who refused to surrender to the infantry, and immediately dispatched an artillery unit to give him the honourable surrender he demanded. It was perhaps the most serious war my grandfather had fought and the heavy casualties on both sides brought home a terrible feeling of futility. He recalled his commanding officer being forced to cremate a large pyre of Muslims – a horror for Muslims – and Hindus together, and when their families came for the bodies, they were given a small urn of ash and told that these were the only remains of their brave Indian dead.

The governments of the two countries parted ways more decisively than the people. My grandfather's best and oldest school friend lives in the Swat valley in Pakistan; in recent years it has become a battleground between Islamic militants and the Pakistani Army. They kept up a correspondence over six decades, even in the days of heavy surveillance, when letters were difficult between the two countries and phone calls virtually impossible.

I came across a recent letter in which, after all the violence, wonder at the passing of time was subject enough:

Dear Amarjit, Many thanks for your letter. I just came down from Swat, where my nephew was killed in a bomb blast. All very sad, a young man of 41 gone for nothing. Things will only change with change in government.

I am not doing too badly for my 80 years. Except that I fell 3 years ago, and developed neuropathy. This has made my limbs very weak and my ears rather deaf. If you had an email, we could correspond more frequently. I am sure one of the children has it. I started using a computer only last year, when my grandchildren began to laugh at me.

If I am 80, you must be 81. Do you realise you're my oldest living friend? So let's communicate more often. Happy New Year. Regards and best wishes, Aurangzeb

'Typical Aurangzeb,' my grandfather said, with glee. 'He's writing from Pakistan to an Indian brigadier and he says, "Things will only change with change in government." Typical Aurangzeb!'

Irony was the great mood of the 1947 Partition of India. The faint, bitter smiles that still cross the faces of that older generation seem like the only fitting response to the friends left behind, the houses and land lost for ever, the wars fought against each other and the two countries made from one shared culture. And though it could be suggested that the same charlatan god who had put up what seemed like absurd divisions between my grandfather and his country was also responsible for landing him after all the violence with a half-Pakistani grandson, he would not have seen it that way. He didn't let the absurdities defeat him. Through his untainted view of the other side, and the hopefulness my mixed birth brought up in him, he cocked a snook at the gods that carved up India. In his hands, the peculiar circumstances of my birth were not strange, unworkable facts but a kind of recompense for all that had been lost, a breach in the historical wall that had put him in one country and his regiment, his house and his 'oldest living friend' in another.

## Syria International:
## Notes from the Translation Room

I left Istanbul the morning after the Love club. My wish to see the city in snow was unfulfilled, but compensated in part by seeing Anatolia in deep winter. I was on the Taurus Express to Damascus, travelling on what had been the old Hejaz railway. It was built by the Ottomans in their last years, with the intention to connect Istanbul to Mecca, and was famous for being blown up routinely by T. E. Lawrence.

The sleeper was blue and white, the only carriage with Arabic letters on it, sharp-edged sickles and dots, which spelt out the equivalent of 'CFS, Chemins de fer Syriens'. It was to fall away from the rest of the train when we reached the south-east. We drifted past a few coastal towns with red-tiled roofs before I fell asleep, making up for the late night. When I awoke it was just after one o'clock and the winter sun was almost hot. Outside, a brown stream was bubbling past rocks in a shallow chasm. The low branches that hung over it would have brought shade in another season, but were now bare and cast a long, thorny shadow over the water. A single white heron gazed indefinitely over at the muddied winter scene. All around, large, round rocks were heaped on top of one another as if in preparation for a child's game, with snow and shrubs competing for the spaces between them. Gradually, the land became flatter and the winter scene more complete. By late afternoon, the train was racing past snow-covered towns, and only the occasional glimpse of a wall or collapsed house of honey-coloured stone spoke of a warm country. A pale, orb-like sun hung overhead and minarets poked out of the thick snow, forging new associations in my mind, unused to linking Islam with winter.

The next morning, after a night in the train, I was in southern Anatolia and the snow was gone. It was replaced by a landscape of grey boulders and gentle hills, with a sparse cover of thin, emerald grass. The rocks stayed, but the earth became red and the grass more lush as we continued south. There were few trees and the land's mild, grassy contours met the sky further than the eye could see. Mid-afternoon. We were unhitched and waited for many hours for a new engine. After a small collision, movement one way and then the other, we set off again.

I stepped out of my cabin to ask our large Syrian attendant, with mascaraed eyes, for some tea when I caught a powerful whiff of marijuana smoke coming from the direction of the engine. I put my head out of the window and it was stronger. I followed the smell, walking the length of the sleeper, until I came to a door with two sealed windows. On the other side, two fine-featured Turkish soldiers with watery red eyes and berets were standing outside their carriage, choking and laughing over a blunt-sized joint.

When they saw me, they bent double with laughter and, arm outstretched, offered it to me. I made a gesture of helplessness: the sleeper doors were locked with a nut and a bolt and seemed not to have been opened in years. More out of courtesy to them than from any conviction that it would open, I tried unscrewing the nut. It slid straight off and the bolt fell into my hands. I pulled at the doors; they divided, but no more than six inches, just enough for the soldiers, now in hysterics, to pass me the joint.

In Turkey, military service is compulsory and they were completing theirs in the nearby town of Iskenderun. They spoke little English so we smoked and laughed, and I, more than them, kept looking behind me in fear of the Syrian attendant catching me. He didn't come so we smoked the fat joint to its filter. At one point, we went through a tunnel and the soldiers took great pleasure in passing the burning end in the darkness. Soon after, the train slowed down and the soldiers shuffled off to duty. A few minutes later I saw them disembark. They waved, then pointed ahead, grinning and glassy-eyed. I put my head out and saw two sentry posts, with small Turkish flags, standing alone on a gently sloping grassy stretch. There was no sign of a town, just the changing gradient of the land. We were at the Syrian border.

The Turkish exit stamp came quickly and the train, passing a barbed-wire fence, rolled in the direction of a complex consisting of a grey building with a green roof, an ochre minaret and a water-tank. The sky was a mixture of rain and evening, and beams of religious light broke through the cloudy kaleidoscope on to the lower country ahead. More trains with Arab script appeared, then a portrait of the Syrian leader, Bashar al-Assad, a boyish, fleshy face and chinless; nothing like the tight-mouthed stare of his late father, Hafez.

They kept us at the border for hours. First, a Swiss consultant was questioned for many minutes about his profession. He appealed to me, but the words that might have worked in Turkish didn't in Arabic. The immigration officer was young and casually dressed. He asked whether I spoke Arabic, if I was Muslim, then offered me a cigarette, and moved on to Leon, a Chinese-American software engineer. He was taken away for several minutes and returned shaken. 'I'll tell you about the little bit of theatre that occurred once we get moving,' he said, with a weak smile. He never did.

The rain that began in Aleppo continued through the day and into the evening, following me to Damascus. An Egyptian film played on the Kadmus bus I had boarded. It was a black comedy of sorts in which the main character, a young man, was afflicted with a skin disease that only he could see; its portrayal was vile. I could barely bring myself to look at the green-black slime that spread over his otherwise pleasant face. The film's garish colours and noise were hard to get away from. A soldier sitting next to me with a crew-cut and severe laced-up boots laughed uproariously at the blighted man's fate.

The countryside beyond Aleppo turned to desert, not soft, sandy desert but flat, hard, gravelly desert. The yellowish-brown hills in the distance were bare and gritty. Every now and then we would pass a large mural of Assad *père* or *fils*. The older man's murals were in 1970s socialist style: the grim-faced leader managing a smile as agriculture and industry, combine harvesters and mills, worked in the background. The colours were faded, and in some the paint had flaked off, leaving powdery white patches. The younger Assad had launched a campaign of his own, consisting of a young Syrian man and woman staring patriotically into the distance, with the red, black and white of the Syrian tricolour behind them. This, I was sure, was a response to the wave of international pressure Syria, after so many years in Arab nationalist sleep, was suddenly facing. As it became dark, the bus passed through the towns of Hama and Homs, both ancient, with rich classical histories. In the early 1980s, Hama had been the scene of a crackdown in which the dictator had levelled a good part of the old city and overnight solved the country's Muslim Brotherhood problem, the Islamist movement that thrived in neighbouring Egypt. People spoke of the crackdown with awe; rumours circulated that the government had chased the Brotherhood into Hama's sewers and electrocuted them.

The Kadmus bus dropped us off at a depot some way out of town. It was a bleak spot, open, unprotected and badly lit. There was little of the comfort or wonder of arriving in a new place, just rain, cement block houses and naked bulbs. The city's skyline was low and indiscernible, green tube-lit minarets and white city lights dotting the gloom. The presence of the minarets in this small, makeshift way, at once shabby and ubiquitous, gave the darkness an unexpected, neon edge. It was Christmas Eve.

\*

I had first heard of the primacy of Syria as a destination for international Islam from Hassan Butt.

'I do believe I've got a bigger role to play,' Butt said, in the curry house in Manchester, 'and when that time comes, I will make my preparations to play that role.'

He'd been hinting at it so I asked, 'It's martyrdom, isn't it?'

'Absolutely,' he replied. 'It's something that makes me really depressed, being stuck in this country, because I know I'm so far away from it. I know that if I was to pass away in my sleep, I would not have the mercy of Allah upon me because I have been such a bad person. And I don't see myself getting into heaven that easily, except through martyrdom.'

'Where would you go if you got your passport back?' I asked.

'Probably Yemen and Syria initially, because at the moment I'm wanted in Pakistan for supposed involvement in an assassination plot against Musharraf.'

'And after Yemen and Syria, the enemy you would finally confront is the US, right?'

'Yes, but maybe America will be destroyed in my time, maybe

I'll have something completely different to do.' Then his face expressed new urgency. 'But I need to learn Arabic! As an English and Urdu-speaking person, I can see the beauty of Islam from the outside, but I really can't access it without Arabic. It's like having a beautiful house and only being able to see through the windows how beautiful it is inside. That is how I view Arabic. I believe the Arabic language will give me the key to the things I don't have access to at the moment. Once I learn Arabic, *inshallah*, I will get myself militarily trained. It's like the Jews in Israel: conscription is incumbent upon every male and female.'

The presence of international politics and of the traditional enemies of international *jihad* were visible in Syria within hours of my arrival. On Christmas Day in Damascus, as I explored the city's bazaars and baths, I saw a series of red banners, hung in a giant sweep across the breadth of the souk. Their yellow, orange and white painted letters read:

From Syria the country of peace and loving to the Aggressive Israel and its allied America . . . We are in Syria the country of self-esteem and homebred we refuse your democracy after what we had seen happen in Iraq and Palestine and how your democracy build on people's bodies which you bombed on civilians innocents and when the matter reached the council of security in the United Nations and how you used the rejection right (the Vito) to save Israel for only a suspicious matter, and how America pursued the council of security to issue a decision against Syria followed by new decision even Syria executed first one, but the Syrian people not afraid and whatever the difficulties could be and they are resistant by leadership of dearest the President B. Al Assad.

On Valentine's Day the year before, a bomb killed the Lebanese prime minister, Rafik Hariri, in downtown Beirut. Hariri had played an important role in rebuilding Beirut after its destruction during the Lebanese civil war and was known for his opposition to the Syrian military presence in his country. The Syrians were rumoured to have been behind the bomb, and after an outcry in Lebanon, they withdrew their army from the country. A UN inquiry into Syria's role in the assassination of Hariri had implicated the Syrian high command, and the Americans, perhaps pursuing ends of their own, were putting pressure on Syria for its meddling in Lebanon and for supporting terrorism in Iraq. The air in Syria that winter was filled with rumour.

The country had been closed for decades. The regime, for most of its existence, had been socialist, intolerant of religious politics, and the people had only received propaganda. With their role in the world suddenly internationalised, the city was plastered with these cryptic, high-pitched messages. It was the government's response to trouble in the world beyond. President Bashar al-Assad and the Syrian people were not kneeling before anyone but God. And so, in the absence of a free press, an intellectual life and a political culture, and under the watch of a fierce secret police, the mosque became the only place for people to congregate and discuss politics.

What struck me on that first day, as I read the banner, was how unusual and desperate a message it was, unfurled over the souk, the most public of public places, in the guise of a private citizen's initiative. In Syria, where an email with sensitive content could get you pulled up by the secret service, the banners could only have dominated the great bazaar with the blessing of the regime. In another society, where it might really have been possible for an independent party to rent space and make a political statement, it would be difficult to imagine a message of its kind: a public shriek directed at international enemies, hanging over the equivalent of Times Square or Oxford Street. In India, I couldn't imagine an international issue with enough following to warrant hysteria of this kind.

The shoppers in their polyesters, eating stringy ice-cream and walking down the covered souk, more reminiscent of a Paris passage than a traditional Arab souk, seemed oblivious to the banners. They were mostly young men with light beards, wide trousers and baggy jackets. They wandered about in twos and threes, often arm in arm, here stopping for something to eat, there for a soft drink, seemingly aimless, smoking at will. The main commerce occurred between women, in dark, heavy coats and headscarves, some fully veiled, and moustached shopkeepers with hard, round stomachs. Only foreigners, the odd group of Italian tourists, still visiting Syria despite darkening clouds, on their way to the magnificent Umayyad Mosque at the end of the covered market, stopped to read it. Indeed, the message, translated badly into both French and English, must have been intended, in some measure, for them too.

Syria that winter, despite the threat of war, was full of foreigners. There were English, French, Danes, Norwegians, Indians, Pakistanis and even Americans. And their presence added to a general air of international intrigue. Syria was the first police state I had travelled in; a wrong step could see me escorted to the border. And so, wishing to stay away from the closely watched hotels and to learn the ropes at my own pace, I decided to rent a flat for two months.

In my early days, I met a particular kind of foreigner, namely the international students at Damascus University, wanting to learn Arabic in the post-9/11 era. Though many were toying with an interest in Islam, it was the language that had brought them to Syria, not the faith. I had difficulty in imagining a man like Butt, who wanted Arabic but also a kind of immersion in the culture of the faith, spending his time among this crowd of foreign students. With him and Abdullah in mind, I wanted to find out what men like these, from freer, more open, more prosperous countries, came to Syria in search of. In Britain, and in Turkey, it was difficult to see them as more than individual voices. But because Syria was where they came to develop their ideas, I hoped to see them in the context of a community and to gain a more real sense of what they asked of the world.

It was in the interest of discovering Butt's milieu that I first asked Even, a handsome blond Norwegian, studying Arabic and considering conversion, where he thought a man like Butt would have gone in Damascus. Having listened closely to all I had to say about Butt, Even compressed his lips and emitted a sound that was at once a sigh of understanding and impatience; it must have been annoying for him to listen to my speculations about where Butt would enrol, knowing all the time about Abu Nour. And as he began to tell me, his elfin face brimming with excitement, of a great Islamic university and mosque, drawing students from Mali to Indonesia, words failed him. He knew what I was looking for and his response now became a faint, secretive smile.

A few days went by before we could arrange a time to go to Abu Nour. Even had Arabic classes in the morning at Damascus University and it was late afternoon when we set out from my flat. We walked up an inclined street in the direction of the biblical Mount Qassioun, a pale, treeless peak with a city of cement shacks climbing its base. We passed the famous Jisr Abyad Mosque, with its rose dome, and the French Embassy where we would find ourselves under very different circumstances in the weeks to come.

Just before the foot of the mountain, we went right. The

walk so far had taken less than ten minutes, but within a few hundred metres the city was transformed. Its wide main roads, apartment buildings and embassies fell away, and a tight, congested neighbourhood took its place. The narrow, crowded streets in this part of town had an authenticity that even the old city lacked. There were no tourists or antiques shops here, and the retail did not seem as much of a performance as it sometimes did in the old city. It was a fully functioning traditional souk, alive with oddities. At a butcher's shop, a whole camel's head and shoulders hung from an iron hook. In one covered section, a man spent the whole day drying trotters with a blowtorch. Near him, scorched goats' heads with gummy grins and little teeth were arranged on a wooden table, decorated with fresh parsley. A small blue lorry ploughed through the crowd, with a man sitting in the back on a heap of pomegranates. Dates, olives, cheese and blood oranges were crammed in next to electrical-repair shops, and perfume sellers promising to replicate any Western scent. Old women rested their heads against the cool stone entrances of the Mamluk mosques with hexagonal minarets and stalactites.

Dressed in a dark Arab robe, his long, blond hair held down by a woollen skullcap and a camera kept discreetly at his side, Even was of a piece with the souk. It didn't matter that he was foreign; the souk was a place of curiosity. He prayed regularly in the souk's mosques and, as a white man, his interest in the faith was met with awe and admiration. He also spoke *fusha*, the classical, literary Arabic, rather than the dialects of the Syrian street, and this, too, must have created an impression.

We continued; the souk narrowed and suddenly, well before the university itself, the characters in the orbit of Abu Nour appeared. A couple of South Asians, in white with small faces and thick, black beards, conspicuous and beady-eyed, scurried towards us. They were like a sort of herald before the full diversity of Abu Nour came into view. Then we saw short Indonesians, with conical hats and wispy beards, vast West African women in colourful veils and European Muslims with red facial hair. There were Ethiopian Africans, with high cheekbones and small mouths, more South Asians, this time with English accents, and South East Asian girls, with diaphanous, rectangular veils. Nationality and race were my markers, but for the people coming to Abu Nour, these differences were trumped by a greater sense of allegiance.

The whole scene culminated in a little square, with an internet café, an Islamic bookstore, a gym and a store called Shukr, which specialised in stylish Islamic clothes for Western markets. Even had bought his robe there. The ingredients were the same as they had been in Manchester's Curry Mile where I met Butt, and on the radical hilltop in Istanbul: the ideological bookshop; the gym, as a social centre, when girls and bars are off bounds; and the internet café, to communicate with Muslims worldwide and to browse Islamic websites. From the little square, the white marble minarets of Abu Nour were clearly visible.

Abu Nour had started as a small mosque seventy years ago, but in the last three decades, under the late Grand Mufti, Sheikh Ahmad Kuftaro, it grew to dominate the small, traditional souk. Three Islamic colleges were added, two Shariah schools and nine floors. Courses were offered in Arabic and religion, and more than twelve thousand students from fifty-five countries attended the university. Abu Nour was the pet project of the highest religious leader in the land; its remarkable growth spoke of the growing role of religion in the old Ba'athist dictatorship, and the importance of Syria as a destination for international Islam. The late Grand Mufti was known for his tolerance and for reaching out to other religious groups; Abu Nour prided itself on teaching the 'correct face of Islam'. On Fridays, its vast chambers, and specialised annexes for foreigners and women, were full. Syrians and foreigners alike came to the mosque, but in the non-Arab Muslim's journey in search of the faith and its language, Abu Nour held a special place.

We were looking for Tariq, a fix-it man known to all new arrivals at the university. Even was asking for him in one of the shops when he appeared on a corner of the square, a big, meaty figure with a friendly manner. Though his face had a dark stubble, it was shaved clean just under the chin, an Islamic fashion. He greeted Even warmly. Then, taking one look at me, said, with his Arab deafness to the letter *p*, 'Are you Indian or Bakistani, brother?'

'Pakistani,' I said, hedging my bets.

'We welcome *beebal* from every country, brother, because everyone was very nice to me when I was in Europe. I can help you here, brother, and unlike a lot of guides I don't want any money.' This turned out to be true and made me even more nervous. In a country where 10 per cent of the population were intelligence informants, including taxi-drivers and waiters, I was worried that Tariq was making his money elsewhere.

I asked him about enrolling at Abu Nour, and he said, 'Yes, yes, brother, I can help you. What do you want? Arabic? Islamic classes? A lot of *beebal* come here from all over the world, Norway, England, Africa, Bakistan, to learn about Islam.' He warned us that we couldn't trust others and told us a story from the Traditions about the second caliph, Omar. 'He was with someone who saw another man braying,' Tariq said, 'and the man said, "He is a good man." "How do you know he is a good man?" Omar asked. "Have you done business with him? Have you travelled with him? Until you do these things, you don't know if he is a good man."'

Tariq was a talker and I felt that if we didn't extricate ourselves we would be listening to him for a long time. He promised to help me the next day at twelve thirty 'before Friday brayers'. His mention of the prayers produced panic in me. What if he asked me to pray with him and he saw I didn't know how?

'Tariq, I need to learn how to pray,' I blurted.

'Don't worry, brother,' he said, in his unhesitating way. 'We will teach you how to bray.'

The next day, I waited for Tariq in the internet café on the little Islamic square. He was late and I was worried that, for all his talk, he wouldn't show up. Next to me, a pale European with patches of a curly brown beard surfed a Chechen Liberation website while speaking through headphones and a mic to someone on Skype. I went in and out of the café a few times and was beginning to worry about the time when I caught sight of Tariq. The call to prayer had sounded and Tariq now looked at me in the way that an Olympic coach might look at a substitute just seconds after his star player has been injured. He took my arm and, moving fast for a man of his size, marched me in the direction of Abu Nour. I reminded him that I didn't know how to pray.

'No broblem, brother,' he said, as we approached the doors of the multi-storeyed marble edifice. 'We will teach you everything.' Hundreds of people of all races were filing into the building and depositing their shoes in little cubbyholes near the entrance.

Inside, I saw that Abu Nour was a multi-dimensional maze of doors, corridors and stairways. I stayed close to Tariq and followed him up two flights of stairs as he wove his way through the closely packed crowd. At the top, we took off our shoes and came into a carpeted gallery. Through a glass partition, I could see hundreds of people arranged in neat rows below.

They sat in an enormous white room around which there were two floors of galleries behind glass. Chandeliers and ceiling fans, attached respectively to long chains and thin white poles, reached down from the high ceiling, to a pointillist sea of white skullcaps.

At the end of the gallery, there was a corner room with wall-to-wall carpeting, a window at one end and a view of the action below. Young men of various ages and ethnicities sat around with black headphones, some in armchairs, others on the floor, watching a filmed sermon on a television screen. This was the translation room, Tariq informed me. He seemed to know everyone and, having scanned the room, touched one man in cream robes on the shoulder. He looked up and Tariq said, 'Muhammad, will you please take care of this brother from Bakistan and teach him to bray.'

Muhammad, small and dark, looked to me like a south Indian. He nodded slowly and said something softly. Tariq thanked him, and flashing a supportive look, he disappeared.

Muhammad offered me a pair of headphones and I sat down next to him. The translation booth asked me if I wanted English (apparently they could do eight other languages). I said, 'Yes,' and a slow voice, with evangelical vocal range, translated the words of the wizened, white-bearded preacher on the screen. He was emphasising the importance of giving alms to the poor, beyond the 2 per cent required of the believer, as a way to show your love for God and His prophet. I didn't know it then, but the preacher was dead; he was Sheikh Ahmad Kuftaro, the late Grand Mufti of Syria and the founder of Abu Nour.

'Should we wash?' Muhammad said, in his soft voice and imperceptible accent, after we had listened for a while.

'OK.'

He rose slowly and I followed him out of the translation

room. Round the corner, there was a bathroom with cold marble floors and a washing area with several metal taps arranged in a row. Muhammad instructed me that I had to wash my face first, then my hands and arms up to my elbows, a portion of my scalp and my feet up to my ankles. 'Make sure the water touches every place,' he said. He began to wash and I, watching him, followed. He washed carefully, prising apart his toes so that the water touched the lighter skin between them. He seemed to notice that I had washed my face only once because he said quietly, 'The Prophet used to wash three times.' I washed some more. 'The reason we wash these parts of the body,' he added, 'is because they are the parts that are exposed, and washing them also keeps the entire body cool.' My body was cooler than cool; it was cold. The marble floors and sharp edges of the washing area made me pick my way out carefully.

I came back into the translation room with wet hands, feet and hair. The video of the late Grand Mufti had finished and there was a break of a few minutes. I took the opportunity to ask Muhammad about himself. He was in Syria, studying Islamic law, he said. He had grown up in Australia. His parents and grandparents had moved there from India to spread Islam.

'Do you like it there?'

'It's very nice,' he said, 'the best country I know.' His dark features were almost African or Aboriginal, and the stillness of his manner allowed them little expression. He asked me why I was in Syria. I said it was out of curiosity for my father's religion, which I hadn't known growing up. 'Islam is needed in societies all over the world in need of peace,' he said, his expression unchanged. 'All religions preach peace, but Islam offers the widest kind of peace.' Before I could ask why, our conversation was interrupted by the arrival of a few figures in the main room below. Their appearance brought many more people into the translation room.

'It's the Grand Mufti of Bosnia,' Muhammad whispered, with excitement.

Because I was new to Abu Nour, I didn't realise what a lucky first visit this was. The university often invited important Islamic leaders to speak from its pulpit but this was, even by its own standards, an august gathering. The men below, three in robes and turbans, were the Grand Muftis of Syria and Bosnia and Salah Kuftaro, the director of the university and the son of the late Grand Mufti. The unbearded man standing next to them in a brown suit was the minister of culture. These attractions were part of the draw of Abu Nour and the little translation room could hardly contain its excitement.

Kuftaro, a corpulent man with a neat salt-and-pepper beard and a prominent nose, spoke first. After Islamic salutations and bearing witness that there was no God but God, and Muhammad, His Prophet, Kuftaro asserted that Islam was a religion of love and tolerance. He mentioned that Abu Nour had never produced a terrorist. But it was outside enemies that Kuftaro had in mind when he introduced the Grand Mufti of Bosnia. He spoke of the terrible and 'arrogant' injustices and atrocities suffered by the Bosnian people. The Prophet had said that Islam would spread from east to west, and so it had, but in Bosnia they had tried to wipe it out. The Bosnian people, though, had remained steadfast: they had kept the faith. Syria, he said, was now facing a similar threat from a foreign enemy and, under the leadership of Bashar al-Assad, she, too, was steadfast.

This was the first time I had heard a *khutba* or Friday sermon and I was surprised by how openly political it was. My few weeks in Syria had been marked by silence when it came to politics. My Syrian friends only ever discussed it in the privacy of their cars, and even mentioning the leader's name publicly was seen as a transgression. And yet here, it seemed, the faith was being used not only to discuss politics but to conflate the enemies of the Syrian government with the enemies of Islam.

The next speaker was the Grand Mufti of Syria, a young, ferocious man with thick lips, a powerful face and build. His short, black beard, along with the gleam in his eyes, made him seem like an old-fashioned grease wrestler coming into the ring. He went over the same formula: foreign enemies of Islam; the great Islamic past; the sense of grievance; praise of the Assads.

Then the Grand Mufti of Bosnia took the stage. He began with a story of an Andalucían princess in the last years of Islamic rule in Spain. During the battle, she was taken captive and was sold as a slave to a Christian family. Her father, in the meantime, fled to Morocco. As the girl grew up, the son of her owners fell in love with her and wanted to marry her even though she was a slave. She had held her tongue until then, but was now forced to speak: 'I am not a slave. I am a princess. I have a father and mother in Morocco. I cannot marry you without their permission.'

'What has the story of the Andalucían princess got to do with Bosnia?' the Grand Mufti asked the congregation. After a pause, he said, 'That princess is Bosnia. One hundred years ago, in Berlin, she was sold as a slave. But when the time came and someone tried to take her for free, she said, "I am not a slave. I have a father in Istanbul, I have a mother in Damascus, I cannot be taken for free."'

I felt unsettled as I heard the Grand Mufti speak. This man of faith, with a measure of dignity and wisdom about him, distorted the history he spoke of. He knew its aims beforehand; the history was merely slotted in. The event in Berlin to which he referred was the 1878 Treaty of Berlin, when the Ottoman Empire had lost a good part of the Balkans. He connected it falsely to the loss of Andalucía several hundred years before. And in the same vein, he went on to join that history to the Bosnian massacres of the twentieth century. The details hardly mattered: it was a long story of aggression and attack from the Christian West, beginning as early as the loss of Andalucía and continuing till the present, in which the sides, as far as he was concerned, were always the same.

It was encased history; I was reminded of Abdullah, in Istanbul, saying that to be a Muslim is to be above history. Nothing in this fixed narrative could be moved or rearranged or made to say something different. Its goal was to forward the idea of the great Islamic past, solidify the difference between Muslim and non-Muslim, and mourn the loss of a great time when Muslims had ruled the world. In the Grand Mufti's account now, the people committing the Bosnian massacres were hardly different from the Americans who allowed them to happen, the Europeans who sold Bosnia as 'a slave' in 1878 and the Spaniards who had pushed out the Moors four hundred years before.

That morning President Ahmadinejad of Iran was in Damascus. The Syrians and the Iranians, both facing pressure abroad, shared a new closeness. The minister of culture had been with him at the Umayyad Mosque before coming to Abu Nour. 'He was on his first state visit,' the minister said, 'and I told him that from this pulpit Islam had spread from China to Andalucía.'

'And so it will again,' Ahmadinejad had assured him.

Kuftaro wrapped up: 'It is easy to get depressed in these times, to see the forces against Islam. The Islamic world, too, is fragmented and divided. It is divided because of the West and the influence of its ideas. First, they rob us economically, then they rob our land, and once they have achieved these objectives, they rob us culturally. They spread their ideas in our society to keep it divided and fragmented.

'But we have our Book,' he added, the message at last uplifting in its own way: it was a long narrative of former greatness and defeat, reversible not through education, new ideas or progress but through closer attention to the letter of the Book.

Then it was time to pray. Quickly, Muhammad described to me what was to be done. We rose. I followed the others, the first part moving quickly, almost like a military formation, putting my hands behind my ears, then across my chest, then on my haunches. And now, the movement seemed to slow, a heightened feeling of privacy crept in and, with it, my own sense of fraudulence. I struggled to keep in time and feared I would fall out of synch. I was up again, then on my haunches, said, '*Amin,*' when the others did, and at last we went down on our knees and submitted. The bowing and touching my forehead to the floor was my favourite part; I enjoyed the privacy it allowed. But there was also a powerful humility in the gesture, which was easily apprehended. After the submission, I sat up with my legs under me, a difficult position that those who prayed regularly took pleasure in prolonging. Through the whole experience, I watched a small boy, sitting at my feet in a white skullcap. He fiddled, then fell occasionally into the prayer position, then got up and looked around. He had beautiful light-coloured eyes. Seeing him near his father, in the all-male environment, it was possible to see how visiting the mosque could become a special rite between father and son.

When the prayers were over, many stayed in the translation room to talk for a while. As if some unspoken connection had formed between us, Muhammad now treated me as a friend and took me round the room, introducing me to the others. I met Fuad, a British Pakistani in his mid-twenties from Birmingham with a serene expression and a thick black beard.

'That's a confusing identity,' he said, his soft mouth and eyes lighting up in a smile when I told him I was half-Indian, half-Pakistani. 'Like us too. When we were growing up we suffered racial abuse. People told us we weren't English. We grew up when racism was still fashionable. I remember Bernard Manning [the comedian], who was very popular when I was growing up, saying about Pakistanis claiming to be British because they were born in Britain: "If a dog's born in a stable that doesn't make him a horse." The choice of dog was not accidental.' Fuad stopped, and as if it had just occurred to him, added, 'He was saying we were dogs.

'Now the home secretary says we're not British enough. We have to be more British.' Fuad worked hard to realise his parents' dream that he enter the corporate world, but he hated it. 'It was so grey,' he said, 'the drive to work every morning, operating on mechanised time, arriving to find you have two hundred emails to answer, no grand narrative. To succeed in that world, you have to serve the corporation. And for what? For money? I decided I wanted to submit to something that was true, something with meaning.'

I asked him where he felt he belonged now: to Britain or to Pakistan?

'I'm both,' he said. 'The ones I pity are my kids. They have a Puerto Rican mother!' He smiled as he said this, an odd, painful smile.

Muhammad was speaking to someone else so Fuad took me up to meet Rafik, a black 'brother' from Connecticut. He was older, perhaps in his early forties, large and jovial. He had moved to Syria with his wife and children after converting to Islam in Florida. He was working as a teacher and advised me not to get married too young and gave me a few tips on how to learn Arabic quickly. I told him about my trip. 'You have to follow the ringing inside you that is Islam,' he said, 'the ringing of what is right and what is wrong. In the West, we learn to question everything. In Islam, we question too, but not just to say, "Ha, ha, you're wrong." You can't prove Allah wrong.'

I took my leave of Rafik and found Muhammad again. He said he would walk out with me. In the gallery outside the translation room, a Koran class had started up and we went through rows of young boys learning the verses. I said goodbye to

Muhammad, the man who had taught me to pray. He took my number and said he'd give me a call later. He and a few friends were going over to KFC; maybe I'd like to join them.

I had come to Syria searching for the world of men like Butt and Abdullah and I had found it, but I had also found something else: confirmation of what about them had interested me in the first place: only thinly hidden behind the curtain of faith were the problems of the real world. The issues raised at Abu Nour were modern, directly related to what Abdullah described as the 'world system'. Kuftaro spoke of feeling robbed culturally and coming under the influence of foreign ideas; the Grand Mufti, of modern genocide seen on television sets; Fuad, of racism, of the clutter of modernity – being bombarded by emails and adhering to drab routines – of children from mixed marriages, and of loss of identity, resulting from the large-scale migrations of the last fifty years, in his case from Pakistan to Britain. They were scenarios the entire world faced, that I faced; they defined the modern experience; there was nothing about them that was particular to Islam, and they made the Book seem like an unrelated solution.

Walking back through the souk, I felt a flatness that was like frustration. It arose from a stifled desire to express myself, from the mosque raising important issues and smothering them with prayer. I'm sure there were spheres of faith in which people find refuge from the troubles of the material world, but Abu Nour was not that. Abu Nour was political. It fanned a sense of grievance and, as it could only ever do, offered retreat as the answer. But, unlike other religions, the retreat on offer was not that of the hermitage or the ashram; it was of the physical completeness of the faith, an alternative world on earth, equipped with sanctified history, politics and culture: 'the widest kind of peace.' It sought to restore believers to a pure historical and political world-order, free of incursions from the modern world. Syria was seen as a good place to begin because it was closed and depressed, with an autocratic ruler who allowed neither a free economic nor a free political life; it was much easier to shut out the world here than it was in Britain or Turkey. But many of the international Muslims I knew in Syria didn't find it pure enough and drifted south to the lawless wilderness of Yemen in search of greater purities and an Islam closer to that of the Prophet's.

In the meantime, the mosque, in its effort to engage the real world, to re-create the time when temporal and religious power were one, dirtied its hands in dealing with bad regimes and cosying up to dictators. Because the faith was such a negative force, because it didn't matter what kind of Muslim you were, just that you were Muslim, because there was never any plan to offer real solutions, only to harness grievance, and because its sense of outrage had much more to do with the loss of political power than divine injunction, it could even find room, as certain decayed ideologies can, for men like my father, who were ready to participate in its grievances but who were also professed disbelievers. It was in the mosque's use of grievance, the way it could make Assad's problems seem like Islam's, but more importantly, the way it could use modern problems to reignite the faith that its great violence was to be found.

And at the end of that cold, tense winter, filled with international fears, what could be easier than to inflame a country in need of release?

# Nail Polish

It was a misunderstanding of giant proportions.

I first heard of cartoons depicting the Prophet Muhammad over lunch with my Norwegian friend, Even. They had been published in Denmark, and then republished in Norway. We hadn't seen them, but they were said to be generating great anger across the Muslim world. Syria and Saudi Arabia had recalled their ambassadors to Denmark. Religious leaders called for a boycott of Danish products. Within days a painful cycle had begun in which every republication of the cartoons elicited more anger, which in turn made the story bigger and forced republication, if for no other reason than to explain what the fuss was about. Rights and, more importantly, the separation of press from government, unknown or hazy to most of the Muslim world, made the offence seem as if it came from the entire country rather than from a single newspaper, an individual cartoonist or editor.

Damascus that Friday morning was like a city under curfew. There were hardly any cars in the street, the shops were closed and the busy road that ran parallel to mine was so empty it could be crossed at an absent-minded stroll. The rain, which began the day before, had stopped but dark, wandering clouds drifted over the city. Their deep colour and low, predatory movement over Mount Qassioun made the mountain seem bigger and paler than I had seen it before. The hoary, Biblical mountain, with its petticoat of shanties, seemed that morning to have regained some of the grit and thunder of old days.

Even had mentioned he wanted to come with me to Abu Nour so I stopped at his flat on the way. We walked there through a souk that was much emptier than normal. We arrived at the translation room to find it full, and as I had come regularly over the past few weeks, I now recognised many faces. We had come quite late and the sermon had begun. Kuftaro stood alone at the pulpit.

'Believers, we are living in total darkness,' I heard, as I put on my headphones. 'The enemies of Islam have been conspiring against the Islamic nation. They are trying to suppress the values of our nation. With the beginning of this century, the enemies of Islam have occupied Iraq . . . and now we have the blasphemous drawings. It is war against all Muslim people! They want to destroy our nation and our faith with all the weapons they have.' Even and I glanced nervously at each other. 'Under the pretext of democracy and freedom, they are spreading such blasphemous drawings! Our Lord demands that we be strong, and our strength comes from our love for our faith and for Prophet Muhammad. We call for good speech, but when our sanctity is oppressed, we are all sacrificing our spirits for your sake, O Prophet. We will sacrifice our souls, spirits and bodies for you, O Prophet!'

When he had finished speaking, it almost seemed strange to pray, like trying to sleep after a heated argument. The mood in the translation room was charged. Kuftaro had made a call to arms. It was hard to believe that, after so fiery and shaming a sermon, the vast congregation of young men in the chamber below would do no more than go home and refuse to eat Danish cheese. Kuftaro would not have risked disturbing the peace without the express permission of the regime, and if he was making a sermon like this, other mosques were too. It was the mosque performing its role of infusing temporal power with divine sanction, and we sensed that some bigger response was brewing.

I went up to Brother Rafik when I saw him come in. I asked him if he ever minded the anti-Western and anti-American stance of the sermon. 'No, because as a Muslim,' he said, as if recalling a principle, 'I am first a Muslim, then an American. Even before I came here I had stopped thinking of myself as American.' Brother Rafik had not met Even before and I introduced them. When he learnt that Even was Norwegian, he became solemn and asked how everything was in Norway, in the way people do if there's been a natural disaster.

'It's fine, but there's not much understanding,' Even said. 'People haven't quite figured out why everyone is so upset.'

'You have to remember,' Rafik said, becoming lively, 'that this is offensive not just to Muslims but also to Christians and Jews who, if they went back to their books, would see that they are forbidden to make graven images.' He seemed to enjoy those last words and spoke them with the power they held for him. 'They are so removed from their books that they don't know they are forbidden it. If you make or replicate creation, you are producing an idol and, inevitably, someone to knock it down. So it's not just offensive to Muslims, it's offensive to everyone.'

But it wasn't offensive to everyone. Rafik meant that it ought to have been, and that it wasn't, was a failing on the part of Christians and Jews. That week, Rafik, born and bred in America, along with others who had grown up in the West, was in a unique position in Syria. He could explain to many of the people around him, including some of the senior leaders of Abu Nour who were in the translation room at the time, something they genuinely didn't grasp: that the offending cartoons did not come from the Danish government or from Danish companies and that they were powerless to stop their publication.

'Do you feel the response is appropriate?' I asked.

'Well, they got their response, didn't they?' he said. 'If it's a response they wanted, they have it. There are men sitting outside their embassies with AK-47s. That's the response. I'm not saying it's a good one, but it is a response.'

'Do you think it's outside the parameters from which the offence came?'

Rafik understood my question to an extent most Syrians would have found hard. But he felt it was more important to educate Even and me about the sin of making graven images. 'You see, for most people in this region,' he said in a quieter voice, 'the newspapers are the government so they can't understand how the paper can print the cartoons without the government's permission.'

I asked why he didn't offer this analysis to the people around him.

'We know that the West has technology and democracy, or whatever else turns your crank,' he answered, 'but they don't have a lot of wisdom. There was no wisdom in publishing those offensive pictures just because you have the right. Well, who gave you that right except God Himself? In the West there is constant movement. You're moving without even knowing why. There is no time for reflection.'

Black rainclouds slipped over the souk like a lid. Its narrow streets were packed with worshippers leaving the old Mamluk mosques. When, at last, rain and thunder broke over the souk, trenches of water formed in the tented entrances of shops. The filthy souk cats were drenched and the mud floor ran like weak dye through sloping streets to the city below. The commotion the rain caused was followed by marvel as fragments of exploding hail beat down. Even and I stopped trying to make our way back and gathered under a rain-filled awning.

The stall behind us served corn soup in white Styrofoam cups, which came with such speed that they were hardly optional. The men who gathered round us were mostly in their twenties. There was a smell of worn winter clothes and cigarettes about them. They were well-built, with prominent eyes and noses, and attentive to fashion. Their facial hair was carefully shaved, their jeans and sweatshirts close-fitting with haphazard masculine touches – a motorcycle, an eagle, bits of fake fur on the collars.

When the hail stopped, we made our way out of the souk. Even picked up some vegetables, saying he was cooking at home, and invited me to join him.

At his small, airy flat, the doors and windows were open and a moist breeze came through. He was on the top floor, and from his terrace it was possible to see cemented rooftops and fields of satellite dishes, like sunflowers, with poised, vacant expressions. Their presence, illegal, but tolerated by the regime, perhaps unavoidable, along with the numerous internet cafés in the city, always full of young people, stood out as the most obvious sign of dissent in a system that had depended on controlling information.

The lunch turned out to be a small feast of eggs, an aubergine and tomato stew, and beef with fennel and salad. We ate sitting on the floor.

We had finished, and a kettle was on the stove, when the response of which Rafik had warned rose up from the street. The cheer of lunch had made me forget the tension in the mosque, and as I had never seen the slightest disturbance in Damascus's streets, the sudden loud chanting came as a surprise.

It took the form of the Muslim declaration of faith: 'There is no God but God, and Muhammad is His Prophet. La-il-la, il-allah, Muhammad-e-Rasul Allah.' That sentence, with its short, deafening music, audible to believer and non-believer alike, and amplified by the many voices from which it came, reached us like an echo. It came alone, again and again. The first time we heard it, our conversation stopped. The second time we listened from where we sat. The third time we ran on to Even's balcony. From where we stood, it was possible to see the entire sweep of the inclined road.

At the bottom, a small but angry crowd was making its way towards us. Far behind them, the remains of the storm settled in a punctured heap of black clouds, bringing out the green and white colours of the biggest banner. They were a mixed group – fifty to a hundred people – of veiled women, children and young men, like those we'd been with moments before at the soup stall. Turbaned sheikhs, just out from Friday prayers at the city's mosques, led the protest. They carried satiny Islamic and Syrian flags. We watched them pass Even's building and stop no more than fifty metres ahead outside the French Embassy. Days before, *France Soir* had republished the cartoons and its editor had been sacked.

The crowd's shouting grew louder, and Even and I ran down to the street. The demonstrators collected outside the steep, curved walls of the embassy. A few red police cars surrounded them and the officers, who stood at a distance, watched calmly.

Now that they had reached their destination, they seemed unsure of what to do next. Even and I stood still at the edge of the demonstration. There was a little scuffling at the front with the embassy guards, but the protestors lacked the momentum to storm the embassy. For a while, they yelled, 'Get out, get out,' in English, and someone threw a sweet wrapper and a milkshake at the embassy wall. Pink liquid dripped down from the point where the milkshake had hit the wall. There were no speeches, no signed declarations, nothing but anger and frustration. And the message was so simple that a young child in a pink sweatshirt led the slogan in a shrill voice: 'La-il-la, il-allah, Muhammad-e-Rasul Allah' and 'Allah hu Akbar' again and again. There was no response from the embassy, just stony indifference to the angry mob. The street was still wet from the morning shower and a light breeze coming off the mountain threatened to blow away their fury.

Just then, a familiar face appeared from the crowd. It was Basil, a Syrian friend of Even, who had followed the demonstration from the Danish Embassy. He pushed his way through to us. He was in a merry, joking mood and was excited by the afternoon's events. He gave Even a big hug and teased him about being Norwegian. He offered to take us deeper into the crowd. We followed him along the edge of the protest, closer to the front, but at that moment the protestors pushed harder at the barricades outside the embassy. I felt the squeeze and stopped, but Even and Basil pressed ahead. Within a moment, I had lost them.

The commotion at the front had made me uneasy, but now separation from Even brought on a wave of panic. The mob was searching for a focus at which to direct its anger. I was scanning the crowd for Even when suddenly I heard Basil address the demonstrators in Arabic: 'This is my friend,' he said. 'He is Norwegian and a good man.' Then he raised Even on to his shoulders and said to him, 'Speak for your country.' Not a sound came from the crowd and the new silence chilled me. Now they have an object for their rage, I thought, feeling all my worst fears answered. Even, if he was scared, showed no sign of it. He took in the crowd, his natural repose undisturbed, and then addressed them in Arabic. 'This is just an embassy,' he began, his face still and serious, his hand raised slightly so that the index finger met the thumb in a gesture suggesting precision. 'It is not actually the country. I think that this conflict is caused by lack of understanding. In Norway we don't know much about Islam, and there are not many Muslims there. Norwegians need to learn about Islam, and through knowledge of Islam, we can learn to . . .' He stopped and bent to ask Basil for the right word. The crowd listened in stunned silence. '. . . respect Islam, and live together peacefully. *Inshallah, inshallah, in-sha-llah!*'

At the time I didn't understand what he was saying, but I tried later to imagine the impact of his words: the surprise of them from a foreigner, their clarity and volume, the classical Arabic in which they were spoken, and the simple, helpful message, the only one, so far, that had been more than a cry of hysteria. The words that came so easily to him, words of sympathy and diffidence, keen not to blame but comprehend, clichés in the West, resounded with freshness on the Arab street.

A roar of approval came from the crowd. Someone yelled, 'He accepts Islam!' A small, withheld smile formed on Even's lips. Hands reached up from all sides to shake his; others took his picture with mobile phones; a TV crew squeezed to the front to interview him. His speech brought the demonstration to an end. I knew a great sense of relief; it could have gone so wrong. I thought that Basil had seriously endangered him, but Even didn't see it that way: he felt it had been an act of trust on Basil's part.

Back at the flat, Basil, in his white cap and over-excited manner, was saying that the Israelis were to blame. They had planted the cartoons to poison the close relationship between the Arabs and the Danes. He heard in the mosque that morning that Muslims themselves were to blame because they had failed to tell people in the West how great a man Muhammad was. He took me aside to tell me of the greatness of the Prophet, his flight to Medina, and how Islam was a religion for all people.

'How do you feel?' I asked Even.

'I wish I could have said more,' he replied, the adrenaline still strong in his voice, 'but I didn't have the words. What I really wanted to say was "We know you're angry, but we still don't know why."'

\*

On Saturday, we knew less. The cartoons had filtered through outraged governments and clerics to the people. And now the street was on the boil. For the first time since I'd arrived in Damascus, nearly a month ago, I felt unsafe. There was something especially unnerving in watching so controlling a state loosen the reins.

I had just had lunch with an American writer friend, Bartle Bull, and was recounting the events of the day before when cries from a new demonstration rang out. We were walking through a small park in a quiet residential neighbourhood when we heard them. Bartle, as if picking up a scent led us in their direction, out of the park, down a main road and finally on to a wide avenue with palms in the centre. Traffic was diverted because thousands and thousands of demonstrators were marching down the avenue. The crowd here was of a type: angry, available young men, unshaven, sullen, with shiny faces and greased-back hair. This was a different, more orchestrated demonstration than the one the day before: young girls and older men marched too, but at its heart was a large group of the dissatisfied young men that all police states have at their disposal.

Unlike the day before, it was a clear, beautiful afternoon. Following the demonstration down the avenue was no more of a strain than taking an after-lunch stroll. The slogan from the day before, 'There is no God but God, and Muhammad is His Prophet', was shouted now and then, but for its size, the demonstration was comparatively quiet, focused and on the move. We weren't sure where it was headed, which European nation had published the cartoons now or, since a demonstration of this size clearly had the blessing of the regime, whether all this anger would be channelled in the direction of 'the big Satan', America. It was only when the leaders turned right into a smaller street that we found ourselves standing in front of the Danish Embassy. At first, it was not very crowded, but barricades had gone up on one side of the street and it was impossible to leave, except by the way we had come. That option was blocked by the waves of demonstrators arriving from the avenue. With every minute that passed, the small area in front of the embassy became more compact and the energy of the crowd, like riotous molecules over a Bunsen flame, surged. I became uneasy at the closeness of the mob, and the sudden ripples of mounting energy that travelled through it, drove Bartle and me to a quieter area.

From there we watched the mob turn their anger on the Danish Embassy's dull beige façade. A few stray rocks began to fly. In places where the rocks hit their mark, a cement wound opened on the beige façade and a cry of satisfaction went up from the crowd. More rocks began to come. One hit the embassy's red and gold crest and the crowd screamed with pleasure. A thin line of policemen in helmets, mostly young boys, stood perfectly still and expressionless with their backs to the embassy.

This was not yesterday's demonstration: preparations had been made and rocks from some mysterious source were now hitting the embassy in a steady barrage. The crowd danced with excitement and a Danish flag was unfurled, burnt, then stamped on many times. Homemade posters were held high: 'We are those who are faster than fate. Vikings beware' and 'We sacrifice ourself, our mother, father and children for you, O Prophet!' A new chant rang through the crowd, and to me, an Urdu speaker, many of the words were familiar: 'Bi ruh, bi dem, rafiki-ya-rasul, With our soul, with our blood, O Prophet, my friend!' It was another of those strange moments in which the crowd's rage submerged the meaning of their slogan, in the same way that it was possible to say that Islam was a religion of peace and compassion, then raise a crowd to fury in its name.

A man ran up to Bartle and me. He would have picked us out of the crowd as foreigners or journalists, and this made me nervous. 'Tell your people in Europe that the freedom of journalists is the freedom of madness. Here, here, write down my name, Muhammad Ghazali, forty-nine.' He was a rotund, cheerful man, sick with exhilaration. 'Look and see these ordinary people, not educated people!' he panted. 'And I am ready to die,' he yelled, over the slogans and the cries of the crowd, 'against those who are saying these bad things against our Prophet.' He ran back towards the crowd and was swallowed up in seconds. He was of a piece with the rest: rage and violence on the surface; euphoria and release below.

It was a little after four and the embassy had been stoned for nearly twenty-five minutes without intervention from the authorities. The thin line of boy riot police stood exactly where they had been. I was observing their expressionless faces when a roar from the crowd made me look up. A young man in jeans had got into the embassy and now stood on one of its balconies. He gloried in the crowd's approval for a moment, then reached over the railing and pulled the oval crest off the wall. It came away easily. He held it up like a trophy and threw it into the crowd. Then he took out a green flag with white writing that read, 'There is no God but God, and Muhammad is His Prophet,' and hung it from one of the embassy's slanted flagpoles.

'They're gonna burn this place,' Bartle said. 'This is huge.'

It hadn't occurred to me that they might; the demonstration

had grown so quickly from a few stray rocks to a full-blown attack. The boy policemen continued to do nothing, and watching them, it became clear that the regime had forsaken the small, besieged embassy. More people broke into its compound and a murmur of anticipation went through the crowd.

The black smoke and fire that started appeared at first to come from the compound, not from the actual embassy. But slowly, the embassy building, rather than being consumed by the flames, seemed itself to breathe fire from its ground-floor windows and doors.

Bartle was on the phone to Sunday editors in London. I called Nedal, a Syrian friend who was helping me in Damascus; he said he'd be there in a few minutes. A pinkish dusk hour set in and the flames and smoke, now reaching out of the embassy, mixed with the fading light in a puzzling and primeval close of day. The crowd danced in jubilation. As if re-enacting some ancient rite, they passed round the Danish crest like a holy relic.

The silhouette of a fire engine appeared past the barricades at one end of the street. The other silhouette, its cross and tower framed against the haze of smoke and evening, was that of a next-door church, now threatened by the fire.

A few minutes later Nedal, short, smartly dressed, with a neatly trimmed beard and bright eyes, appeared from among the crowd and we began to make our way out of the crush. I asked him to help me talk to a few people, who were now also moving in the direction of the avenue.

One man shouted, 'They started it. It will not just burn, but be blown to pieces.'

A young girl in a headscarf, called Heba, said, 'This is nothing for us. They have insulted our Prophet. What is an embassy?'

A twenty-six-year-old, bespectacled student, called Muhammad, heard us talking and interrupted her, 'This is wrong. We can protest, we can demonstrate, but we can't do this. Our Prophet would not like it. It is our fault because we are not good Muslims. If we were good Muslims, no one would dare insult our Prophet and our faith. When we were good Muslims, the language of the world was Arabic, not English.'

When he had finished, Heba was silent and nodded. The pain the student expressed was not uncommon: many felt that the insult of the cartoons could only have been inflicted on a defeated people.

The street emptied quickly. The façade of the embassy was charred and soaked where the firemen had doused the flames. On the avenue, a woman with streaked hair and an elegant blue jacket walked past the embassy with her shopping. 'Oh, good, good,' she squealed in English. 'They've burnt it.'

A forty-year-old man, calling himself Jihad, stopped me: 'If you are aware of the Jewish conspiracy, you will see the stamp of Mossad all over this. This is a trick of the Jewish people because they know the Prophet is a symbol of all Muslims in the world.'

'If you know it's a trick, why did you fall for it?'

He wouldn't answer, but wanted to list the wrongs Israel had done. Nedal was visibly upset. He was worried about how this would damage Syria's place in the world and its relationship with the Scandinavian countries that, until now, had been allies and supportive of the Arab cause. He kept asking me how it was possible to have a right to insult the Prophet.

On the way home, I noticed that the violence was spreading from the embassies to the neighbourhood round my flat. Mobs of young men ran from street to street, kicking over dustbins and attacking anything they could find. Now real riot police, with faceless helmets, black uniforms and batons, roamed the streets; a water cannon was brought out. News came in that the Norwegian Embassy had also been burnt and it was at this point, with riots spreading through our part of the city, that I became worried about Even. In Damascus, most people knew their neighbours and could easily point out where the Norwegian who had addressed the demonstration the day before lived. Even didn't have a mobile phone, but I finally got hold of him on Basil's phone. He sounded frantic. He had been at the Danish Embassy and after that at his own. He said he was coming over to my flat.

He arrived twenty minutes later with Basil. Soon after, the police chased a small mob down the street at the end of ours. We saw them like a screeching flicker in the corner window. After a tense few seconds, an expression of relief passed over our faces. Even could hardly think beyond his nerves and excitement. He told me of his afternoon in broken sentences. Outside the Norwegian Embassy, a man had grabbed him and screamed, 'Where are you from? Where are you from?' He had answered, 'Sweden,' and some of the others there had pulled the man away. The demonstration was tear-gassed and Even went with the demonstrators to wash their eyes in a mosque, but the detail that impressed itself on him was that the call to prayer had sounded as the demonstration approached the embassy. The demonstrators had stopped, prayed in the street, then risen and charged the embassy. 'I can't believe they prayed first!' he gasped.

That night the Norwegians in Damascus were meant to have had dinner in the old city, but as rioting continued into the night, it was cancelled. News of the burnings had already made its way from the street to the world beyond and Norway announced it was evacuating its citizens. By four a.m. the first planes were leaving.

*

On Sunday morning, drinking Nescafé on my slim balcony, I looked out on a city in bright sunshine. The neighbourhood was not just calm, it had been cleaned. No trace of the riots remained. There was traffic on the intersection, the shops were open and the baker, just past the traffic-lights, was churning out hot mincemeat pizzas. So much had happened in the last few days, a whole cycle of religious ecstasy, and the final hours of violence had felt almost ritualistic. The mood that morning in Damascus was like the day after a festival in India.

The passions spent, it felt strange to think of their cause: cartoons.

The offensive cartoons could not have been understood Islamically. The democratic rights and interlocking institutions that protected them were outside the faith's compass. Nedal was right: I couldn't explain to him how one could have the right to insult the Prophet unless I was to step outside the circle in which it was written that it was wrong to make graven images. Indeed, to explain to Nedal how one had the right to insult the Prophet, I would have to ask him to suspend his faith for a moment and believe in sanctities greater than that of his Prophet and his Book. But the reverse was not true. Europe had lived through an ugly history of religion intruding on the public sphere. It knew about religious injunctions, and also their dangers. It could be said that the systems that protected the cartoons now had been set up in part to protect public life from the excesses of religion. The cartoons came from places that considered it an achievement for religion to be able to take a joke. It had not always been that way.

In coming to Syria, I had hoped to see the rhetoric of Butt and Abdullah put into practice. I got more than I bargained for. Abdullah's notion of Islamic completeness, a negative concept, possible only as opposition, was already being expressed at Abu Nour before the cartoons had came along. As it was, they provided the ideal grievance: here was an offence from the hostile, alien world, and the faith, for once, knew how to react. But if there hadn't been cartoons, they would have had to invent them: all that preparation and frustration needed release.

What happened in Damascus can be explained in miniature by a story a Syrian friend told me. Its small domesticity hides the hysteria in the background. It is a story of a man who goes to his priest to ask if his wife is permitted to wear nail polish. Expecting the answer to be no, he is surprised when the priest says that of course she can: why shouldn't she look beautiful? However, it is written that when she washes for prayer, the water must touch every part of her body, including her nails. 'The company that invented the polish,' the priest smiles, 'also invented a nail-polish remover.' So, yes, she can wear nail polish as long as she removes it every time she is at prayer: five times a day! And so, the faith deals with the nail polish in its own way but never confronts the real offence: the triumph of the other society, the 'world system', of which the appeal of its nail polish is so soft yet potent a symbol.

# Bhutto's Footprint

My parents met in March 1980, in Delhi. My father was in India promoting a biography he had written of his political mentor, the Pakistani leader Zulfikar Ali Bhutto. My mother, a young journalist on a Delhi newspaper, was sent to interview him.

'Which one of you is Salmaan Taseer?' she said, as she entered the room my father and his publisher were staying in at the Oberoi Hotel in Delhi.

Their affair began that evening. My father took my mother's number, they had dinner at a Chinese restaurant called the House of Ming, and for a little over a week, my father disappeared with my mother.

My parents met at a point in their lives when they became politically involved in countries that were experiencing political cataclysm. The state of emergency that Mrs Gandhi declared in 1975 – a month after my mother joined the *Statesman* newspaper – jailing the opposition and silencing the press, had come and gone. Mrs Gandhi had returned to power, and the terrorism in Punjab that would take her life was about to erupt.

In Pakistan the year before, the same year as the Iranian revolution and the Soviet invasion of Afghanistan, Zulfikar Ali Bhutto, to many the great hope of Pakistani democracy, had been hanged. And now General Zia, the military dictator, was settling into the blackest decade Pakistan would know.

My father, who loved Bhutto, could not turn away from these events. He had heard Bhutto speak for the first time as a student in London in the sixties and was moved to his depths. Afterwards, he followed him to the Dorchester and approached him as he sat with a group of friends at the bar. Bhutto invited him to join them for a beer. It was a gesture that meant a great deal to my father. He had lost his own father when he was six – around the same age that I became aware of the absence of mine – and grew up in Lahore with very little money. He was in London studying chartered accountancy, and on most days had little more to eat than a bar of chocolate. Bhutto's generosity and openness at that time in my father's life left more than a strong impression: it was the beginning of a lifelong love for the leader and his family, and excited in him the desire to be involved in Pakistani politics.

For my father, the events of 1979 brought in a time of both uncertainty and possibility. Bhutto's daughter, Benazir, had entered politics and Zia had to be fought. For a man of thirty-six, touched by unusual idealism, the trouble in my father's country had also come with a ripening of purpose. His biography of Bhutto, begun before Bhutto's death, was in many ways a political entry-point.

My parents' affair lasted little more than a week, when my father left Delhi for Lahore, where he already had a wife and three small children. A month later, my mother discovered she was pregnant. The scandal of it was too great to assess. My mother was from an old Sikh family still carrying the pain of Partition. For her then, to become pregnant out of marriage by a visiting Pakistani was at the time, and still today, incalculable scandal. In a week when she was considering an abortion, my father called unexpectedly from the Club Marbella in Dubai. She told him what had happened.

'What are you going to do?' he asked.

'What do you think I'm going to do?' she replied.

My father asked her what could be done to change her mind. She replied that they would have to at least pretend to be married, and over the course of their conversation, they came to a tenuous agreement to continue their relationship for as long as they could.

The months that followed were defined by secrecy. My parents met again in April, in Pakistan; they went to Dubai; they spent a summer in London, full of bright evenings and the bustle of people in pubs and open-air restaurants; and, all the time, their relationship and my mother's pregnancy were kept from her parents and from my father's family in Pakistan. It was this pact of secrecy that made their relationship possible, and it was from this period that one of the two objects I linked with my father as I grew up came into my mother's possession: a copy of his biography of Bhutto. The inscription, dated '17/5/80', read: 'With love and love, Salmaan Taseer.' The other was a browning silver frame with two pictures of him. In one he's holding me as a baby and in the other he's at a Mughal monument, dressed in white, wearing large seventies sunglasses.

News of my mother's pregnancy was kept from my maternal grandparents until weeks before I was born, in November that year, when my mother's sister presented it to them as a *fait accompli*. They were conservative and old-fashioned and the news would have come as a terrible jolt. But they showed immeasurable bigness of heart when they were told. And with my grandfather, of course, there was the nostalgia for his Punjab. Though it was unsaid, there would have been some secret pleasure in his murmuring, 'I always thought one of you would go back to that side.' Despite the scandal, despite the shock it caused, despite the fact that there was something malicious and teasing in the way the news was kept from them, their first instinct was to get on a plane to London to help with the baby.

It was their first time in Europe and they never went again. They used the trip as an excuse to travel in Europe and always presented it to me, with their many photographs, as something they were grateful to me for giving them the opportunity to do. In Spain my grandfather, with his pointed moustache and turban, was mistaken everywhere for Salvador Dalí.

They returned with me to India in the spring, and that April, they held a reception for my parents in Delhi, publicly acknowledging and legitimising their relationship in front of their friends and family. A few weeks later, events in the Bhutto family intervened. A Pakistan International Airlines flight had been hijacked and forced to land in Kabul. Bhutto's son, Murtaza, was involved in the hijacking. The BBC interviewed my father, who was by then aligned with Benazir Bhutto – herself under house arrest – in the fight against Zia. My father was in Pakistan and told the interviewer that, while Murtaza had only hijacked a plane, Zia had hijacked all of Pakistan. Within hours, my father's house in Lahore was surrounded and a warrant had been issued for his arrest. It was no longer safe for him to be in Pakistan. He managed to escape the country and get to Dubai, where my mother joined him, leaving me with my grandparents.

The hijacking brought my father into the long fight against General Zia, and soon after, our small, makeshift family felt the first tremors.

## Mecca Reprise: 'Muslims Only'

I left Syria in the aftermath of the cartoon riots and took a car and driver south to Saudi Arabia. The Kingdom's border was a vast complex of warehouses, a mosque with a white minaret and a high shelter with square pillars, also white, which cast strips of welcome shade on the blinding tarmac. The flat, arid land was dotted with barbed-wire fences and tall, stooped steel lights. The glare seemed to suck the colour out of the landscape, and the painted yellow and black paving stones that ran round the square pillars stood out as the only shred of colour. A mid-morning quiet prevailed. Since Syria, the land had turned to desert. Almost everyone was now in full Arab dress, the women heavily veiled, and the Levant's racial mixtures had faded. It was more than a border: it was the ancient boundary between the classical world and Arabia. Visible beyond a narrow stretch of brilliant sea was Egypt.

But for a few men in white robes and pickup trucks – familiar with the routine, arms outstretched with papers – there was hardly anyone at the border. Our SUV drove up to the immigration window as if it were a tolbooth. A man, with a boyish face and a light beard, looked hard at my passport, then glanced at me. Saudi Arabia was a closed kingdom and I was lucky to have the visa. The immigration official seemed impressed and called a colleague to take a look.

'Riyadh?' The colleague smiled.

'No, Jeddah,' I said, smiling back.

He stamped an inky black oval with a little car and the Kingdom's sword-and-palms crest into my passport and waved us through.

'Saudiya,' the driver whispered, as the SUV rolled out of the shade of the border.

My first view of the Kingdom was a hard, arid mountain on whose gritty surface the words 'La-il-la, il-allah' – there is no God but God – were written in huge white chalky letters. Soon after a sign read 'Makkah 1171 km'.

*

Jeddah was the historical gateway city to Mecca. I waited for Hani in a square in its old city. I hardly knew him, but a mutual friend had put us in touch, and when he heard of my plans to go to Mecca, he offered to take me. He also arranged a guide for old Jeddah. 'You don't have to touch the stone,' the old guide advised, after I told him of my purpose that evening. 'People push and shove, but it is enough to salute the rock.'

Around us the maroon and black rugs of the Grand Mosque in Mecca hung outside shops. Jeddah's old city lacked the bustle of markets in other places. The afternoon pall that I now associated with the Kingdom in general prevailed here too. There was also the conspicuous absence of Saudis and women. The men carrying boxes or wheeling carts were Pakistanis in grubby *salwar kameez*. The only woman I saw was a large African, covered, but for her face, entirely in black. She sat in the shade of a *neem* in the middle of the square. Her head was in her hand, and her elbow rested on her knee. She was dusty and her stricken expression spoke of destitution. The complete, virtually enforced absence of women made her, with no male escort and exposed to the gaze of all the men who walked past, seem still more wretched and alone.

A breeze from the sea made its way through the square. Among the tall old buildings and the semblance of trade, it was possible for the first time to think of old Arabia in the Kingdom, and of Jeddah as it had been before the discovery of oil, a major Arabian port and the gateway to the holy city.

The guide said I would enter the mosque from the south-east gate. But first I had to announce my intention to complete the *umrah*, an off-season pilgrimage to Mecca, and to wear the pilgrim's clothes. For this, I was meeting Hani within the hour.

Like many young Saudis, he appeared in his national dress, an off-white robe without the scarf. He was well-built and hand-some, with a prominent jaw and cheekbones. His slightly gapped teeth gave him a fierceness unsuited to his warm, friendly nature. He had just finished work at a bank and said that we had to make a few stops before we prepared for Mecca.

The first was at his family house, which, like many, was in a compound where different members of the family also had their houses – low bungalows, spread out over a big lawn. Hani's grandfather's bungalow was a dim, spacious place with a sparsely furnished drawing room, and large windows, overlooking the garden. It had the decorum that elderly people's houses some-times do, of old upholstery, furniture and framed photographs. No one was at home and the reason we stopped there was so that Hani could pray. I wouldn't have thought this about him, this strict adherence to the hours of prayer. Earlier, he had produced two neatly rolled joints from his pocket.

The prayer stop made me a little unsure. We were going to Mecca, but we hadn't discussed my religious credentials, and it would have felt strange for me to join him as if I, too, kept the hours of prayer. Besides, I was still unsure of my co-ordination, especially without the security of other worshippers. So I wandered into Hani's grandfather's study, a comfortable, well-lit room of dark wood and leather, its walls covered with books, many on politics, energy and religion. Through a crack in the door, I caught sight of Hani, his large frame and classically Arab features, kneeling and submitting, muttering the prayers. His ease as he prayed, his comfort with the faith's liturgical language, set against my own unfamiliarity and the impending pilgrimage, gave me a pang of exclusion.

The pilgrim's clothes, a stack of white towels, were already in the car. When Hani had finished praying, we drove to his friend Kareem's house to put them on. It was turning out to be a cool February night.

Kareem was unusually good-looking, in a pale, wolfish way, with light eyes and hair. He had a cynical manner and a mocking smile. The house's high walls were painted a reddish-orange colour. It was modelled on a Spanish *hacienda* with stone arches and a swimming-pool. Kareem's little brother was at home and sauntered past in shorts and a sports jersey. The house had all the comforts of life in the Kingdom – flat, wide-screen televisions, large refrigerators, low, comfortable sofas. We made our way through a den of sorts into Kareem's room, which seemed unchanged from his childhood.

'Should we have a last cigarette?' Kareem asked.

The state we would be assuming was called *ihram*, which literally meant 'prohibiting'. Once we were in it, it was unlawful to do a whole list of things, of which I thought, mistakenly, that smoking was one. As I finished one of Kareem's Marlboro Lights, I had a strange feeling of adolescence. I don't know if it was Kareem's pre-college room or the pleasure of a stolen cigarette or, in a deeper sense, the fraternal connection the faith inspired. There was some current of macho comradeship and familiarity that I'm sure I didn't exude, but felt obliged to slip into when I was with Muslims. That fraternal feeling, whatever it was, was amplified now by the generosity of the two men I hardly knew, who had opened their houses to me and were taking me to Mecca.

This feeling of adolescence was reflected in my awkwardness. I felt a fraud: for not being versed in the meaning of the prayer and rites we were about to perform, but also for being curious, rather than believing. I had a fear of being exposed, which turned out to be well-founded. A few moments later, after we had washed ritually – faces, part of the scalp, hands to the elbows and feet to the ankles – in Kareem's bathroom, we dressed in the pilgrim's clothes, two seamless white garments to be worn with nothing else. One was tied round the waist, the other thrown loosely over the left shoulder. It was important that the right shoulder was exposed as this followed the Prophet's own example. The problem was that, from another far more adolescent experience in Goa, I had a tattoo of Shiva, the Hindu god of destruction, on my right arm. Kareem and Hani looked at it in shock, and then with some amusement. Tattooing was not only forbidden in Islam – 'Muhammad forbade the custom of the idolaters of Arabia to prick the hands of their women and to rub the punctures over with wood, indigo, and other colours', Mishkat, Book 12, Chapter 1, Part 1 – but to have a tattoo of a Hindu god would spoil more than a few pilgrimages and possibly land me in trouble with the religious establishment. It was decided that I would make the pilgrimage with the second white garment wrapped round both shoulders, closer to the example of an old woman in a shawl than the Prophet.

When we were dressed, we prayed together, announcing our intention to make the visit to Mecca. I fell into an easy rhythm in which I paid no attention to my movements in relation to the others'. I took as long as I wanted for the submission, which I liked, and though I had no prayers to say, I enjoyed the privacy so soon after the anxiety the tattoo had caused. By the time I sat back on my legs and felt the ligaments at the top of my feet stretch painfully, my breathing changed and I was aware of a new undeclared ease that had formed between the three of us.

We left Jeddah in Hani's Lexus on an elevated highway. The city's poorer areas were visible below, an expanse of single white lights punctured by dozens of green, tube-lit minarets. Once the road cleared Jeddah, it levelled into a wide, multi-lane highway. The Kingdom's unlikely fusion of grim desert mountains and American chain restaurants gathered close to the road. When their coloured signs grew fewer, we were left with the darkened shapes of hills dotted with floodlights. There was hardly any traffic and the desolation the desert brought on emphasised the security of the fast-moving, air-conditioned car. It was strange, in this prudish country where one could be pulled up for wearing shorts, to be out and about wearing little more than a towel.

On the way, Kareem asked for the story of the tattoo. I told it to him and Hani, complete with details of beer consumed, the little Goan hut besieged by monsoon and the drug-addict tattoo artist who was now dead. Then the solemnity of our present purpose intervened, and I felt uneasy. Hani and Kareem seemed near to me in many ways, but there were aspects of the religion that were written into their cultural framework, such as the visit to Mecca. And, as my exclusion grew, I felt like I implicated them in my discomfort.

My unease must have been apparent because Kareem soon asked the question that had hung over our undertaking since it began. 'So, do you think of yourself as Muslim?' he said, the question's seriousness masked by the lightness of his tone and an artful smile.

'Well, I'm not sure if this is the best time to get into it.'

'No? Why not?'

'Well, sort of,' I answered weakly. 'Culturally.'

A cultural Muslim: a term my father gave me when I asked him the same question. I used it now, not fully knowing what it meant, more as an out than as an honest answer to Kareem's question. I had learnt from my experience with my father that the term meant more than just a lax approach to religion: it contained political and historical allegiance to other Muslims. In the Kingdom, I could see how cultural Islam on the sub-continent would once have been something quite apart from the Islam of Arabia, but I was also aware of a changing balance. In a world that was less local, less particular, Islam, to the detriment of cultural Islam, also became more global, more homogeneous; men in Beeston and men in Istanbul, less far apart.

The journey to Mecca took less than an hour, and before the city, the highway split into two: one was for 'Non-Moslems', known as the Christian bypass, and the other was the one we took, for 'Makkah-Moslems only': an exit for the faithful.

'Where does the other go?' I asked.

'Off a cliff,' Kareem laughed.

The car passed under two vast intersecting concrete slabs that formed a cross.

'What was that?'

'Oh, that's just for tourists,' Kareem said.

It was only when we drove a few hundred metres past the overturned concrete cross that I could make out its shape: it was a colossal Koran stand.

Soon after, Mecca's hills and skyscrapers came into sight. A curved road brought us into the city with unexpected speed. The skyline I saw was nothing like what I imagined. Even though I was prepared not to see an old city, I had imagined a lower city, more scattered. But the city we entered was like the financial district of a metropolis. There were cylindrical, tin-can skyscrapers, with little balconies; white apartment buildings, many storeys high; hotels with reflective-glass windows; and twin-tower office buildings. I imagined businessmen in hotel suites surfing the web while looking down on the Grand Mosque, or Meccan executives swivelling in chairs as they planned development deals and handled pilgrim tours: their food, their lodging, buses to the different holy points, an apple and a soft drink as a morning snack. We passed one mountainside covered with low, expansive dormitory housing, a sprawling shanty rising from the base of the mountain and reaching close to its summit.

'Many of those houses will be demolished by companies such as Jabal Omar,' Kareem pointed out. 'The whole mountainside has been bought over. Development in Mecca is proving problematic.'

As we got nearer to the centre, Mecca's commerce – dozens of little restaurants, religious bookshops, clothes stores, shopkeepers sitting idly outside them, airline offices, a sign for Pakistan International Airlines – cluttered the bases of the towers. Some of the buildings had Islamic touches, a colonnade of little pointed arches at the base or geometric designs on the façade while others were Marriott-style fronts of blue glass and beige stone. Much of the architecture was from the seventies and eighties: heavy, four-square buildings that gave off a whiff of damp carpets, dim lighting and plywood furniture. At this evening hour, even though it was low-season, there was bustle and bright lights. Men ambled across the road freely and robed figures queued at a fast-food restaurant with a bright yellow and red sign. Descriptions of the old Mecca suggest a similar clutter of tall buildings, but of stone and more along the lines of Jeddah's old houses, narrow with little windows. I felt some sadness at not seeing that old city gathered tightly round our destination, the city's nucleus and main public place.

The other surprise was how African Mecca felt. Everywhere I looked I saw African figures in white, sometimes with skull-caps and sparse, kinky beards. Their sudden presence in Mecca expanded my notion of the Arab world, reminding me of countries like Chad and Mauritania, and Sudan, only a narrow strip of sea away. I felt I entered the deepest sphere of Arabia, where the peninsula faced Africa rather than Asia. It was this proximity that allowed members of the Prophet's family and early Muslims, persecuted by the pagan Meccans, to seek refuge in Abyssinia. There were so many Africans that at last I asked Kareem about it.

'It's a big problem,' he replied. 'They're west Africans who come for *hajj* and stay. Half the domestic help are *hajji*s.'

We drove into a plaza of humbling proportions, composed of white light and marble. Behind us, cranes hung over the skeletons of partially completed towers, their unfinished silhouettes vanishing into the night sky.

'Bin Ladin.' Kareem grinned, referring to the construction empire the al-Qaeda leader's father founded. Relishing the surprise that name brought to the face of a foreigner, he added, 'See? You need to be very close to the royal family to be given a job like that.'

Once the car had driven away, and we were half-naked specks on the marble plaza, Hani said, 'I'll read and you repeat after me.'

*

The Prophet of Islam was born and lived his entire life in what is today Saudi Arabia. There was so little that was old in what I'd seen of the Kingdom that I had to remind myself of that fact. Neither Islam nor the Prophet ventured much further than Arabia during his lifetime. In fact, the entire orbit of

Islam in those early days was concentrated within a radius of a few hundred miles from where I stood. The details of the Prophet's life, unlike Jesus's and the Buddha's, are rich and well documented. He was born in Mecca. He worked in the caravan trade with his uncle, Abu Talib. When he was twenty-five, he went to work for Khadija, a rich, forty-year-old widow, married twice before with children, whom he soon married. The young man without means and the rich, middle-aged woman spent the early years of their marriage trying to have children; the boys died in infancy. During this time, Abu Talib's son, Ali, came to live with the Prophet and Khadija. Ali, the Shia hero who later married the Prophet's daughter by Khadija, was also his cousin and the Prophet himself had lived with Abu Talib when he was a boy.

When the Prophet was forty he had his first revelation. Five years later, he received divine instructions to become a full-time Prophet. The twelve years that followed the first revelation were spent in Mecca and the verses revealed in this period are very different in content from those that come afterwards in Medina, a town a few hundred miles away. The later verses are more specific and grounded in the particular concerns of seventh-century Arabia while the earlier ones concern the universal questions that men face. The years in which these verses were revealed were not easy for the Prophet. The pagan Meccans persecuted his small band of followers and they were beset by financial troubles. In 619, the Prophet lost his wife and his uncle-surrogate father, Abu Talib. Over the next couple of years, his life was threatened and he was driven from his hometown and took refuge in the oasis city of Medina. Ten years later, after another set of revelations, a triumphant return to Mecca and the consolidation of an Arabian empire, he was dead. The glorious years of victories against the world's great empires came later. In the time of the Prophet, the champions of the faith were a small, rag-tag group on the run. The world of Islam was confined to oasis communities, desert valleys and battles between warring tribes.

All this for me was a revelation. Many of the hard facts from the Prophet's personal life make their way into the Book and Traditions. 'Islam has many rules about this world,' Abdullah had said to me in Turkey. 'We say that for a person who is a Muslim, the religion will have something to say to him at every second of his life.' This was one aspect of the faith's 'completeness', its detailed control of the believer's life from his personal habits to his food choices.

In Arabia it was possible to see these commandments as organic, suited to the place, the way Hindu ritual can seem in India. And it was their old tribal past that the Prophet had in mind when he gave the Arabs their religion, a well-balanced reform of the existing way of life and of which the pilgrimage to Mecca, a pre-Islamic custom common to all the warring tribes of Arabia, was an abiding symbol.

Even though the Prophet's family had been custodians of the Kaba, it was not his first choice as the new religion's direction for prayer. Thomas Patrick Hughes wrote, in the nineteenth century,

At the commencement of Muhammad's mission, it is remarkable that there is scarcely an allusion to the Ka'bah, and this fact, taken with the circumstance that the earliest Qiblah, or direction for prayer, was Jerusalem, and not the Ka'bah, seems to imply that Muhammad's strong iconoclastic tendencies did not incline his sympathies to this ancient idol temple with its superstitious ceremonies. Had the Jews favourably received the new prophet as one who taught the religion of Abraham, to the abrogation of that of Moses and Jesus, Jerusalem and not Makkah would have been the sacred city, and the ancient Rock and not the Ka'bah would have been the object of superstitious reverence.

But the Jews did not welcome the Arabian prophet. Mecca itself only came in the last years of his life. In 629, the idols were still there and the Prophet, according to a treaty with the Meccans, was permitted a visit of three days. At noon, on one of the days, his companion, the slave convert Bilal, climbed on to the Kaba and sounded the first Muslim call to prayer. The next year, the Prophet and his armies occupied Mecca and destroyed the idols in the Kaba. It was then – two years before the Prophet's death – that the ancient pagan pilgrimage common to all the tribes of Arabia was recast in an Islamic mould. Hughes continued, quoting Professor Palmer's Introduction to the Koran:

> Here, then, Muhammad found a shrine, to which, as well as *at* which, devotion had been paid from time immemorial; it was one thing which the scattered Arabian nation had in common – the one thing which gave them even the shadow of a national feeling; and to have dreamed of abolishing it, or even diminishing the honours paid to it, would have been madness and ruin to his enterprise. He therefore did the next best thing, he cleared it of idols and dedicated it to the service of God.

This was another revelation about the pilgrimage to Mecca: it had very little to do with Islam and everything to do with Arabia. It was a pre-Islamic Arabian custom refashioned by the Prophet to unite the Arab tribes and celebrate the fathers of their race, Abraham and Ishmael.

And, just as it was possible to imagine Islam as organic in

Arabia, it was possible to imagine it as alien in places where the faith went. Hybrids would have formed between Arabian Islam and the cultures of the places to which the faith spread. Cultural Islam was the result of these mixtures and it was this, rather than the letter of the Book, that was followed. This Islam, with its mysticism, its tolerance, its song and poetry, its veneration of local saints, often common to Muslim and Hindu in India, was the religion that gave me the string I wore round my wrist. But in modern Saudi Arabia, this type of worship felt like a religion apart from the literalism that was followed. The dark, fleshy pilgrim had approached Hani and Kareem expressly to state his objection. Hani had replied to my weak defence: 'Don't say that. That's even worse. The Wahhabis hate Sufis.'

But even in Arabia it wasn't always like that. The historical events that had made our short exchange possible were also behind the growth of a more global, literal Islam.

In the first years of the nineteenth century, the Wahhabis invaded Mecca. Most of the Hejaz region at the time was part of the Ottoman Empire and the Sultan was perturbed by their success in the region and by the doctrine they propagated. Its founder was Muhammad ibn Abd al-Wahhab, who had made a religious and political pact with Muhammad ibn Saud, a local chieftain and ancestor of the present Saud family, half a century before. The objections of the Wahhabis were to the excesses they felt had come into Islam, indeed to cultural Islam, and taken it away from the pure simplicity of the Prophet's example. In the years they controlled Mecca, they attacked sacred shrines, superstitions, idolatry and luxuries, such as silks, satins and Persian pipes. They attacked shrines like the one from which my string had come, places of music, dance, amulets and comparatively tolerant, flexible doctrines. At the time these attacks were taking place, a large part of the Muslim world would have known faith of this kind.

The Wahhabis' stern rules led to a sharp drop in the number of pilgrims to Mecca. Soon after, they seized Medina, the second of the holy cities, and their reforms were so complete that even the Prophet's tomb, with its ornate dome, was destroyed. The Ottomans at last sent a strong army to retake the holy cities, and in 1818 Saud's descendant Abdullah, who had become the Wahhabi leader, was executed in a public square in Istanbul. After that, the Saud dynasty and the Wahhabi doctrine seemed to vanish for nearly a century, and when the Englishman Wilfred Blunt wrote the *Future of Islam* towards the end of the nineteenth century, he described the Wahhabis as characters from the past:

I believe it is hardly now recognised by Mohammedans how near Abd el Wahhab was to complete success. Before the close of the eighteenth century, the chiefs of the Ibn Saouds, champions of Unitarian Islam, had established their authority over all Northern Arabia as far as the Euphrates, and in 1808 [*sic*] they took Mecca and Medina. In the meanwhile, the Wahhabite doctrines were gaining ground further afield. India was at one time very near conversion, and in Egypt, and North Africa, and even in Turkey, many secretly subscribed to the new doctrines. Two things, however, marred the plan of general reform and prevented its full accomplishment. In the first place, the reform was too completely reactive. It took no account whatever of the progress of modern thought, and directly it attempted to leave Arabia it found itself face to face with difficulties that only political as well as religious success could overcome. It was impossible, except by force of arms, to Arabianise the world again, and nothing less than this was in contemplation. Its second mistake, and that was one that a little of the Prophet's prudence, which always went hand in hand with his zeal, might have avoided, was a too rigid insistence upon trifles.

It was strange now to be in Arabia, more than a century later, and to see that the Sauds and Wahhabis had triumphed. Once again the doctrine had wide international reach, once again it sought to Arabianise if not the world, then the Muslim world, not by force, but by the tremendous wealth at its disposal. And here, once again, I was being pulled up for trifles.

Blunt, writing then, was more forgiving. He saw in Wahhabism similarities to the reforms brought to the Christian Church. He felt that an 'unquiet attitude of expectation' had been an 'unintended result' and 'that Islam was no longer asleep'. A 'wiser' Wahhab, he thought, might 'play the part of Loyola or Borromeo with success'.

An 'unquiet attitude of expectation', Islam 'no longer asleep' but the Wahhabis stronger than ever: these were the mixed, but still potent, still pregnant ingredients that, more than a hundred years later, made the passion, zeal and inevitable frustration in the Muslim world seem as though it was on the verge of some undisclosed outcome. The Muslims themselves, more religious than the rest of the world, closer to the idea of a precipice, gave the impression that something had to give. But what Blunt saw as a failing then was a failing now too: literalism instead of reform.

On the train back from Beeston, I had felt short on Islam, that the small sense of being a Muslim with which I had grown up was not enough. Now, mid-way into my journey, after Turkey and Syria, after much time spent with men of faith, I no longer felt that my idea of the religion was a great negative space. I now had a detailed sense of how the faith's injunctions on dress, food, worship and individual behaviour, as well as in the context of family and society, could form a complete way of life. But learning more about the faith had also extinguished my interest in it. I didn't believe any more that knowledge of the religion, especially its Book, could explain its modern revival. Men like Butt and Abdullah and the people I met at Abu Nour had re-found the faith, but even they thought more about the 'world system' than the Book. And men like my father, who couldn't have been further away from the Book, stood up in surprising ways to defend the faith. So I felt that if I were to understand these emanations of modernity, I would have to look outside the closed circle of faith. And for this I would need a wider view of the societies I travelled in.

It was also for this reason that I felt Mecca had been a wrong turn: Mecca was about faith, faith and tribal Arabia. For the second part of my journey, the journey away from Arabia, through Iran and Pakistan, I didn't feel I needed to be among people of faith. It was more interesting to see how Islam worked on men and societies in ways deeper than the faith, to see how it worked on men like my father, and on countries like Iran where Islamic revolution had redrawn the landscape.

*

After we finished the re-enactment of Hagar's search for water, Hani's Lexus met us directly outside. The Meccan barbers were sitting there and cut a symbolic strand of my hair, bringing the visit to an end. A mood of fatigue and inadequacy hung over our small group. Though full of clues for the journey ahead, it had been a sad, ill-advised undertaking, a wilful misstep on my part, embarrassing for us all. Hani apologised for it not having been a very orthodox *umrah*. I thought of my father who had also performed an *umrah* but hadn't worn the towels;

he had done it in a suit. I apologised for not being a very orthodox candidate. Kareem asked if I would do the *hajj* with him the following year. I thought he was joking, then saw he was quite serious. I wasn't sure if I would, but I was happy to be asked.

It was hard not to be affected by the fraternal attitude of other Muslims towards me. Having grown up without the faith, I was perhaps more aware of this. In a sense, being seen and treated as a Muslim because my father was Muslim constituted the biggest part of whatever Muslim identity I had. My father was also Pakistani, but that didn't automatically make me Pakistani, even in the eyes of Pakistanis. But being Muslim was a different matter.

We took the curved, descending road out of the city. Mecca was quieter now, its lights dimmer. A corresponding gloom grew in the car too, interrupted by flashes of street-light. Then, just before the city limits, I saw two golden arches with no Islamic influence.

'A McDonald's?'

'Yeah,' Kareem said. 'A Muslims-only McDonald's.'

# PART II

## Stranger to History

'That's Tehran,' Mr Sadeghi said, 'if you can see it through the pollution.' I couldn't. The sun was at a tilt and seemed to make solid the brown skin that hung over the city. The vague shapes of sunlit buildings lost their outlines to the wobbly vapours of heat and haze. There were snow-capped mountains in the distance, above the film that covered the city, and their soiled edges, like dirty bed sheets, produced a special squalor. We came in from the south and the girdle the mountains formed in the north made Tehran seem like a city built in a crater.

'Tomorrow will be clean. It's the birthday of Muhammad,' he sniggered, 'the Prophet of Islam.'

We passed a great golden dome with minarets, bronze now in the murky light.

'What's that?'

'It's Khomeini's . . . Khomeini's whatever,' Sadeghi said, his tired, drooping eyes lighting up. 'Khomeini's palace,' he added, with a chuckle, pronouncing it with a French accent.

With his education, Sadeghi should not have been driving a taxi. And at his age he should not have had to drive more than four hundred kilometres to Isfahan that morning to pick me up, and then the same distance back. But when he told me he had been an economics student in India when the revolution happened, I realised I had misread his age. The lines in his face, the droop of his cheeks and his pulpy, lidded eyes made me add fifteen years to his fifty-something. His master's in economics was interrupted by the revolution. Like many Iranians he came back to take care of his parents. He started a garments business with a friend, but it failed within a few years. 'I had problems with my partner,' he said in a barely audible voice, 'but, besides, those were difficult times for business. It was the time of the war.'

A varied scene opened up before us: apartment buildings with murals of martyrs in poppy fields from the Iran-Iraq War in the 1980s; a detailed digital gauge showing red levels of pollution; a green plastic cactus and a neon-orange coconut palm; a network of highways choked with traffic; and a mismatch of four- and five-storey buildings. Some had reflective silvery squares between blue borders; others were colourless and rectangular with dusty aluminium windows. One rust-coloured giant grew outwards from a circular base and had no windows except a thin, hidden strip at every level. As the city went north, the buildings grew taller. There was more reflective glass, mostly ice blue, sometimes black, and many clusters of white towers. Nothing seemed old, nothing especially modern, nothing particularly Iranian, nothing so Western; it was a bleak, unplanned vista without landmarks, a city on the edge of history, free of the stamp of any one culture, free of design, guided only by human multiplication. Urban snobbery was written into its geography. It was built on an incline: the rich lived at the top and the poor at the bottom where the pollution seeped deepest.

The traffic was hypnotic. The overspill from the main arteries, tar gashes with lush traffic islands, reached the avenues, and from the avenues, the smaller streets, so that the city seemed always either paralysed or spasmodic. At the traffic-lights where we waited for many minutes, I rolled down the window and let in the warm, smoky air. A girl walked by, wearing huge oval shades with a yellow and black polka-dot headscarf. The only other flashes of colour came from yellow taxis and pink buses.

I had been delayed by my travelling in Arabia, then by the two-week-long Iranian New Year and lastly by my journey north to Tehran from the southern city of Shiraz. It was April, and I had a month-long tourist visa.

My relatively trouble-free experience in the Arab police states – Syria and Saudi Arabia – made me feel that my work could be done more easily than I had thought. I had managed to fly under the radar in these countries, and so long as I didn't ask about politics or approach people connected with the state, a renewable tourist visa had been the best way to operate.

An Iranian journalist friend lent me his flat, leaving his keys and mobile phone with Sadeghi. It was off Shiraz Avenue, a road devoted to bathroom fittings. Down its entire length, and even on the streets leading off it, all the shops sold gold-plated taps, four-spray shower heads, shallow basins, toilet seats, cisterns and bowls. It seemed impossible, even in this city of fifteen million, for demand to match supply.

The flat was in a large building complex, overlooking the city on both sides: mountains, some greenery and taller buildings in the north; low, boundless sprawl and smog to the south. Around me, there were cemented rooftops with a busy organisation of air-conditioner exhausts, blue coolers on stands, television antennae and discreetly positioned satellite dishes. Besides the congestion, the roar and the greyness of Tehran, something else, like a drone, an alloy of noise, fumes and concrete, tapped against your equilibrium. It was a city you longed to turn off or escape. The only visual respite, indeed the only reason for building a city in this spot at all, was the mountains. Below, but for three feet of wretched green water in the deep end, the building's swimming pool was empty. Graffiti in red, on the boundary wall, read, 'Life = A Sexually Transmitted Disease'.

*

For me, even in those first few days, Tehran was addictive: a modern crisis city, full of energy, anonymity and menace. It was also a city full of talk. Summer was on its way and there were rumours of girls rounded up for not being correctly dressed, cars stopped for playing Western music, raids, confiscations, a general tightening of the belt. At the same time, the news carried reports of women being allowed to enter stadiums for the first time, despite the religious men in Qom creating an uproar about it. The regime was keeping people busy interpreting these mixed messages.

My guard was down in Tehran for no other reason than that the Iranians I met spoke openly and freely, and were so trusting that I stopped feeling as if there was anything to be worried about. In Syria, even people I knew for weeks remained guarded and never spoke in public places or on telephones. But in Iran, people not only seemed to speak without fear, they seemed to take special pleasure in the volume of their dissenting voices. On the way north, a student I met at the university in Yazd relished telling me, 'Our revolution has expired.'

This mood suited my ambitions. I was at a turning-point in my journey. Rather than meeting specific people of faith, I wanted to gain a sense of what kind of society the Islamic Revolution had created. I wanted to know what the desires of men such as Butt and Abdullah looked like when they were realised in a larger, more macro sense, when they became more than just voices in Manchester and Istanbul. I also felt that this would be a preparation, or rather a coalescence, for the second part of the challenge my father's letter had presented me: to know Pakistan better. But first, I wanted to meet a man who had made good under the Islamic Republic.

\*

Muhammad Rahimi was twice as old as the Iranian Revolution. The first half of his life was spent under the Shah, the second under the Islamic Republic. Like my driver Sadeghi, he had been a student in India. He attended the Indian Institute of Technology in Delhi, a highly competitive university, in the late 1970s – interesting years in India, cataclysmic years in Iran. His level of involvement in the events of 1979 was unique. He was politically active, had been anti-Shah, and when the revolution came, he was part of a small group of Iranian students in India who took over the Iranian Embassy in Delhi and proclaimed the new Islamic Republic. Nearly a quarter of a century later, he was a private-sector businessman who had thrived in the post-revolution years. On paper, he was a sort of golden child of the Islamic Revolution.

I knew very little about his student years when I met him on one of my first days in Tehran. The building he owned, in a stylish section of town, and the dark, wood-panelled board-room where I waited for him, showed signs of his prosperity. At even intervals, there were framed photographs of ricefields in Bali, desert sunsets in Arizona and other natural vistas. Muhammad came in wearing a tan linen jacket over a blue shirt. He was large and pale, with a goatee and a warm, jovial manner. His easy self-confidence and personal style, the finely made gold glasses he wore and his diving Breitling spoke of his success. I had known him as a child in India, and his warmth and laughter were what I remembered about him.

I had barely reintroduced myself when the conversation turned to politics, and the summer crackdown on women's dress. He screwed up his face and became serious: 'We were more moderate before, under the Shah, but it is still a moderate country and will be again when this regime is gone.' To hear him speak in this way, knowing he had supported the revolution, brought an unsettling personal note to the remark, like listening to someone you hardly know speak of a family feud.

'I hear this a lot,' I said, 'talk of when the regime is gone. Do you think it will happen soon?'

'It is the younger generation who will change it,' Muhammad said, 'and they could do it very soon, even in, say, one or two years. But the foreign powers mustn't intervene. If they don't, it will happen very soon. If they get involved, these guys will stay because they will be able to unite the people. They mustn't do here what they did in Iraq.'

There was a strong air of the self-made man about Muhammad and perhaps this, along with his political past, reminded me of my father. He spoke in a lecturing way, a little pleased with himself, certain of all that he said. The conversation created a premature intimacy between us. Then he seemed embarrassed to have begun on so serious a note. He suggested we walk to a restaurant for lunch and ushered me out of the boardroom. The quiet side-street where he had his office led on to the city's main avenue, Vali Asr – where I would find myself again for less appetising reasons, in the days to come. For now it was painted in the spring sunlight that came in patches through the *chenar*s, the Oriental plane, a magnificent tree, redolent of the Kashmir Valley, with a broad canopy and leaves like the hands of a child. At one end of Vali Asr were the mountains, so close that morning that they seemed part of a film set. The avenue was lined with coffee shops, women's clothing stores, small businesses, hotels and embassies. It also housed the Discplinary (*sic*) Force of the Islamic Republic of Iran. On certain nights cars would collect in a line along the avenue and car-flirting would begin. It was a Tehrani activity in which carfuls of boys rolled past carfuls of girls, looks were exchanged, smiles, paper chits, and if the bearded men showed up, the scene scattered.

The restaurant was called Bistango. It was down a short flight of stairs, a smart, well-lit place, with crisp white tablecloths, heavy glasses and peach-coloured wallpaper. The manager knew Muhammad and, greeting him warmly, seated us at a table in the centre of the room. Muhammad scanned the other tables quickly, as people do when they're having lunch at a place where they're used to running into people they know. The other diners were mostly older men in dark suits and I could almost have felt I was in a corporate lunch place in mid-town Manhattan. It seemed natural to reach for a wine list.

I hadn't seen Muhammad since I was a small boy in India, but when he said he had returned to Iran in 1980, between revolution and war, I realised I must have known him as a visitor to India, and not when he was living there. In 1980, the entire Muslim world was in spate: events from the year before – the Soviet invasion of Afghanistan, the attack on the Grand Mosque in Mecca and the execution of Zulfikar Ali Bhutto – would bring a decade of political Islam sponsored by the Saudis, Pakistani intelligence and the CIA.

'So, right in the middle of things?'

'Yes.' He smiled, as if surprised himself by what an eventful year it was. 'Seven days after I came back the war started.'

The war with Iraq became the instrument by which Khomeini was to enforce the Islamic Republic, eliminate all opposition and extend the war into the carnage it became. Half a million Iranians died. It was started by Saddam Hussein and prolonged by Khomeini. The Iraqis, backed by the Americans, lost half a million people too. Those numbers, and so recently, had to be remembered; it was the event that touched people's lives even more than the revolution.

But 1980 was still a year of possibility in Iran: the Shah and Savak, his vindictive secret service, had gone the year before; a wide political spectrum was still in play; the religious regime had not begun in force and some even believed that Khomeini might step down now that the revolution had come.

'If I had entered politics at that time,' Muhammad smiled again, as if withholding a secret, 'I could be at the level of a minister now, you know. The guy who's the foreign minister today was also Indian-educated, but I realised from an early age that politics was a very dirty business and I never wanted to enter it.'

Muhammad returned to Iran with an Indian wife and a small child. The foreground of his young life mapped perfectly on to the drama of Iran's revolution and war. But despite his own success, financial and personal, against the toughest odds, he became disenchanted with the revolution he had proclaimed in India. Looking at me from deep within his finely made glasses, he said, 'You know why we had the revolution?'

'Why?' I asked, after some silence, in which his mood seemed to change from combative to maudlin.

'Because the people had nothing else to do,' he said. 'There was so much money from oil that even a teacher could take his family on a tour of Europe. The people had everything. Every one of us students had scholarships to go abroad for university. We didn't understand the meaning of any of it! The Shah was introducing democracy. We thought democracy meant standing outside his palace yelling, "Down with the Shah!" We were moving too fast. The Shah considered himself a modern man and he was moving the country too fast with President Carter behind him, yelling at him to go faster.' Muhammad had been one of the people outside the palace, yelling, 'Down with the Shah!'

'You know I spent forty-five days in prison here under the Shah?' He grinned, relishing the surprise it caused. 'Yes – because we stormed the Iranian Embassy in India and took the ambassador hostage. There was a student demonstrator who had come from Iran to India. The Iranian government wanted him and had asked the Indian government to extradite him to Iran. So we broke into the embassy and took the ambassador hostage in his office.

'The ambassador swore to us,' Muhammad went on, after a dramatic pause, 'in this fatherly voice, on his dignity and honour, that it was not him who had issued the extradition order. He said it in such a nice and fatherly voice that we believed him. We let him go. There was nothing we could have done anyway. We didn't have any guns or knives or anything. Only after we had let him go did we get hold of the records of who had issued the order.' He paused again. 'It was him!

'Some time later, I was at a celebration in Tehran and I saw him. He saw me too and sent for me. When I went up to him, I reminded him that it had been me in the embassy that day. He said, "I know."

'"Why did you swear on your integrity and lie?" I asked him. And, do you know what he told me?'

'What?'

'He said, "Politics does not understand integrity. Take my word for it, you have a bright future ahead of you. Stay out of politics." Before I left, he said to me, "If you're ever in the same situation as me, please remember my words."

'I was so angry!' Muhammad cried, reliving the feeling from that time. 'I went around saying, "Our leaders are terrible."

'It was only later,' he said, a touch of sadness entering his voice, 'when the revolution happened and we stormed the

Iranian Embassy . . . It was me who suggested we do it, by the way, and declare the revolution. You know we held the embassy the entire night until the Indian government recognised the Iranian revolution. That night I was around people who were drinking and partying; the next day they stood at a formal ceremony in front of the embassy reading the Koran! It was then that I remembered what the ambassador had said to me.'

He stopped to gauge my reaction and, perhaps feeling I had misunderstood him, glowered at me. 'I have nothing against drinking – but then to stand there and read the Koran! I didn't stay. I told them that my university was very hard and that I had to go back. It was then that I decided to stay away from politics.'

Muhammad was shocked that the religious revolution had been a cover for something else. I was less surprised. Before the revolution, Iran was bombarded with a wide distillation of foreign influences, the onslaught of the world beyond. Very quickly that world came to be linked with Tehran nightclubs, half-dressed women on television and the excesses of the Shah and the wealthy Westernised circle around him. It was oil money that brought the sudden wealth to Iran, and yet Iran was not Saudi Arabia; it had a significant educated and professional middle class; its collapse was not easily explained. Neither, once the old system was dismantled, were the religious ecstasies and retreat that followed.

But hearing the innocence of Muhammad's story, it was possible to believe his description of the almost childish wilfulness with which the world was taken apart. I was not nearly as appalled as Muhammad by his fellow revolutionaries drinking at night and reading the Koran the next day. But for Muhammad, who might truly have believed in the faith as providing the guidelines for a new world, this was the first wrong step. It was as if what had been rejected would always have been more

128

powerful than what was meant to supplant it. But could any Islamic Utopia have been pure enough? His idealism, his religious idealism increased my eagerness to see the country the revolution had created.

In Muhammad, that idealism had been replaced with a kind of Islamic doubt, a world of cobwebs, oil companies and the foreign hand; a suspicion about the work of men. The Iranian Revolution happened in part as a response to this meddling foreign hand, but even now, after the country's closing off, he felt it had not been complete enough; he still felt his country was being played with.

'You know,' he said, 'we had everything, but I sometimes wish we hadn't had oil because that brought all the attention from outside. Even now with this atomic-energy business, the Chinese and Russians support the government because they want oil. The Americans have put up with this Ahmadinejad because he makes it possible for them to play a role in the region.'

'You think he's their guy?' I asked, with some wonder how Muhammad could believe that the Iranian president, Mahmoud Ahmadinejad, the man who with every passing day came to seem like America's nemesis, was an American stooge?

'One hundred per cent,' Muhammad replied. 'You have to look at his political career. Where did this guy come from? Nowhere. Nobody supports what he says. Wipe Israel off the map? Who are we to wipe Israel off the map when even the Palestinians haven't been able to do it?'

Seeing the scepticism form in my face, Muhammad said, 'It's like when I was sixteen and in love with a Christian girl. I wanted to get to know her so I arranged with my friend that he would push her. The plan was that when I saw this I would slap him, and like that I'd be able to get close to her. So, when the moment came I really slapped him hard and the girl and I became friends.'

The friend in the story stood for Ahmadinejad, Muhammad for America and the girl for Iran.

'This is how it is with America,' Muhammad went on. 'They need a problem in the country so that they can get involved.'

'But isn't the president in Iran just a puppet of the mullahs?' I said, playing along.

'Yes, but they're in with the Americans too,' Muhammad returned.

'You think Khomeini was?'

'Absolutely. Otherwise, how did he fly into the country on a private plane from Paris? We have such a great country,' he spat, 'but it's just this bloody politics.' It was remarks like these that could make conversations in the Islamic world seem to contain an element of fantasy.

Then, with no warning, Muhammad asked me if I knew who Cyrus, the classical Persian king, was. It was a shift in conversation that reflected the extent to which the new regime was a reminder of old, historical wounds.

'The Achaemenian king? Yes.' Cyrus the Great in the sixth century BC founded what became a vast global empire, the first of its kind, and whose further expansion led to the legendary wars with Greece.

'Cyrus two thousand five hundred years ago had laws that today are displayed in the United Nations!' Muhammad exploded. 'He set out human rights and said that no human being has the right to enslave other beings. This was two thousand five hundred years ago! And these mullahs try and tell us that if the Arabs hadn't come and saved us we'd be eating ants now.'

Muhammad was talking about much more than politics now. I was amazed by the freshness of this fifteen-hundred-year-old history, resurrected by the Islamic Revolution in Iran. The awareness Iranian Muslims had of the time before Islam, and their conversion, didn't exist among the sub-continent's Muslims, most of whom believed they came with the Muslim invader.

Muhammad spoke with such passion about distant history that it seemed his words contained some other, hidden meaning. In Bistango's air-conditioned seclusion his tone, and not his actual words, seemed to speak of a more real and closer threat.

'And you know what's worst?' Mohammad cried. 'They burnt our libraries and books. They tried to kill Farsi!' he ranted. 'Avicenna was a Persian writing in Arabic!'

Returning finally to the regime, he said that in textbooks they were shortening the country's pre-Islamic history. 'And this is what I always say,' he continued, his voice dropping. 'The youth of today are strangers to their history. I met one of the people from the regime the other day – they had invited me to represent the private sector – and I told him that you can't make the youth strangers to their history. You can't build a country like that.'

In the end, he came full circle back to despair. But his earlier urgency and the hint of hysteria in his voice lingered. They took hold of this last idea of his, haunting as it was, of being estranged from history. And from this big, jovial man I had not expected so abstract, and shrill, a cry of loss.

# *Rupture*

A pact of secrecy had made my parents' relationship possible, but soon after they went to Dubai, leaving me with my grandparents in Delhi, this pact began to unravel. News of my birth was travelling.

In Dubai, there was a false alarm. My father was cooking dinner when his sister's husband walked up to him and said, 'How's Aatish?' My father dropped the pan he was holding and recovered himself only when he realised that his brother-in-law didn't in fact know of my existence, but was using my name – not normally used to mean 'fire' in a banal sense – to check the stove's fire.

But soon after, real transfers of information began. Uncles of my mother who had been at the reception in Delhi went to Lahore for a rare school reunion at Aitchison College where they made enquiries about the Pakistani she was said to have married. My father's eldest daughter, a teenager by then, heard about me from an aunt and confronted him. Until that point, my father might have believed he could lead two lives. He had said to my mother – in that time before mobile phones and email – that there had been no contact between the two countries for so long, why should there be any now? But as news spread, my father, more determined than ever to be in politics in Pakistan and knowing it would be impossible with an Indian wife and half-Indian son, began to lose his nerve; and, as secrecy unravelled, so did my parents' relationship.

After they had spent a short time apart, my mother rejoined my father in London, bringing me with her. She found him changed. He was colder, more aloof, and as she walked about their flat off Baker Street, she saw from the long, black hairs strewn around the place that he had had an affair. It was a public affair with a well-known Indian actress, and my mother felt sure that he had wanted her to find out about it so that she would end their relationship. Many years later, my father's sister told me he had written to the papers himself to publicise the affair. He wanted his relationship with my mother to seem like part of the excesses of a Pakistani playboy, rather than a serious involvement with an Indian woman. He calculated correctly: his affair with the Indian actress ended their relationship.

My father left, and my mother and I stayed on for a few months at the Baker Street flat. They saw each other only a few times after that, once formally to decide what would be done with me. My father's approach was 'Either you take him or I do, but it must be a clean separation.' My mother was clear that she would have me, but she hadn't anticipated how ugly things would become over money. My father had given her a thousand pounds, but when she wrote to him asking for more, he accused her of being a 'bottomless pit'.

By 1982 my mother, still in London, was borrowing from friends. She sold the diamond earrings her grandmother had given her – one of the few family heirlooms to survive that sudden departure in 1947 – at a shop off Bond Street. In the spring of that year, my father let her know through a mutual friend that she had to leave the Baker Street flat. 'Where should I go?' she asked.

'I don't know,' the friend replied, 'but you have to go.'

My father had told her that the flat had been bought for me, and at first she resisted leaving, even changing the locks, but when he threatened to inform British Immigration of irregularities in her visa, she gave in.

By the summer, she had moved back to Delhi and my father to Pakistan. Soon after, he was married again, and the following year he had the first of three more children. What I heard of my father over the next two decades came from my mother. She supported us with her career as a political reporter in India, covering secessionist movements and terrorism, first in Punjab and later in Kashmir. Because she was a political journalist we followed my father's progress across the border closely, through multiple imprisonments in the 1980s, to the restoration of democracy and Benazir Bhutto's landslide victory in 1988, to the failed governments of the 1990s and his eventual exit from politics. His fears of being politically harmed by his connection to me were perhaps real, and despite our separation, his opponents would distribute copies of my birth certificate to undermine his bid for election.

It was during the years that I was growing up in Delhi that I had my first questions about my father, but like so much else about that early absence, they were lost in confusion and laughter. One day, my second-year teacher telephoned my mother, concerned that I was suffering from some kind of emotional disturbance. When my mother asked her why she felt this, she said I showed a tendency to tell wild, obviously untrue stories. My mother pressed her and she said she had asked the class what their fathers did for a living and I replied, 'My father is in jail.'

'It's absolutely true,' my mother said, and left it at that.

Then, aged seven, I met a friend of my mother's, and discovering his name was Salman, asked him, to my mother's great embarrassment, whether he was Salmaan, my father.

We lived at first on our own in a small terrace flat, for which my grandmother paid the rent, and later with my grandparents in the small house, past the flyover, from which I would go to the Lutyens bungalow on the *neem*-lined avenue.

When I was very young, my mother explained her separation from my father in terms of a fight with a friend, not unlike those I had routinely with my friends. When my questions became more sophisticated, she told me about his political career and how it would have been impossible if we had been in his life. And though I didn't have a good impression of my father, I don't think I had a bad one either. My mother was always very clear about who he was. She supported my interest in meeting him, and made sure that I saw the Pakistani friends they had in common whenever any came to India. She seemed also for many years, and I don't know how I know this, still to be in love with him, or at least thought of their relationship, as the big love affair of her life. She often said, 'Sometimes people come together for a reason, to create something or someone, and then they go their own ways.' This made me think, at least when I was child, of my father's departure as something unavoidable for which no one was to blame. My grandfather, of course, made it seem like just one more chapter in the Partition saga he had lived through.

When I was eight or nine, I wrote my father a letter, expressing my desire to see him, which I sent with my mother to Pakistan where she was covering the election. 'If I see him, I'll give it to him,' she said, 'but be prepared that he may not reply. What will you do if he doesn't?'

'I'll leave it and never get in touch with him again.'

As it happened, with my mother covering the election and my father contesting it, they did run into each other. My mother gave him my letter. He took it and told her he would reply, but never did. And for years I made no effort to contact him again.

## The Tyranny of Trifles

At the start of my third week in Iran, I sat with Muhammad's son, Payam, in the food court of a mall. The regime had taken away a friend of his.

'Disappeared?'

'Yes, for one year.'

The mall had been shut down by the government for promoting 'mingling', but had recently reopened. Its top floor had brightly painted walls and brushed-steel chairs and overlooked a park. It seemed to commit no more offence than offering bad world cuisine, but I soon saw that it attracted undesirables in the Islamic Republic. As we came in, an effeminate boy in low jeans and a black tank top, with spiky hair, dozens of earrings and glittering blue mascara kissed three times a more discreetly dressed figure with greasy coils. They giggled at the entrance for some minutes, then vanished into an alcove. The Islamic Republic had put homosexuals to death and it was in little glimpses like this – from a yellow and black polka-dot scarf to my driver, Hussein, insisting I play 'Like A Prayer' from my iPod at top volume as he rolled down his windows – that I saw gestures of dissent every day in Tehran.

'Yes, there was a student demonstration,' Payam continued, 'and he just happened to be in the area. He wasn't taking part, just buying something nearby. They started rounding up students and they took him along because he was there. His family, his friends, no one knew where he was.' Payam was an industrial-engineering student in his early twenties. Unlike his father, he was quiet and soft-spoken. He had large, sorrowful eyes and dark skin, inherited from his Indian mother. He seemed protected and young.

'And then, a year later, they just released him on a road somewhere. He's so scaredy now, he doesn't go out after seven. He's scaredy of everything. He told us what they did with him.'

'What?'

'They would make him and the other guys stand in a half-filled pool of water up to their waists. Then they would put on a cooler, an air-conditioner, over them and if they moved out from under it, they would hit them . . .' His English wasn't good and he reached for the word. 'With cables,' he said unsurely.

'Where is he now?'

'He's in Tabriz. He's so scaredy of everything. He came back really thin. He used to have perfect eyesight. Now, he wears glass that are this thick.'

Payam left half an inch between his thumb and index finger. I asked if I could meet his friend and he said he would speak to him, but he thought there was little chance; he had become paranoid. Listening to Payam, I was struck by how unlikely a character he was to be near a story like this. In another country, it would be possible to describe him as a nerd or even a mama's boy, but in the Islamic Republic, no one's innocence was spared. Everyone had stories like this.

In Syria, I felt that when the faith was made to explain aspects of the world beyond its circle of completeness, such as how rights and judiciaries worked in a modern society, it could force the faith into trifles. I also felt that it could force the faith into hypocrisy. But I was really saying the same thing: that when the faith was made to understand a world that was beyond its grasp, a world that could feel like an affront, for reasons other than faith, it could end up, as it imposed its simplicities, in doing the little right at the cost of committing a greater wrong.

But while Abdullah in Turkey was just one man, and Abu Nour in Syria just one mosque, the Islamic Republic was an entire country that had been passed through an Islamic filter. The emphasis on trifles, and the hypocrisies that came with it, had been institutionalised, turned into a form of control over the people who posed the greatest threat to the republic: its young.

In my optimism, I had missed something important. When I saw that Iranians were no longer looking to religion to solve their problems, I concluded that they were on a healthier path than other Muslim countries I had visited. But though the mosques were empty in Tehran, though I hardly ever heard the call to prayer, never saw a woman fully veiled or a man with a beard, unless he was a government man, the revolution had not been kind; it had brutalised its children. And where religious feeling had departed, new psychoses had crept in. People had been twisted. There were small signs of this as I made my way up from the south, but it was only after seeing Tehran and the shrill panic it could awaken, that it was possible to know how bad the revolution had been.

\*

Amir only ever wore black. He wore loose black trousers with a collarless black shirt. His hair was long, as was his beard, and he wandered about barefoot. We shared a taxi one day and the driver asked why he was wearing black.

'For me, every day is Ashura,' he replied, referring to the tenth and most bloody day of the Shia mourning.

Amir was a film director and lived with his beautiful actress wife, Anahita, in a small house in a residential colony in northern

Tehran. The couple were part of the country's loudest collective dissenting voice: its film industry. Over the past two decades, it had produced some of the strongest films anywhere in the world. But the industry, which grew in the brief spring it had been allowed under President Khatami, was now being suppressed. Ahmadinejad's government had given permission for no more than two or three films in the last year and Anahita's most recent film had been shot without permission, secretly, in Kurdistan. 'I feel as if I'm starting to censor myself,' she said, her almond-shaped eyes widening. 'My thinking is changing. I don't think of things outside the censorship because I know it won't be possible. It's terrible because I know that this is what they want.' We sat in their small, cluttered kitchen. Its colourful cabinets, little stove, solitary table and weak light from bulbs and candles gave it a protected atmosphere. A big spring night came in through an open door that led onto a paved veranda. Anahita, her thick black hair in a plait, talked between preparing yoghurt, kebabs, salad and Iranian smoked rice.

Amir poured us red wine and a newly invented cocktail called Whisky Albaloo. Alcohol was banned in the Islamic Republic, but could be bought fairly easily through bootleggers and in grocery shops once they knew you. 'The people suffer from a kind of schizophrenia,' Amir said, 'because in the day even a little girl has her head covered in school and has to learn about religion, but when she comes back there's no religion and she takes her headscarf off.' I realised I had heard the same words in reverse from Abdullah in Istanbul. 'For example,' he had said, 'I would go to school, and Atatürk was in school, just in school. Outside there was no Atatürk.'

'Have you seen the mosques?' Amir said. 'They're empty except for a few people and Basiji. People use them as bathrooms!' The Basiji were a militia of young Iranian men whom the regime allowed to enforce religious morality. 'They're like a different species of people,' Amir said. 'If you look in their eyes, they seem like a different species. We call them *Homo Islamicos.*'

Anahita's father was a theatre director whose plays the regime suppressed. On one occasion the censors showed up three hours before his play was to go on and made him perform the play, itself three hours long. When it was over, they proposed cuts and revisions. He said he couldn't possibly introduce them at this late stage. They said he would have to or they would stop the performance. The actors did the best they could, but the regime's inspectors were not pleased and during the interval, the theatre owner appeared to say that there had been a power cut. The director turned to his audience and asked if they would mind the actors performing the rest of the play in the dark, using light from candles and torches. There was a roar of approval. But the owner declined, stating a security risk. He turned them out on to the street where they saw that the entire neighbourhood, but for the little theatre, had lights.

Amir told the story not to show artistic repression in the Islamic Republic but to point out the sophistication of the regime's methods. 'You say Syria is a police state,' he said. 'In Iran, they've planted the police state in our heads.'

A candlelit sadness lingered in the kitchen as Amir and Anahita spoke. My heart went out to the young Iranians I met. Anahita described Iran as a place where she felt she kept hitting her head as she tried to grow: 'There is no appreciation for what I do here, no appreciation, and that's why I'll have to leave one day.'

I didn't think she would. Her resistance was like a kind of addiction. It would be difficult to feel as worthwhile elsewhere. And, besides, there must have been some appreciation because everyone knew her name. For people with no outlet, it was a different matter.

\*

In Tehran, I reconnected with Reza, a young vet I had met on my journey north. He was a light, jovial character with floppy black hair and teeth that clambered over one another, but when he spoke of the Islamic regime, his lightness vanished. 'It'll be the death of this religion at least in Iran. Seriously, if they continue like this, religion in this country is finished. Do you know how many spiritual groups are cropping up now? There are Hare Krishnas, a man who teaches the *Mahabharata*, three hundred followers of the Sai Baba. People understand they need spirituality, but they are sick of this religion.'

Hare Krishnas in Tehran! I couldn't believe it. In the Islamic Republic, and in Islam, to convert out of the religion was apostasy, for which the sentence is death. I couldn't believe people would take risks like that. What interested me was not the rejection of faith – I had met many Muslims without faith – but the potential rejection of its political and historical character.

Reza roared with laughter when I said I wanted to meet the Hare Krishnas, making me think I had fallen for an elaborate joke. But then he assured me that the Hare Krishnas did exist and said he would speak to his friend, Nargis. He warned me that he thought her teacher, Gulbadi, was a fraud. 'He teaches celibacy!' Reza cried. 'The whole country is exploding with sexual frustration and he teaches celibacy!' A few minutes later he rang again with Nargis's number, saying she was expecting my call.

The voice on the telephone seemed much older. It was slow, languid, and though the words came, there were no extra words, no colloquialisms, to iron out the discomfort of a first conversation. Nargis wanted to know what my project was, and though I was happy to tell her, I was nervous for her sake and mine about speaking on the telephone. We arranged finally to meet at her flat early the next morning. She said she would speak to the taxi-driver and explain where to come.

For the rest of that day a sly, superstitious uneasiness crept up on me, as if I had been right to be nervous about talking to Nargis on the telephone. It began at a lunch appointment with Violet, a half-German, half-Iranian ex-journalist who came to me through the Rahimis. I had found no equivalent in Iran of Eyup and Nedal, the students who helped me in Turkey and Syria, and I was beginning to need help, especially as I planned to travel to the religious cities of Qom and Mashhad in the next few weeks. Violet had been a reporter in Iran for a major Western news agency for many years and I thought she might be able to suggest someone safe and reliable.

I met her at her house in a dim room with heavy carpets. She was a pale, watchful girl, who had spent the last few years surrounded by sickness and death. She and her German mother had nursed her Iranian father who, after many months of illness, had just died. Violet was still finding her feet, still seeming to take solace from the endless duties that arise when someone dies. She had quit her job in the hope of writing a book, but found herself too tired and 'burnt out' to begin. The story she wanted to tell was semi-autobiographical and linked to other Iranian women's stories, but the material was sensitive and she didn't have the strength for it. The other reason she had left her job was because after 9/11 her employers pressured her to come up with certain angles and stories that amplified the dangers of radical Islam. It had been too much of a strain. I felt more than her fatigue in her: in that low, dark room, still heavy with the late presence of death, I felt her disturbance.

In the taxi on the way to lunch she asked me not to talk because it made her feel sick. She rolled down her window and looked out. We passed Vanak Square, at this hour crowded with buses, taxis and pedestrians. Even in bright sunshine, Tehran had a vertical, gassy quality; the light didn't burn away the city's black edges, or its fever. Violet stared at a green patch in the middle of the square, then turned to me and said she could recall when public floggings happened there; they had stopped under Khatami. It was hard to graft that image onto the square: it was so ordinary and congested, like a bus terminal. There was special menace in thinking of that desert cruelty transposed to the drab, municipal atmosphere of Vanak Square, with its crowds and traffic.

We went to an air-conditioned windowless restaurant decorated with mirrors and Persian scenes of banquets and the hunt. Once we sat down, Violet became more relaxed. She said she knew a few people she could call about my work in Tehran. She suggested Jasib, a young Iranian who had worked with her at the press agency. She said that when he arrived he had been very religious and conservative, but had opened up at work and improved his English. He was now working night shifts at another news agency and she thought he would be an ideal guide for me.

As she described her work as a journalist in Iran, I began to feel that Violet, with a foot in and a foot out of the Islamic Republic, was even more damaged than the people whose stories she recorded. She was over-exposed. I could see why she was having trouble with her writing. She was like an artist who had begun a creative work that took more and more out of her until she was too implicated in it to continue. She covered the 1999 student protests, which had led to a severe crackdown from the regime. Earlier that morning I had driven past the dormitories where it had taken place. I had wanted to stop but it was forbidden. The regime's men had forced students to jump from their windows and the site had become an unmarked memorial to those who died. 'They had thought a revolution would happen,' Violet said, 'and basically it didn't. They counted on Khatami coming out in support of them, but there was just a neutral statement from his office. It was very disappointing.' Violet added that though many felt Khatami hadn't gone far enough, a great deal was accomplished in those years, especially in the area of press and individual freedom.

Jasib called while we were still at lunch. Violet suggested a few coffee shops and restaurants where we could meet but he insisted on a public park. We paid and left the restaurant. A taxi took us down an avenue, then on to a long, quiet street running next to the park. We stopped in front of a small kiosk that sold internet cards, chocolates, soft drinks and magazines. The park at this mid-afternoon hour was quiet, except for a few lone figures strolling down its paved paths. The foliage, still new and bright green, seemed almost to glow against the blackness of the branches.

I wandered up to the kiosk and was looking at an Iranian magazine with an Indian film star on the cover – the always amazing reach of Bollywood – when Violet gestured to me to come over. A man on a bike had dropped off Jasib, then driven off without a word. Jasib was a large, friendly man, heavyset and broad-chinned, but nervous. He smiled and looked behind him, smiled and scanned the street, the park and the kiosk. He managed to say hello to Violet in Farsi, but could hardly focus enough to greet me. I put out my hand for him to shake, but he offered me his wrist. He flicked his thumb up for a second; it was covered with blood. The sight of blood, breaking the afternoon stillness, made me recoil. Jasib kept shrugging his shoulders and smiling. I focused on his thumb. I had assumed at first that he had cut it on the bike, but now, as I looked closer, I could see that the thin stream of watery blood was not coming from a clean gash but from a cuticle; it was the worst I had ever seen. A whole piece, about a millimetre thick and wide, was bitten fresh from a torn cuticle.

His nervous, unfocused manner, interrupted by unprovoked bouts of laughter, made me uneasy. Also, his English was not good enough to interpret. He could barely understand me and was trying to hide it by answering me with a quick phrase, a nod, a laugh, then a full sentence in Farsi to Violet.

Violet looked sternly at him. She had insisted I keep up formalities and call him Mr Jasib. 'Mr Jasib,' she now said herself, 'you haven't been practising your English. It used to be much better.'

'No!' he said, with emphasis to imply fluency, and smirked awkwardly. Then, picking his words carefully, he said, 'It – wasn't – better.' His large, ungainly figure shook with laughter.

'Yes, it was!' Violet scolded. 'That was why I suggested you for this work.' She seemed to be speaking more to me than to him.

'I didn't promise my English was perfect!' he burst out.

'No, the fault is mine. I thought it was much better. You haven't been practising, Mr Jasib,' she said again, in a tone of matronly reproach.

Turning to me, she said that it was a shame about his English because his contacts, especially in Qom, were very good. I made a last attempt to explain my interest in Qom, the Islamic Republic's clerical capital. I could see he wasn't following so I stopped.

'I'm sorry,' Jasib murmured, like an overgrown child about to start writing lines. 'I am very sorry I haven't been practising my English.'

In the car on the way back, I said, more out of politeness than sincerity, that I wished it could have worked because he had seemed ideal otherwise.

Violet's pale face became serious. 'You know,' she said, 'I'm beginning to think he wouldn't have been. In fact, I think it's a good thing it didn't work out.'

'Why?'

'You have to watch these guys very carefully to see if they change when they join these agencies. Once the government knows they're working for foreign publications, they come to them for information. Did you notice how agitated he became when you were putting your number into his phone?' I did remember. He wrote down the wrong number so I corrected it and entered my name. He had jumped at me. 'What are you doing?' he exploded. It was one of his few fluent sentences. 'And his insistence,' Violet said, 'that we meet at a park. It's very strange. You see, they can't obviously go to the foreign journalists so they go to these guys.' I couldn't understand why Violet, if she had known all this, hadn't warned me of this in advance or met Jasib on her own first.

It was almost evening now. I was seeing some people for dinner and wanted to do some exercise at the gym I had just joined. I got out of the taxi and caught another one to Shiraz Avenue. Violet gave the driver clear instructions on how to get there. He nodded as she spoke, then, looking over his shoulder, stared with aimless intensity at the roaring street behind him. He was a lean man in his twenties. He wore a loose shirt through which his hard, wiry frame was visible. His collarbones were exposed and jutted out, seeming to hold up the rest of his bent torso. His eyes were small and sunken with a vacant polish, like billiard balls, and his stubble, though almost a shadow, was black against his unhealthy skin. He looked at me for a moment, thin-lipped and smiling, as if he knew me from before.

Once we were moving, he said in English, 'I don't know where Shiraz Avenue is,' and laughed. 'These women are driving me crazy.' For some reason I thought he meant a private domestic situation, but I soon discovered he meant the women of Tehran. On the heavily trafficked avenue, his eyes fixed on a pretty, made-up face under a light pink and blue scarf in a nearby car. She was worn out by the traffic delays. Her head rested against the car door and her delicate wrist hung out of the window. As soon as the traffic moved, the driver inched his car up to hers and slammed noisily on the brakes, making her look up.

He asked her where Shiraz Avenue was, but as she collected her thoughts to explain to him, he leered at her. He was uninterested in what she said, and when the traffic moved, he made a sucking sound and a kissy face and drove on. He drove fast, in an unsettling, predatory manner so that he seemed almost disappointed when his risk-taking did not cause an accident. After the first woman, there were one or two more. All the time, despite his speed, he didn't seem to know where he was going. I began to question him. He dismissed me with a nod. Then, absent-minded, his eyes scanning the traffic, he found himself channelled on to an exit for a multi-lane highway.

Sloping, grassy traffic islands came into sight, the familiar tall buildings of the avenue fell away and the road veered up ahead. Now I knew we were going in the wrong direction and raised my voice. He nodded and braked, causing the cars behind us to erupt into angry honking. Then already fifty metres or so up the exit ramp, he rested his arm on the seat, turned to face me and began reversing into the oncoming traffic. I started screaming at him, but his face was expressionless. He ploughed through the traffic, the other cars now as hysterical as I was, honking and swerving to avoid him. People rolled down their windows and hurled abuse at him as he went past, but he seemed untouched by their anger. His face, after the leering and the frustration, was serene, as if he had found the release he was looking for. When he reached the point where the road had forked, he swung the car back on to the avenue.

I called an Iranian friend, explained what had happened and passed the driver the phone. He spoke to my friend and now seemed to know where he was going. He made a few swerves, a jolting progress down an avenue, and soon a familiar blue-glass tower came in sight, the row of mountains swung to the right and before long we were going past bathroom-fittings shops on Shiraz Avenue. When we reached the multi-storey concrete blocks where my friend's flat was, the driver asked for no more money than we had discussed. He just looked on as I paid him, one arm on the wheel, distracted again, frustrated, of a piece with the traffic.

I had barely arrived at my friend's flat and was checking

emails when the phone rang. It was a friend of Jasib. He spoke fluent English with an American accent, rattled off his CV and said he was the official stringer for ABC News in Iran. 'I had a seminary training myself,' he said, unprompted, 'so I've been good for a lot of sensitive stories. I think because you're writing on religion Mr Jasib suggested me.' His constructions seemed to be from Farsi, but the language came easily to him.

'Where did you learn English? Did you live abroad?' I asked.

'No.' He laughed a cheesy American soap-opera laugh. 'I've not had the opportunity to go abroad. I learnt my English right here in Tehran.' He pronounced it Teh-*ran*.

'How old are you?'

'Thirty-six.'

I thought Violet should speak to him first. He said he'd call her and get back to me. I went to the gym, and by the time I returned to the flat, its windows showed a dark sky with bright city lights beyond.

I was in the shower when the phone rang again. The cordless lay on the bed and I came out to answer it. It was the translator. He said he'd spoken to Violet, and began to give me the names of some people he'd worked with. He mentioned Jeremy someone from a news agency, then Daniel Pearl.

'Daniel Pearl?' I said, feeling a sudden chill.

'Yeah,' the translator breathed, in his American fraternity accent, 'and then he went off to Pakistan and got himself killed, which wasn't so cool.'

Daniel Pearl, of the *Wall Street Journal*, had been beheaded in Pakistan while chasing a lead. His story was among the most grisly in recent memory. To hear it referred to in this casual, artificial voice, here in Tehran, scared me profoundly. It was fear of my own inexperience, of coming into a milieu of foreign journalists and stringers with dark cameos that I knew nothing about. I wanted to get off the phone. I had no taste for the journalist's thrills, not even a good writing style for it. I thanked him and put down the phone. For the first time since I arrived in Tehran, I was aware of being alone in the flat and of its quiet, broken by the cyclical groan of a lift.

I called Violet back. 'You know, I don't think he should be working for anyone,' she said. Apparently he had also worked for an old news-agency chief who was forced to flee the country with his wife, who later wrote a book scattered with suspicious Tehran characters. He was banned now from working with anyone other than ABC, and Violet assured me that he was watched.

She could tell she had unsettled me and asked if I would like to come over for some take-away food. I cancelled my other plans and went because I thought I might feel more at ease if I could go over the day with her, the day with its ambiguous sense of danger and unexplained premonitions.

That night in Violet's drawing room, lampshades casting low-voltage parabolas across the walls, she began to tell me a story from when she was a child in Tehran.

Her parents had gone out to dinner, leaving Violet and her sister alone at home. The girls had a white West Highland terrier called Emily, and after their parents left, they took Emily for a walk. The streets around the house were quiet and residential. They would have been familiar to Violet, and walking the dog was a nightly ritual, which held perhaps, the possibility of bumping into neighbours. But that night the moral police were patrolling the streets and came down Violet's.

When they saw Emily, their car stopped and a few men got out. Dogs, according to a Tradition, are unclean animals, but while the Tradition only discusses how many times a vessel should be cleaned if a dog drinks from it, the Islamic Republic incorporated the Tradition as another aspect of its tyranny of trifles. The men, despite appeals from the sobbing girl, arrested Emily.

Violet would not let the car go. One of the men said, 'It's

either you or the dog.' If they took Emily, they said, they would kill her. Just as the girls surrendered the little West Highland, an uncle or a friend appeared. He knew how to speak to the men and succeeded in arranging a bribe for the dog's life. The weeping girls went back into the house with Emily. That night, Violet said, perhaps thinking only of the bribe and not of herself, 'I wrote in my diary, "Tonight was my introduction to corruption."'

People made corrupt, people stunted, twisted, criminalised by the tyranny of trifles. That was what the faith had become available for in Iran. The faith that Abdullah described as having something to say to the believer in every second of his life had been turned against the people of Iran; the regime used it to deal obsessively, almost voyeuristically, with the private details of people's lives. Though Iranians had not known the great machines of socialist and Fascist repression, they knew a subtle, daily harangue. That it was conducted in the name of Islam was a great pain: the people's deepest allegiances were used to subdue them, their religion turned to nonsense. It left a terrible vacuum. The young, who suffered most, didn't remember a time when Islam was not in the hands of the Islamic Republic. The Book was not clear on the varied meanings drawn out of it. As in the case of dogs, some obscure Tradition, locked in the context of the Arabian oasis, was used to control everything from satellites to hairstyles, music, dress, socks and even elbows – in the worst days, men had been pulled over for wearing T-shirts because their elbows were considered attractive to women. At a time when people might have needed religion most, a hybrid of the world's two most pernicious varieties, the bureaucrat and the cleric, was in charge of it.

\*

It was pouring the next morning when I went to see Nargis, spring rain washing clean the city's smoky air, its sooty buildings, making the fumes vanish in swirls of cold mist. The traffic was worse than normal and I spent many minutes behind a green van with 'yah Mahdi!' written on the back. We were on an avenue festooned with political slogans.

'Imam Khomeini's supporters are always supporting Palestinians and fighting their enemies' was painted in white letters on a black background next to an American flag and a blue Star of David. Then we passed a powder-blue mural on the side of a grey building with blue-glass squares on the front. Half a dozen young faces with short beards, some smiling, others wistful, one with spectacles, gazed over the street. A huge billboard several feet high showed the famous Palestinian mother suicide-bomber against an astral background that made her look more like an astronaut than someone entering the afterlife. The words below said: 'My children I do love, but martyrdom I love more.' The Islamic Republic enjoyed provocations.

Nargis lived in a small flat in an angular white building, five or six storeys high. It was on a narrow street, with hardly any traffic, and large over-hanging canopies. She waited for me on her landing as I came up. In her twenties and strikingly beautiful, she had tight coils of thick black hair, bronze skin, round, slightly bulging eyes and a slim body, with heavy breasts. She wore a white net sweater with a purple skirt, and bits of turquoise dangled from her ears.

It was very early in the morning and I felt a little confused to enter a flat painted mauve, powder blue and beige with streams of incense smoke rising rapidly into the air. The room was full of things from India: little colourful stuffed birds and dolls, chimes, Krishna cushion covers, a standing rack of clothes with glass and stitch work. Hindi phrasebooks and India Lonely Planet guides lay about; a Krishna temple had been constructed near the kitchenette. Electronic music played in a monotonous cycle in the background. Nargis wandered into the kitchenette and put the kettle on for tea.

It was easy to see the effort that had gone into making the flat a cheerful place. Nargis was someone with an idea of how she wanted to live. She had realised this as fully as it was possible to do in the little space, down to its colours, the fittings, the choice of stone for the kitchen counters. There was a touching attention to order, detail and the *objets* from India that made the place distinctively hers. My feeling for it must have come in part from hearing that it had been ransacked not so long ago. It was only when I thought of the little flat's plants ripped up, its temple broken, the clothes thrown everywhere, its careful, new-age serenity overturned, that I was moved by the optimism with which it had been restored.

'They didn't like us having a satellite dish and receiver so they broke into the building,' she said, eyes wide, reliving her surprise at their arrival. Tehran was full of satellite dishes and the crackdowns were more a moneymaking enterprise than a concerted effort at stopping their spread. 'They came in and broke everything,' she continued, looking about the place as though making an inventory of what 'everything' meant to her. 'When they began to search the flat, I said, "If it's the satellite dish you want, then take it, here." But they said, "Maybe you have guns or something." Then they took my husband and made him spend the night in jail. We had to buy his lashes. Forty lashes. The government has a little package.'

'Buy his lashes': the phrase brought back the feeling from Vanak Square, the anachronism of Islamic punishment, so clearly outlined in the Book, and its savagery amplified by the modern bureaucracy that dealt it out. Her husband managed without faith, but Nargis, naturally inclined to spiritual quests, rejected it for a philosophy derived from Hinduism. Nargis grew up in a religious family. Her mother was a believer and her aunt a servant in one of the most sacred mosques in the country, the Shrine of the Imam Reza in Mashhad. It wasn't easy for Nargis to reject Islam. 'She cries for me,' Nargis laughed, speaking of her mother. 'She doesn't understand why I would worship what she thinks of as pieces of wood. She tells me she prays that I won't go to hell.'

'What drew you to Hinduism?' I asked, watching her put teabags into mugs of hot water.

'Before we were Zoroastrians,' she said, 'and that is so close to Krishnaism and so far from Islam. Both use nature. Krishnaism is more natural in its eating, its culture. It uses the sun and the moon, and for me that is so much more comfortable than the government's version of Islam where they just do whatever they want and say it is Islam.'

Nargis was too open, too spiritual in a real sense, to damn any faith, but she couldn't have gone on with the republic's religion. The tea made, she stared at it vacantly, and shrugging her shoulders, said, 'Real Islam is not like what we have in Iran. We have Shiite Islam here, which people made after the Prophet, and it's totally different from the real Islam. During Muharram [the Shia month of mourning] we have half the Muslims celebrating and the other half beating themselves and crying. It confuses me. Just because some people did something fifteen hundred years ago we don't have to go on doing it. Shias don't like to be happy, they prefer to be angry.' My amazement made her smile. One really needed to come to the Islamic Republic of Iran to hear a Shia Muslim speak in this way. The ability to look hard at your own faith, to reject it, to consider another: I sometimes thought I must have travelled through a good part of the Muslim world in search of this intellectual openness and not found it until now. It made it possible for Nargis to think of herself as once Zoroastrian and to care as much about Tibet's freedom as Palestine's; it made it possible for her to overcome the agony at the deaths of Ali and Hussein; it freed her judgements from the motives of faith.

Gulbadi, her teacher, had reached her through vegetarianism. He gave cooking classes in extreme vegetarianism in which eggs, onions and garlic were prohibited as well as meat. Nargis didn't seem to know it, but the diet was classically Jain, a derivative religion of Hinduism that practises extreme non-violence. For fear of the regime Gulbadi devised an ingenious way of reaching people – ingenious because the emphasis on eating meat, especially red meat, was part of the culture of the faith, part of its seemingly limitless compass. And yet, vegetarianism was not prohibited; it was just unusual for Muslims. Gulbadi, knowingly or not, walked the finest line between the commandments of the faith and its culture. He drew people to his classes who, if considering extreme vegetarianism, would in all likelihood have also had doubts about Islam.

'What is the punishment for apostasy?' I asked Nargis, who was watering the plants now. I was trying to broach the subject of the risk she took in embracing 'Krishnaism'.

Her eyes showed white. She looked at me in disbelief as if *I* were considering this path. 'In Iran,' she whispered, looking up from a money plant, 'they kill you for it. If Muslims change their religion, they are killed. They believe here,' she added, by way of gentle explanation, 'that Islam is the last religion, so if you are a Muslim, you have the best religion. That is their mentality.'

Nargis slipped on a white muslin 'manteau', a long coat with buttons down the front, and threw a purple scarf over her springy black hair. She was ready to take me to meet the other Hare Krishnas. We went down to the ground floor in a very small lift, then raced across a cemented driveway in the rain. Nargis drove a jeep, which was parked in the street. The sight of her wet, white manteau clinging to her, the coils of black hair pushing up the purple scarf and the dark, delicate Nargis behind the wheel made me wonder if we weren't committing some kind of offence; cars had been pulled over for much less.

The rain made the traffic worse and I stopped paying attention to where we were going. On a busy main road, Nargis veered left and parked at the side. A gushing open drain, clean as ever, divided the main road from a narrow service lane. Nargis moved stealthily across the lane. I followed her as she slipped behind a black gate on to the paved drive of a low, double-storey bungalow with tinted sliding doors. The rain fell lightly around us and there wasn't a sound. It was still very early and it felt as though everyone was asleep in the house. We made our way round an empty swimming-pool in the garden towards the sliding doors. Outside them, on a veranda, were the first signs that the house was not asleep: dozens of shoes and sandals were strewn about.

As Nargis approached, the doors opened and we were ushered into a dark anteroom by a tall, smiling man with a short grey beard. The little house was crowded, and after the silence outside, I suddenly found myself in a warren of rooms alive with murmurs, chanting and clashing cymbals. My eyes had not adjusted when I lost Nargis. The man who showed us in took my wrist and led me into a blue room with a dim green chandelier. Inside, forty or fifty people sat, rotating rhythmically, in front of a painting of the blue god, his head cocked to one side, a peacock feather in his crown. At one end of the room, two women in white, one with a drum round her neck, were singing and gently rocking forward and back on the balls of their feet. 'Hare Krishna, hare rama' went through the room again and again. Some faces watched the women, feeding off their ecstasies, others looked ahead at Gulbadi, a little bespectacled man with a greying crew-cut and a youthful face, chanting behind a low desk with a book on it. Outside, through the tinted glass doors, the garden was quiet and wet, revealing nothing of the warmth and throng within.

From Nargis, I had gained the impression that the Hare Krishnas would be like her, young, rebellious, slightly new age.

But the faces I saw in the blue room were nothing like what I expected. Though there were several young people, there were also older women, mothers and wives, some fully covered. On the other side of the room, I saw balding, middle-aged men, who looked like bankers and shopkeepers, in beige trousers and checked shirts, with gold rings on their fingers. The average age of the men was well over forty. Somehow the middle-aged, middle-class aspect of the crowd, the men's slightly embarrassed faces, brought vulnerability to the group – the vulnerability of people making a great change late in life. As though submitting to some hidden desire, balancing something that felt right yet seemed wrong, they let their voices catch the increasingly rapid pace of the chanting. One or two eyed me with suspicion. The energy between Gulbadi's chanting and the two musicians was building.

The room was covered with stylised pictures and icons in vivid colours, of Swami Prabhupada, the twentieth-century founder of the Hare Krishnas; of Krishna as a child playing with butter; Krishna, in a Bollywood-style love scene with his girlfriend, Radha; Krishna with his flute; Krishna in grand format; Krishna in a small, makeshift temple with fake yellow flowers placed outside; and, most significantly, a picture of Narasimha, the god Vishnu's half-lion, half-man incarnation tearing to pieces a king who won't allow his son freedom of worship. It was not an image I had seen often, even in India, and I couldn't help but think that its presence in Tehran was Gulbadi's own private stab at the Islamic Republic.

Gulbadi, caught up in a chanting fever, was now hardly able to separate consonant from vowel. The 'Hare' had gone and the blue god's name was now just a breathy whisper: 'Krish-na, Krish-na, Krish-na, rama, rama, rama.' Just at the point when it seemed the momentum had to break, it got faster and louder. I was watching Gulbadi when someone walked into the room behind me. It was the expression on his face, of fear and resignation, that made me turn. I saw a tall man, with a stoop, and a short, salt and pepper beard, come in and sit down. His entry coincided with Gulbadi upping the ante: 'Krishna, Krishna, Krishna, rama, rama, rama, Ali, Ali, Ali, Allah, Allah, Allah.'

What?

I didn't know it then but the man who'd just walked in was the regime's spy. Gulbadi had been closed down, put in jail, faced court trials, but he hadn't given up. The Islamic Republic, at last, acting always with the subtlety of which Amir had spoken, decided to use him rather than silence him.

Soon after his arrival, the chanting died down and Gulbadi began a sermon in Farsi. I got up and went to find Nargis. A number of people were sitting round a dining-table next to a refrigerator, listening to the sermon; it was just an ordinary house when it wasn't a temple. Nargis was listening from just outside the room. When it was over, Gulbadi fielded questions. He made a comparison between Kalki, the final incarnation of Vishnu, who comes on a white horse to bring in a better age and the Shia Mahdi, who also comes on a white horse at the end of the world. A schoolteacher was asking if, perhaps, they might come sooner. 'No,' Gulbadi said, and Nargis translated, 'He must take his time.' With this, the meeting was dismissed and tea and sweets were served on the dining-table. Nargis took the opportunity to introduce me to Gulbadi.

He was nervous. He gave me a long, involved speech on how he hadn't rejected Islam. 'People in India ask me if I converted,' he said, 'but Prabhupada's instruction is about the love of God and he has many names. I am a Muslim, I love God and Muhammad. I didn't reject one for the other, I accepted them all.' Then he came out with what was really on his mind. 'He is a judge of the courts,' he whispered, looking at the man who had come in late, 'and a very Islamic person. He became interested in our classes. I had a case in the courts, but by his mercy he talked to the other officers and saved us.'

This was not quite true. The man was a government monitor.

On the way to Gulbadi's vegetarian restaurant, Nargis told me that the judge often disrupted Gulbadi's sermons by saying that Islam was superior to Krishnaism and suggested books that showed how the Koran was more powerful than the Bhagavad Gita. That morning his presence led Gulbadi to make an energetic sermon cast in Hindu terms against democracy, America and the material world. 'How can they bring democracy when they don't even have it in their own countries?' he had asked. 'They are in passion, and passion makes anger, which makes war. That's why America makes these wars against Afghanistan and Iraq.'

Gulbadi's vegetarian restaurant was on the veranda of an attractive red-brick building, near the embassies. This was an older part of town, with wide boulevards and low, heavy bureaucratic buildings. The old American embassy was just next door, its walls now covered with vivid, anti-American murals and slogans, the faint outline of its defaced crest still visible at the gate. Houshmand, a friend of Nargis, had joined us. He was a slight, fine-featured student with dark, intelligent eyes.

'In this country, the government can do what they like,' Nargis explained, referring to the earlier episode of the government spy.

'Did Gulbadi switch to saying "Ali" because he came in?'

'You can make this connection,' she laughed.

Houshmand looked at me intently. Minutes ago he had also been laughing, telling me how they had picked up his brother and given him a full eighty lashes because they had found a picture of him at a party from the year before in his car glovebox. 'We have a thousand experiences like this. Maybe I do a business with the government and make them whips for lashing.' Now, becoming serious, he said, 'You must understand the difference between the real Islam and what you see here, which is not Islam, and the real Muslims and these Muslims you see here. All religions try to give you inner peace, but only a few intelligent people understand the real religion. Even with Hindus, you have the bad ones, who tell me to go out of the temple, but with our Muslim religion, we have more of a problem.'

'Why?'

They talked between themselves for a few seconds, Houshmand arranging the words he wanted to give me. Then he looked up and said, 'I think Muslims are more strict because, I don't know when this happened, they started to feel danger from other religions, maybe three or four hundred years ago. And the father started telling his son that you must fight the other religion and the son tells his son the same thing. And now, today, we have this.' Arm outstretched, he pointed at the city around us, still drying after the morning shower.

The 'other religion' was the growth of the West and the dates were roughly right: between two and three hundred years ago European powers, charged with new learning, grew stronger and Muslim empires everywhere began to fail. The faith's response was to retreat behind the purity of its Book and Traditions and to assert its simplicities more forcefully. Wilfred Blunt, writing in the interim between what seemed like the end of the Wahhabis and their resurgence in the twentieth century, had seen in their literalism a spirit of reform, but felt that their two mistakes, which were really the same mistake, were an over-insistence on trifles, the letter of the Book, and the attempt to Arabianise the world. But to be in Iran, and Saudi Arabia, more than a century after Blunt was writing, it seemed as though the trifles, rather than holding back the literalist imposition of Islam, had become the instrument by which regimes that sought to execute these programmes could control their population. But an entity like the Islamic Republic, perhaps many hundreds of years in the making, had, in imposing the modern tyranny of trifles, opened itself up to the charge of not representing the 'real faith' and, more importantly, of being mired in the corruption that lay behind the insistence on trifles.

*

Nargis wanted me to meet another friend, called Desiré. We drove over to her flat later that evening. Desiré was always in trouble with the regime, and within minutes I could see why: she was eccentric and outspoken. I could barely make out her features because her flat was in darkness. The whole place was lit with dim ultraviolet light. The walls were painted white and mauve, and the seating consisted of several fat saffron-coloured cushions. All the colours glowed. On the wall there was a huge painting from the Hindu epics of Krishna driving Arjun's chariot into war. Incense sticks burnt in the fireplace, a wide-screen Panasonic TV sat darkly on one side of the room, and under a reading lamp, the only real light, a DJ's mixing equipment was laid out.

Desiré was dressed in a red, sleeveless vest and tight beige tracksuit bottoms that followed her legs closely to the knee, then flared. Her hair was short, but with bleached dreadlocks tied into it. In another country, she might have gone to music festivals and raves, or hung about on beaches in Goa, been at Burning Man, or known full-moon parties in Bali, but in Iran the tyranny of trifles had made something of her. She was far too essential to their programme to be ignored and she, as if addicted to the attention, violent as it was, couldn't get away. They picked her up all the time, sometimes just for laughing in a public place. But the most recent episode had been the most serious.

Desiré spoke in a torrent of chaotic accented English, stray laughter and impassioned exclamation marks. 'So many times! So many times, I'm telling you!' she cried, when I asked her if she'd been picked up before. 'But the thing is that every time I knew how to get away. I look like a foreigner, I don't look that much like an Iranian, and so many times I would start pretending that I am French, that I am Indian maybe, too. I knew how to bribe them and talk to them, but this time it wasn't talkable.'

'Why did they come?'

'Because my friend and I, we wanted to go and party in Shemshak.' The place she spoke of was a ski resort north of Tehran. 'And my friend, she wanted some drugs, you know, and there was this guy who used to always come and give it to her. But this time he arrived at her house with the police because they had taken him.'

'This is the dealer?'

'Yes, they took the dealer and came to my friend's house, and they were there waiting when I arrived, waiting, talking, speaking to my friend. My friend had called before to say, "Come pick me up and we'll go party in Shemshak for my birthday." So I went to pick her up and suddenly I come in and see this guy with a gun to my head.'

'Was your friend also in the room?'

'Yes, they were searching her house when I rang the bell.'

'She didn't call to say don't come?'

'She couldn't! She can't! They don't let you do anything. So, anyway, they're standing there all rough and tough. You see, most of these people, they grow up in these houses without their mother and father . . .'

'Orphanages?'

'Yes. Or even if they have parents, in their . . .' she paused in search of the right word '. . . culture, beating a woman is very easy. From the time a boy is a little boy, the father says,

"Beat your mother," so he starts beating his mother, his sister, anybody. So, beating us is nothing for them.'

'Did they beat you?'

'Of course!' she said, with near-jubilation. 'Once we were in Shemshak. Nargis was there.' Nargis, sitting on a saffron cushion, looked over. 'We were walking,' Desiré continued, 'it was night time, and we were going from my house to Nargis's house. I had a car, but I just felt like walking. And a car, not even a Komiteh car or a police car, just a white Pride, came near us. We saw them, but thought they were these guys who say things to girls. OK? Suddenly we see four big guys come out of their car and come to take us. They take one of my friends and they want to put her in the car. She was like, '*Aein, aein . . .*' She emitted a girly nasal noise to indicate that she had put up no resistance. 'But I wasn't . . . I said, "Leave me alone! Don't touch me! Don't touch me!" I wanted somebody to help us because I didn't know these were police.'

'Were they Basiji?'

'No, no! They were so clean, in their white shirts, nothing. Normal people. I tell you, after that night I was scared of every-body because those men were so normal. You might even party in front of them.' Desiré said 'party' with special emphasis, drawing out the word, as if the world was divided into people who partied and people who didn't. 'We didn't know where they were from! I was scared that these were people who wanted to steal us and rape us, you never know! I was screaming, "Show me your paper, show me something," and they were like, with their big batons, beating us! Nargis was funny,' she chuckled. 'She's big, you know, so when they wanted to put her in the car, I was screaming, "Nargis, don't get in, don't get in!" So she put her hands up and they were pushing and pushing, but they couldn't get her into the car.' Desiré laughed out loud, and for the first time I could make out her features, her strong, square jaw, her red lipstick, her light, tanned skin. She was right: she could have been from anywhere. 'And they were beating me and beating me like hell!' She said it with so much energy and lightness that it didn't feel real.

'With a baton?'

'Yeah, with baton. I swear if I didn't do this,' she said, raising her arms over her head, 'I would be dead because my arms were black. Suddenly I saw Nargis was getting away and the baton guy was going to hit her on the head. I jumped in front of him because I thought maybe it would hit me somewhere but not on the head. So I jumped in front of him. I screamed, "Don't touch her, don't beat her," and I went in front of the Komiteh. Nargis was smart, she used that, and she started running. Running and running! The Komiteh was yelling, "Stop, stop," and she was running. I was yelling, "Run, Nargis, run, Nargis," and – and, oh, stupid Nargis! After running, she comes back! Running back! I said, "What the fuck is she doing? She's coming back!"' Desiré was reliving every second, laughing now, sipping vodka and cranberry juice with ice, standing in front of her refrigerator. 'She came running back to me, screaming, "Listen, listen, your car is there, I saw your car." I said, "Fuck the car, just run, man, run." And she was worried about my car!'

It was disturbing to hear Desiré speak this way. There was something hard and desensitised about her. She seemed to boast, her voice full of bluster; her eyes were frazzled and glassy.

'What did they want?' I asked, hoping to ground her story a little.

'It was a football thing,' she answered. 'Everyone was celebrating in the streets. There were so many people in the street and, oh, I think it was the time the Americans came into Iraq and TV programmes started to say something.' She meant the American-based Iranian TV channels that broadcast anti-regime propaganda to the Islamic Republic. 'And they [the regime] said,

"Fine. Wherever we go, we're going to do this." And that was one night in Shemshak that they did this.

'They knew that Shemshak was an easy pick-up for them. Anyway, Nargis ran away, I don't know, but she ran away. Me, I was getting beaten because I made her run away. They beat the shit out of me. I was numb. I said to myself, "Just cover your face and head." Their boss was down there and they were taking all the young people and they were beating them. They beat so many people that night, it was like, I can't tell you, it was like a disaster! They would scream, "Whore, you mother-fucker whore," and I was saying, "Oh, I get it, it's because your mother was a whore that you think I'm a whore. Don't fucking beat the shit out of me." And he would beat the shit out of me.' She laughed uproariously.

'I said to one of them who was beating me so hard, "Do you have a mother? Do you have a sister? Do you know that beating a woman like this hurts so much? Don't, please, have mercy on me!" And he wouldn't have mercy. I was bloody and down on the floor.'

'They must have given some reason? What do you think was their reason?'

'Nothing. They didn't have any excuse. They never have any excuse.'

'If you had to say . . .'

'They just wanted to show, "What's going on here? It's like Europe here? What is it? What is this? Girls and boys walking in the street, very cool, it's not possible here. You're not allowed to have fun. You have to always cry, beat the shit out of yourself and be in misery so they would love you." You're not even allowed to look nice. I had a nice picture of myself, I gave it for my passport. They gave it back! They said, "This picture looks nice, we don't take it." And they took such an ugly picture and they put it in!' Desiré laughed.

The regime was the biggest figure in Desiré's life; it seemed to consume her.

'I tell you,' she said, 'when they beat me, they pulled me on the floor because I couldn't walk any more. They dragged me by the hand and put me in the car. It was a bus full of young people crying.'

They had put up roadblocks and were stopping cars, making people get out. They went from door to door, raiding chalets. Nargis and Desiré said the police took thirty busloads of people to Tehran that night. Influence in Shemshak got Desiré off the bus, and one other thing, the horror of which must have registered on my face, because she said, with some anger, 'I am not a young person. Why? What did you think?'

I tried in the half-light to see her face more clearly. I had put her age somewhere in the late twenties, perhaps early thirites. But now as I looked closer, I could see that her skin was slacker than I first thought, and lined. She was forty with a son of twenty. It was not that she looked young; it was that her growth was stunted. She was an absurdity. She dressed and behaved like a teenager. Her whole life had been given to fighting for the right to party.

Coming back to her original story, I asked her what happened after the gun was removed from her head. 'Did they take you to prison?'

'No,' she answered. 'They told me to give names of people. And they had this electric thing, this shocking thing. They would put it to me and ask me to give names. I would say I don't know any names. They would say, "No?" and shock me. "If you want us to free you, you have to give somebody's name."' Desiré claimed she gave no names so they took her to her house and searched it.

'Did they find anything?'

'Of course, of course,' she smiled, more sedate now, 'grass, drink, satellite. Whatever's good in life is not good here in Iran, man. My house was not good! When I was in court, the guy was saying to the judge, "Judge, you have to see her house. I have to go and film her house and show you. If you see her house, you will give her six months in Evin."'

She was referring to Evin Prison, renowned for its cruelty both under the Shah and during the Islamic Republic. A trial of sorts followed, in which Desiré was allowed neither lawyers nor family. When her father came looking for her, he was told falsely that the trial was over and that his daughter had been given six months in Evin.

In the courtroom, Desiré was accused of making pornography and of living as a kept woman. Her accusers' vendetta was so obvious that the judge became suspicious. 'What do you want?' the judge finally said. 'Do you want me to stone her? Do you hate her so much?'

Five minutes later, Desiré's father walked through the door, furious at having been lied to. By this point Desiré had already spent four days in jail.

'They didn't try to get you out earlier?'

'You can't,' she said. 'Four days is nothing. That's the pre-prison. The real prison is Evin.'

'What were the four days like?'

'Oh, fine,' she said. 'It was dirty, there were druggy people, heroin people, vomiting everywhere. We were all in a small room, we slept together. The sheets were smelly and dirty, everyone was smelly and dirty. I was able to take a *hijab*, which was like a kimono, and I would crawl into that at night so that nothing would touch me.'

When she came out of prison none of her old friends would see her. They hung up the phone when she called.

'Why?'

'They were scared.'

'Of what?'

'That I would give their names. And because my best friend told everybody that I had given her name. She wanted to run away from Iran and needed an excuse. Afterwards I said to her, "What were you thinking? How could you do this to me?" She said, "I thought your ass was on it so a little bit more wouldn't matter."

'"What?" I shouted. "Do you know that little bit more was the worst part? You have to take pain away from me, not give me more!"'

'So I stayed home. I started not to call people. I started not going anywhere because I would go places and people would be uncomfortable. They would think I was working for the government. Because most of the time when they take you, if your punishment is a lot, they make you work for them instead. In this way you never know if your friend is an informer or not. Everybody becomes an informer. You have to be scared of everybody.'

I believed Desiré when she described this as the worst part, and yet I couldn't help but feel sympathy for her friends too. Not everyone was capable of Desiré's heroism, and one of the most treasured aspects of a state that didn't brutalise and spy on its own people was that it allowed people without a hero's courage to live with dignity, without the guilt of having betrayed friends from fear. Heroes, then, were saved for when they were needed, for truly heroic acts, and Desiré's heroism, if it was real, would not have been squandered on the freedom to 'party'.

'Why do you stay?'

'My land,' Desiré muttered. 'I don't know. It attracts me wherever I go. I speak French, I speak English. I am an English resident. I had a husband, my son is in England, some of my family is there. Everyone asks me, "Why are you here?" I go there, I spend time there.' Then, as if telling me a great secret, she whispered, 'But then I want to come back. Krishna always says, "Wherever you were born is your root, and wherever else you might go, you always come back.' She stopped, and those frazzled eyes glistened with a few stray tears. 'I don't know why. Shit, I hate it. But I'm comfortable here.' Then, choking with fresh laughter, she added, 'And it's not comfortable.'

\*

Desiré mentioned the word 'Islam' only once to me. At her trial she had asked, 'You don't know anything about me so how can you judge me? Is Islam something that has to judge people like this?' Houshmand also differentiated between the 'real Islam' and the Islam of the Islamic Republic. It was true that, as I encountered the Islamic Republic in the lives of its people, I made no separation between the republic's Islam and the 'real faith'. Did it really matter whether the Islam of the Islamic Republic was the 'real Islam' or not? Did it matter whether the socialism of Stalin or Mao was the real socialism?

The rush of sudden oil wealth, 'the country moving too fast', unstable, undemocratic governments interfered with by foreign powers: these were the components of the Islamic Revolution. This was what had mattered before the society was put through the Islamic filter. It was a distortion of the faith's rule now, always happier dealing with trifles, to shut out those questions and to choose instead to harass Desiré.

Even as I heard these stories, my own luck was running out. It was as if tales of this unseen regime made certain our meeting.

# Phone Booth

I didn't try to contact my father again until I was seventeen. I was in my last year of boarding-school in the hills of south India and about to go to college in America.

The school had been started by American missionaries in the early part of the last century and grew into a 'Christian international school', drawing a bizarre mixture of Midwestern missionaries and hippies who wanted to spend time in India. The school therapist was an old American hippie who had set up a peer-counselling programme that I joined. She trained us in one-to-one meetings in her sunny office near the chapel. Together, we would invent hypothetical problems and work through them, employing the methods of parroting, paraphrasing and open-ended questions to arrive at a made-up solution. She was a large, blonde woman, with protruding blue eyes and thick spectacles. She listened carefully to everything I said, her lips adjusting themselves over the braces she had recently started wearing to take in an overbite. 'I'm sorry, they still cut my mouth a bit,' she would say, if she saw that I was distracted by the movement.

On one of these afternoons, playing shrink and patient, I found myself recounting the real facts of my life to the therapist. I suddenly felt awkward, but found it comforting to talk to someone so removed from my life. I also liked showing off my surprising indifference to my father.

'But wasn't it difficult for your mother to marry a Pakistani?' the therapist asked.

'Oh, yes, it really was. She was a total outcast,' I exaggerated.

'That must have been hard for you to handle those social pressures at such a young age.'

'Well, yes, but I had a lot of support. You know, the Indian family system, so strong, so inclusive.'

'And what was it like to grow up in Indian society without a father?'

'Well, as my mother always says, it was the biggest favour he could have done me.'

'Who? Your father? Why does she say that?'

'She's only joking.'

'Oh, I see. Do you have any memory of him?'

'No, none at all. He jumped ship when I was two.'

'When you were two? And you never heard from him, no letters, no phone calls?'

'I think he wanted it to be a very clean separation.'

'And how does that work for you?'

'It's fine. See, the thing is that while a lot of children get messed up because of fathers that are there and then not there, for me the idea of a father never took root at all. And since these things are all social constructs, it's possible to do without them just as long as you get love and attention from somewhere else.'

'Uh-huh. And who were those people in your life?'

'Oh, lots.'

'Grandparents?'

'Yes. Grandparents, aunts, uncles, cousins. You're never alone.'

'Uh-huh. And now?'

'Now what?'

'How do you feel about your father today?'

'Nothing. I mean, the man is obviously a shit. He abandoned my mother with a baby to bring up on her own in India. Everyone gets shitty people in their lives. Some have shitty mothers or grandmothers, some even have shitty children. You take advantage of the good ones and let the bad ones find each other.'

'You seem to be very decided about it. How did you come to feel this way?'

The therapist had an awful way of depriving any experience of its uniqueness. I felt threatened by the equalising character of her questions. I realised then that the particularity of my story had been a refuge and that much of what I told her was related to the peace my mother had found, derived in part from the thrill of the cross-border romance, the love-child, the challenge and excitement of an unconventional life. These things could get her through, but they would never have been enough for me because they were not of my making. Rather than comfort me, they made me feel the absence in my life more acutely, as though someone else had lived and I hadn't.

The therapist's technique prevailed; the seclusion of her office was too great; for once I shrugged off my stock answers.

'And why,' she continued, 'leaving your mother's problem with him aside, have you not tried to contact him?'

'I honestly don't think my mother would like that.'

'Yes, but, Aatish—' She stopped.

'What?'

'No, I shouldn't. It's not for me to disturb whatever equilibrium you have come to. It's really moving to hear you talk with this resolve about what must have been such a painful side of your life, but I feel you must also consider yourself when you make this decision about your father. It is your right to know him. It is your right not to have to live with his ghost.'

The therapist chewed her braces for a moment. 'You are not betraying your mother by seeking out your father.'

'Oh, please, stop it. This isn't America. What am I going to do after all these years? Just call him and say, "Hello, Abba, this is Aatish"?'

'No, deciding the best approach is another matter. First, you have to be willing to address the subject.'

That day as I left her office I knew I would do it. Her words had binding force; it was harder not to act.

I took advantage of the free period after my meeting with her to go back to my dormitory. Everything felt vivid and new: the wooded road leading up to the dormitory, the occasional views of blue eucalyptus hills, the old colonial club where retired army officers gathered in the evening to play bingo. Why should this hill station in deepest south India, full of hippies and Christians, be the setting for one of the most important decisions of my life?

I slipped into the dormitory building without my housemistress noticing and went into my room. Leafing through my address book, I already felt a tinge of guilt. I was looking for the number of an old friend of my mother, an ex-friend, really, because he had remained friends with my father after the split. He was the friend who had asked my mother to leave the Baker Street flat. I chose him because my mother wouldn't find out. I found the number and scribbled it on to a phone pass. Then, to avoid coming back for another, I changed the 'number of calls' from one to two, and in place of my father's telephone number, I put the country code for Pakistan. It was all I knew of his whereabouts. I approached my housemistress who spent several minutes searching for her spectacles, then examined the pass closely.

'First call, England. And second to which country, please?' she asked.

'Ma'am, to my mother's mobile phone.'

'Mobile phone?'

'Yes, ma'am.'

'Mobile phones require international standard dialling?'

'Yes, ma'am,' I lied.

'Oh, God, please save us from this new technology,' she said, and signed the slip.

I made my way along the uphill road, past the chapel and the therapist's office to the telephone operator in the main administrative section of the school. There was a ten o'clock assembly and a degree of commotion in the normally quiet corridors. There were two phone booths: a cramped wooden one with graffitied walls and a naked yellow lightbulb, and a newer one with a window and stool.

I handed the signed phone pass to the operator and asked for the wooden booth. I was reading the graffiti when the phone started ringing. I answered it and the operator's voice bellowed, 'Trunk call from India. Mr Nath? Mr Nath?'

A sleepy voice answered, 'Yes.' I realised that in my excitement I hadn't taken into account the time difference.

The man, though surprised to hear from me, was friendly and gave me my father's number so quickly and with so few questions that it felt as though he had been expecting my call for years. I wrote down the numbers and apologised for waking him up.

The assembly was still going on when I left the phone booth. I walked in its direction hoping to find the therapist. I caught sight of her in a far corner, leaning against a pillar. When the assembly was over, I rushed up to her and asked if I could see her in the next class period. I would have to miss Hindi, but was sure I could get away with it. We agreed to meet back in her office in ten minutes.

Sitting again on the sofa in her office, I asked, with new purpose, the same question: 'So what am I going to do? Just call him and say, "Hello, Abba, this is Aatish"?'

'Well, first,' she began, 'it's important to establish that he's in a position where he can speak to you. He has a new wife and more children, right?'

'Yes.'

'Do they know about you?' she asked.

The question stung, but I could see that she hadn't intended it to. 'I don't know. Maybe.'

'Well, then, you're going to want to make sure it's a good time. You don't want to phone him just after he's had a big fight with his wife and suddenly say, "Hello, it's me, your long-lost son."'

I heard her out, then left her office. My only thought was that I would telephone my father later that day, and that I had to convince the operator to connect the call with my dormitory. I hoped my father, like my mother, was better disposed to dealing with important matters in the evening.

The operator said his colleague would be taking the evening shift, but that he would pass on the request for the nine-fifteen call.

'Operator, one other thing,' I said. 'When you connect the call, could you not say where it's from? It's a surprise of sorts.'

The operator didn't object so I left the slip with him and headed off to my classes.

It was a difficult day to get through, with a double-science period in the afternoon, during which my thoughts were fixed on the evening call. Practical considerations troubled me most. How would I make sure that my housemistress or friends wouldn't interrupt me? Would I take the call in the corridor or in the housemistress's apartment? If a servant should answer, who would I say was calling? How would I greet my father? Surely not 'Abba', but by his first name then? I'd never addressed any Indian adult in that way.

I decided to return to the dormitory early and make some headway with my homework as I was sure it would become harder to do as nine fifteen approached. I met my housemistress on the way and told her I was expecting a trunk call that evening so that I could wish my mother a happy birthday.

'Your mother's happy birthday today?' She grinned.

'Yes, ma'am.'

'Good, good. Please also convey my very best wishes to her. Please feel free to speak in my apartment.'

'Thank you, ma'am,' I said, sidling off to my room.

The study hour began, and my two roommates came in. I wished I could tell them of the error I was making. I felt in unsafe hands with the therapist, yet in a day she had reduced the greatest gulf in my life to a tantalising two-hour wait. For all that I didn't trust her, I was excited and willing to believe. My caution was just fear of disappointment.

By nine, the study hour was over and I escaped the clamour of the corridors for the quiet of my housemistress' apartment. In the fifteen minutes I spent by the phone, I took in every minute detail of the apartment, from my housemistress' shrine to the late Princess Diana to the needlework pastoral scenes, with religious messages.

At ten past nine, I focused on the task ahead, as if I were doing last-minute revision for an exam. I prayed the call wouldn't go through. But the operator was following a simple instruction, and the line was connecting as it had before, and the phone rang.

I answered it, expecting to be flung straight into conversation with my father, but the operator's voice spoke instead. 'Call to Lahore, Pakistan. Should I connect?'

'Yes, please,' I managed, shuddering at the mention of Pakistan.

Then, as if performing a magic trick, the operator's voice was gone and a gruff voice at the other end of the line, said, 'Hello.'

'*Salam Olaikum*,' I said, recalling a Muslim friend of my mother teaching me the greeting. 'Is this Salmaan Taseer's house?'

'*Olaikum*,' the gruff voice replied, with some puzzlement. 'Yes, who's speaking?'

'May I speak to him, please?' I asserted.

'Speaking,' the voice said in English.

'This is Aatish Taseer,' I said, blushing at my own heroism.

The voice did not respond. I imagined the comfort of an evening at home ruined.

Then the therapist's suggestion came to mind, and I said, aware that I had not banished the flutter from my voice, 'Is this a good time to talk?'

'No,' the voice said. Then, as if explaining a hard concept to a child, 'This isn't actually a very good time.'

'Will tomorrow morning be better?' I offered.

'Yes, it will be better.'

'Should I try the office number?'

'Yes, do that. Where are you?' the voice asked, with sudden concern.

'In India, at my boarding-school in southern India. It's in Tamil Nadu.'

'OK,' the voice said, losing interest.

I said goodbye and hung up.

The next morning I rushed into the therapist's office, furious at the disappointment. She was engaged in another one-to-one peer-counselling session, but she asked the person to leave. She listened to every last detail about the sound of his voice, his choice of words, the way he had said goodbye. Then she asked, like a mantra, 'How has it made you feel?'

'Extremely disappointed.'

'Have you thought yet of why?'

'Yes, I've been thinking about this man all my life and I got the courage to call him only to be told that it wasn't a good time.'

'Maybe it wasn't,' she said stubbornly.

'What? Do you mean you think he was telling the truth?'

'Perhaps not, but we have to take people at their word.'

'You think I should call him back?'

'What harm is there? If nothing else, you'll hear his voice again, which will only affirm that he is a creature of flesh and blood, and not some over-built-up myth.'

She was an infuriating woman to share a secret with, but she had one unique quality: she was never dissatisfied with an outcome, no matter how far it was from what she expected. It made me want to call my father, if only to throw it in her face.

Later that day, I returned to the original wooden booth and waited to be put through to my father's office. My mood was not unlike that of someone calling a customer service or IT help desk for the tenth time. When the number finally rang, I could tell the operator was still on the line. He said, in a heavy south-Indian accent, 'Hello? Hello? Stand by for trunk call.'

The voice at the other end was quiet. I said, 'Hello, can I speak to Salmaan Taseer?'

'Who's calling?' the voice said. I recognised its gruffness as my father's.

'His son,' I said firmly.

Then the voice changed. The gruffness was gone and the tone was meek, like a servant's. 'He is not in at the moment,' the voice said, now in Urdu.

I hadn't planned for this. 'What?' I said, certain that the voice sounded like my father's, but unsure how to proceed.

'He is out,' the voice, still servile, repeated.

The cowardice enraged me and I felt a strange sense of power over the voice. I wavered between pressing on and giving up. Then, a sense of fatigue took over. I made the owner of the voice write down my number and hung up.

I never found out if it was really my father.

# The Discplinary (sic) Force of the Islamic Republic

In the Name of God. As Long as a Tourist is in an Islamic country, the Islamic government is responsible to guarantee his safety and comfort. If a Tourist in an Islamic country loses his properties, the government should support and provide him with the lost property.

*Imam Ali, from a sign in a travel agent's office*

The Discplinary (*sic*) Force of the Islamic Republic of Iran and Department of Aliens' Affairs in Tehran had a bad reputation for inefficiency and unpleasantness. I was thinking of going out of town to renew my visa, but as it was about to expire I had little choice. I still had a lot more to do in Iran. I wanted to go to Kurdistan and to the holy cities of Qom and Mashhad. Reza, my vet-friend, and I organised our train tickets to Mashhad at a travel agency on Tehran's congested south side. Then, to renew my visa, we took a taxi north into cleaner air and *chenar*-lined avenues, with glass-fronted boutiques and coffee shops.

In that hour before lunch, the office was empty. I followed Reza in past a guard; we signed our names in a visitors' book and dropped off the forms. I was requesting a month's extension but was willing to settle for a fortnight. The man who took them said I could pick up my passport on Saturday, the night before we were meant to leave for Mashhad. It seemed straightforward enough.

Saturday came and, as instructed, I returned to the Discplinary Force of the Islamic Republic on the long, tree-lined avenue. This time, the office was airless and crowded. The main room was full of Africans, South Asians and Asians standing around for varied consular services, such as visa extension, pick-up and delivery. Many had dazed, puzzled expressions, showing the effects of indefinite waiting. The usual religious decorations and instructions hung on the walls: 'Honourable aliens, Islamic *hijab* is necessary,' 'Yah Fatima' in gold letters and a romanticised portrait of Ali's son.

In a far corner of the room behind a glass partition, I saw a sign that said 'Visa Pickup and Interview Box'. A couple of Europeans were standing near it and I made my way over. The man working behind the partition with two stars on his epaulettes was bald, with a moustache and a cold, stern mouth. His eyes darted from person to dossier to person, giving the impression that the two were interchangeable. After a short wait, I handed him my pickup slip. He fingered a few dossiers, then went away, came back and searched again for mine. I saw it before he did and gave him some indication of where it was. He picked it up and scanned its contents quickly. Then his eyes rested on something in it.

'I can give you two days,' he said blandly.

'Two days?' I blurted.

'Two days,' he replied, paying no attention to the emphasis in my voice.

'But I asked for a month.'

'I'm sorry, I can't help you.'

'But why? Why have I just been given two days?'

'I'm sorry, I can't help you.'

'But I haven't even made transport arrangements to leave in two days.'

'I'm sorry I *can't* help you,' he said, then turned to the next person.

I had prepared myself for a variety of surprising outcomes, but two days was less than my lowest estimate. It would not give me time to travel by land to Pakistan, which was my plan, let alone to the religious cities of Qom and Mashhad. It was hardly any more time than my visa already allowed so I didn't bother to ask for the two days he offered.

Panic rose from my stomach. There was so much I still needed to do in Iran! The bald man's answer didn't just alter my plans but altered me, bringing me into line with the level of distress in the room. I pushed my way out of the window-less office and on to the street.

I walked up and down the block, past a pastry shop, and crossed the black metal rails that bridged the clean waterway, bright from light driven in spokes through the *chenar*s above. In the other direction, the incline took the eye past the broad stretch of avenue, culminating in the snow-capped mountains that, despite the dark layers of pollution, gave Tehran an aspect of spring. This strange city could turn like a hologram: at one instant it was spring, greenery and white mountains; at the next, traffic, pollution, black outlines and hazard.

I was still under the impression that my two-day extension was the result of a bureaucratic accident and could be amended with the help of someone who knew the country and the language. I couldn't decide who to call. Most of the people I knew in Iran were young and would have no influence. The only older people I could think of were Muhammad Rahimi and his Indian wife, Sita. She had been away since my arrival in Tehran, but had returned in the past few days and I was meant to be meeting her anyway.

'I'm sorry to call you with this, Sita,' I said, 'but I have a bit of a problem. They've given me forty-eight hours to leave the country. I have a lot of work still to do. Is there any way you can help?'

'Well,' she answered, perhaps a little put off by the urgency in my voice, 'Muhammad's office is always getting visa extensions for people who work for the company. You should have let us know you were doing this. Let me call him and then I'll call you back.'

Sita called back within minutes and sounded reassuring. She asked where I was, then said she would have their son, Payam, who I already knew, pick me up and take me to Muhammad's office, which was off Vali Asr.

Payam's arrival was a comfort after the large and inscrutable government apparatus, but the doubt I had sensed in Sita must have been playing on his mind too: had I only been offered a two-day visa because of a bureaucratic error or because I had run into trouble with the regime? In the first case, it made sense to contest the decision; in the second, it would be reckless to do so.

Muhammad, sitting in his elegant, wood-panelled office, squinting through his gold-rimmed glasses, traced my story back to the flat I was staying in. He was certain that my friend's links with the press had brought me under scrutiny from the Islamic Republic. 'Is your friend Iranian?' he asked.

'Yes.'

'Then be sure he's an informer,' he said, with the special confidence he reserved for expounding conspiracy theories.

'He's hardly ever lived here,' I protested. 'I know him from England. He's only just started to work here. Besides, he's not even in the country.'

'Be sure he is an informer,' Muhammad said, shaking his head from side to side.

We waited for Mr Valaie to show up. He handled Muhammad's business visas for his foreign employees. He was someone who, Muhammad said, 'knows how to speak to those people'. I liked the description: it was exactly the kind of knowledge I felt I lacked. I was still more comforted when Valaie arrived. He was a tall, burly man, with a quiet but substantial presence, and wore the short, stubbly beard of the Basiji. He had the appearance of an insider. We recounted to him the morning's events and he suggested we go directly back to the office and speak to them.

Soon we were back in the car, finding openings in the giant traffic formation heading down Vali Asr.

Using back-streets, and side-streets, and outmanoeuvring other cars, we arrived at the Disciplinary Force of the Islamic Republic of Iran. Again we went straight past the bearded sentries into the main room, which had cleared since I'd last seen it. The bald man, with the hard mouth, was immediately visible, and I pointed him out to Valaie. Valaie told me to stand back and moved his large, impressive form in a swift, self-assured step toward the man, who was now standing up but looking down. When Valaie approached, he glanced up for a second to take him in, as if he had been expecting him all along.

Valaie explained himself, then asked, 'May I take some of your time?'

'I have no time,' the man replied, and returned to his work.

'Could you just say what the problem is?'

'No, I cannot, and you must not ask me.'

As soon as he had said this, he moved away from the desk. Valaie appealed to him again as he withdrew. He did not answer, but when the appeal came again, he snapped, in a louder voice so that his other colleagues heard, 'Two days and don't ask for an explanation.'

A woman came up to the desk, like an apologetic wife, and explained politely that a Mr Rashidi had denied the visa; we had to speak directly to him. When Valaie asked where Mr Rashidi was, they said he had left for the day.

Valaie looked as if he was unused to being spoken to in this way. It was as if a kinsman or relation had insulted him. He advised that we take the two days and try again for more days tomorrow when we came to collect the passport. Since the extension fees were paid and the two days would give me at least one day more than my visa allowed, I agreed. Valaie took the slip back to the counter. This time someone else dealt with him.

My relief at having escaped the government office, and its bitter disappointments, was so great that it was some minutes before the realisation of what had occurred sank in. I had a two o'clock appointment with Hosseini, who had recently returned from America and was a senior administrator at Tehran University. He was to help me in the religious cities of Mashhad and Qom. Now I was not sure if there was any point in seeing him. I still wanted to complete the trip by land and had already begun to calculate how long it would take me to reach the Pakistani border. Iran's border with Pakistan, in the southern region of Balochistan, is a heavy smuggling route and rumoured to be dangerous. It was the riskiest part of the entire trip, and while I could muster the courage to do it in normal circumstances, I wasn't sure I wanted to cross it if I was already in trouble with the Islamic Republic. I called Hosseini to tell him what had happened. 'I think I can help you,' he said. 'Let's meet as planned, at the hotel.'

The Homa had once been the Sheraton. Like many Iranian hotels, it was trapped in the past, a past that was once not a bad present but today showed its backwardness. The lobby was dark, musty, and seemed to reflect the state's enthusiasm for foreign visitors. Old cutlery and plates from the Sheraton days remained, but the coffee shop was run like a college canteen.

The place was teeming with staff, but the service was hopeless. As I entered, the sofas in front of the reception desk were filled with people waiting. None could have been Hosseini so I veered off to the left to inspect the bookshop. It sold soft, old paperbacks, outdated guides for Iran, airport thrillers, James Baldwin's *Another Country*, with the *Spectator* calling him 'the greatest Negro writer'. If I hadn't grown up in the frozen socialist days of India in the 1980s, I don't know if I could have placed the exact year when the clock stopped in Iran. As it happened, it was familiar and stirred a degree of nostalgia.

When I went back to the lobby, I saw a small, elderly man sitting in a corner with one leg outstretched. We caught each other's eye and he rose with difficulty, then walked with a limp in my direction. He was clean-shaven and distinguished, and didn't look like a government man, but his being in a senior position at Tehran University, which had only just received a mullah as its president, made me wonder. But even as these judgements became harder to make in the rest of the Islamic world – people you never expected to be religious, surprising you with their piety – in Iran, the positions became always clearer. As I would come to learn within the next twenty-four hours, Islam in Iran was not religion; it was politics. And my having confused this landed me in trouble.

I spent a few hours with Hosseini. He told me he had been appointed to a position that dealt specifically with international relations for Tehran University and he would let the people at the government office know I was a former student of his, working on academic research in Iran. 'But I don't have a visa for that,' I said. 'I have a tourist visa.'

'That's OK, but don't say anything about religion. Say you're working on a thesis about the cultures of people in the East.'

It sounded vague to me, but I guessed that was the idea. It was evening and Tehran's main arteries were clogging when

Hosseini dropped me off at Shiraz Avenue. On the way I asked him why he had left Iran. 'I didn't like this government,' he said. 'Also, I wanted my children to grow up in a free country. One goes to Harvard, the other to Stanford, and my son goes to Northeastern for engineering. They wouldn't have had those opportunities here. I value very much freedom of expression, freedom of thinking. I value these things very much.'

Hosseini's family had owned a construction company, which they lost in the 1979 revolution. He spent many years in America and had only recently come back after being offered a senior position at the university. Like so many other Iranians, a sense of loss and love of his country brought him back. His main reason for leaving, as he said, was his children and how growing up in the Islamic Republic would limit them.

'You know what happened in Iran?' he said, after the traffic slowed again, 'People were very connected to religion even though the government was not religious. But now that the government is religious, most of the people want to get away from religion. They see it as killing people, putting journalists in jail. That is the true religion. It is very hard for me to say I am a Muslim. Most of the terrorists today are religious. I prefer to say I have no religion.' Then, as if in an afterthought, he said, 'We are a talented, enthusiastic people, but with a bad government.'

'It's funny that everyone always says "government",' I said, 'when they mean "regime" or "state".'

'Yes, because every year we say this is the last year, but they're still here.'

We agreed to meet the next morning at nine fifteen outside the office of the Disciplinary Force of the Islamic Republic of Iran.

That evening I had an urge to go out. Nightlife in Tehran happened at private houses, and as my absent host once said

185

to me, 'It's filthy.' Most of the time I was too busy or un-prepared for its excesses, but that night, like many young people in Tehran, I felt in need of release.

I called Amir. When I told him what had happened, he became quiet. I still expected Hosseini to perform a miracle, but Amir smelt trouble. 'This can also happen,' he said, after a long silence. 'Don't push too hard.' We talked of other things and I said I'd like to see him in case I was leaving tomorrow.

'Yes,' Amir said. 'In fact I'm taking you to a party. It's the birthday of an actor friend and I think it'll be fun.' I readily agreed and he said he'd pick me up in a few hours. I was stand-ing on the balcony when I spoke to Amir and caught a glimpse of the lights coming on in the city. My eyes had fixed on this view so many times over the previous month and, despite its ugliness, it was a captivating and dark urban vision.

Amir and Anahita arrived in high spirits. They drove an elegant, cream 1970s Paykan – Iran's Volkswagen – and Anahita was holding a large tambourine. The party was in another high-rise building, which, like mine, was constructed in the time of the Shah.

At the party, beautiful made-up girls threw off manteaux and scarves to reveal *décolleté* tops and long, flowing hair. The room was dark, the music loud; a famous Iranian hit song played; a light came from the kitchen where several kinds of spirits and beer lay around the sink.

Most of the crowd were in the film business, and when I told them I was Indian, they tittered about Bollywood. A girl in a red and white satin blouse danced close to me, a man smoked a joint on the balcony and Anahita beat on a drum while others, including the host, who was bearded, with clear blue eyes, danced round her. Fun of this kind in Tehran always seemed to be had with the accompanying awareness that it could land you in trouble. Almost everyone present had had a brush with the law; almost everyone had been at a party that was busted; many of the girls had been picked up for stretching decency laws. An entire urban youth had been criminalised. Most of the people there were almost exactly the same age as, or slightly older than, the revolution. They had lived through times when T-shirts, Western music, certain haircuts, the mingling of the sexes, dancing and, of course, intoxication could have you hauled in. And yet they took their chances – in fact, too many; they were hooked on dissent.

Leaving the party, two girls reeled ahead of us, carrying a giant ten-foot sandwich from the party on their shoulders. They rocked from side to side and their headscarves slipped off. One climbed drunkenly into our car. Anahita, who had been drinking through the evening, drove and sang. She tore down highway after highway, veering the car towards traffic islands, then pulling away with a laugh at the last minute. Amir looked serene. It was behaviour that would have got us arrested in London, let alone Tehran. I leant over to him and said, as if consoling him, 'Fuck the Islamic Republic of Iran.' He laughed, and Anahita and he stuck up their elbows and rotated them, a jeer at the regime from the time when elbows were sexy.

We ended up at some house, sitting about the floor, drinking cheap vodka in plastic cups. A painter friend of Amir, a dark man with a shaved head, began a story. Addressing me, he said, 'I was the most religious guy. I believed in Muhammad and Ali for years. But I have seen all the propaganda in schools and now I don't believe in religion. One day I started thinking and I stopped believing.'

'How?'

'I was driving with my friend and I had a Koran kept in that . . . How do you say it, the sun thing in the car?'

'Visor?'

'Yes, visor. And the road was very bumpy and the Koran fell down. So I picked it up and kissed it. And my friend, he saw me, and he said, "Oh, your Koran fell down. Let me kiss it too." So I give it to him and he takes it, kisses it and throws it out of the window.'

The room erupted in laughter, but the painter withheld his smile, eager to continue. 'And . . . and my friend says, "This is nothing." And I start to think, How can he and how can't I? How can he and how can't I? All night I lay in my bed, thinking, How can he and how can't I? All night. And then it came to me: Islam was nothing but history written by victors. So before, when I was religious, I was a big fighter. Now I give a prize to anyone who can make me fight.'

No one laughed now. They smiled knowingly at the painter, nodding and sipping their drinks. He described Islam as 'history written by victors'. He made a haphazard connection between being a 'big fighter' and religion. His description of himself reminded me of Muhammad Rahimi's student days. Religion overcome, the painter knew a kind of peace; he saw empowerment in his transformation from believer to thinker. His tracing his former rage to the religion's view of history was the most significant thing I heard on my journey. It was at the heart of my problem with my father, with whom, but for religion, it could be said I shared a single history.

The next morning, I felt the effects of the night before. Payam was downstairs at eight fifteen, alert in a crisp white shirt. The highways had burst their banks and even the exits were filled with slow-moving traffic. Our maddeningly slow pace, leagued with my dehydration, brought on nausea and sweatiness. When we reached Muhammad's office, Valaie was already there but was caught up with work and took many minutes to come down. I was anxious not to keep Hosseini waiting, but when I called him, he was already outside the government office. We were fifteen minutes late for him.

This time Hosseini, dignified despite his limp, led us into the office. It was as crowded as it had been the day before. I caught sight of the man whom I had dealt with previously. I pointed him out to Hosseini and he signalled to me to stand back. Watching from afar, I could see that the man had spotted the large figure of Valaie slouching towards him behind Hosseini. He looked irritated, but when Hosseini approached and introduced himself, his manner became courteous and helpful. It was the first encouraging sign so far.

The man retrieved my file and began to leaf through it as Hosseini, occasionally throwing a glance in my direction, stood in front of him. After the man looked over the file carefully, Hosseini and he had a short exchange. Then Hosseini nodded and limped slowly back to me.

'There's nothing wrong with your application,' he said. 'He says he'd give you the extension right now, but since Mr Rashidi has denied it, he says we must speak to him to find out why. He's from a different agency.'

'Where is Rashidi?'

'He's not in yet, but should be here soon.'

A moment later Valaie came up to us. He had enquired about Rashidi and been told that he would be in at eleven. It was ten o'clock and we decided to take a break for an hour and meet back at eleven. I hadn't had breakfast so Payam took me to the former Miami Hotel. We went to a breakfast room on the top floor and I fell upon a plate of fried eggs, cheese and cold meat. Two cups of coffee later, I felt much better.

When we met up again with Hosseini at eleven, Rashidi had still not arrived. We decided to wait for him outside. A couple of Pakistani women in *chador* were slumped on a bench with their chins in their hands as if in grief. A heavyset man in Pakistani *salwar kameez* stood in front of them, staring in bewilderment at a set of pink forms. Hosseini and Valaie were deep in conversation. Hosseini was saying how in the past you could send someone to pick up your US or UK visa for you but now, since the revolution, it was different: if you hadn't been in the Islamic Republic for a long time, it was important not to lose your cool when dealing with bureaucracy.

Then he grew impatient and moved towards the office again. I was going to stay outside, but decided to follow him in so that I could take a mental note of what the office looked like. The crowd had thinned, but the windowless room was still almost full. I had barely an instant to take it in when across the room past dozens of people and behind the glass partition, I saw a man who could only have been Rashidi. The words 'He's from a different agency' shot into my mind and, guessing which agency it was, the blackest fear sprang up in me.

I had seen an intelligence man only once before. It was in Damascus and I remember I was struck then by the certainty with which I recognised him. Rashidi, too, was a breed apart from the other officials in the room. In plain clothes, he wore a dark blue jacket over a dark blue shirt, had a short salt-and-pepper beard and his eyes gleamed from behind a pair of silver spectacles. There was an air of extra-legality about him. He looked like a man who had been sent to override the system, to get the job done quickly and efficiently. He spoke rapidly into a mobile phone, and though I'd never laid eyes on him till that moment, the instant he saw me he knew who I was. His eyes burned and he made a violent gesture with his arm for me to come over. Payam, who had followed me in, saw the gesture, and it was only when I recognised the fear in his face, like a man made aware he's bleeding by another's reaction to it, that my heart sank.

I grasped for Hosseini. He had seen the gesture too, and continued to walk at a steady pace ahead of me. His presence shielded me from the anger that Rashidi was ready to direct at me. When he saw that the small, elderly man was with me he seemed to show the disappointment of a dog restrained by the appearance of his master. We went up to the window together. Hosseini and Rashidi began to speak energetically to each other in Farsi. I could only make out the odd word in common with Urdu: '*saval*', question, '*javab*', answer, 'Afghanistan' and 'Pakistan'. They spoke for many minutes, Rashidi shaking his head vigorously and answering the professor politely, but assertively, and Hosseini stubbornly persisting. At last they came to an impasse and Hosseini turned to me to say, 'He won't give it because apparently you filled in your visa application incorrectly. You have to review it before you apply again.'

At the time, Rashidi's sarcasm was lost in translation, but the extension was the last of my concerns now. I wanted to take my passport and leave immediately. Hosseini said, 'I told him you were my student.'

To which Rashidi had replied, 'Don't get involved with these foreign students.'

It was an easy lie to uncover and it scared me more.

'I'm already involved,' Hosseini said. 'I represent the international relations of Tehran University. He is doing research for a humanities thesis on Eastern peoples.'

Rashidi gave the old professor a long, cold stare, then picked up the telephone and made a call. When he hung up, he gestured to two young military recruits in dark green fatigues to take us somewhere. The bearded men, with sunken eyes, came up to us. Only Hosseini and I were to go. We followed them out of the office and into a small lift. The building was not just that one office, but a complex. The recruits pressed the button for the fifth floor and the small lift made a slow ascent. When the doors opened, we were met with a series of green arrows. Four pointed left, indicating services such as passport renewal and licence-plate registration. A single arrow pointed right. It read

'Offend'. Hosseini looked at me and shrugged. For the second time that morning I felt sick.

We were brought into a lobby of sorts, with rooms leading off it, and were seated next to two European men. We waited in silence again. A few minutes later, three plain-clothes men showed up and *salaam*ed everyone before vanishing into different rooms. One of the Europeans was called in. They began to speak and I heard something about a camera. Photography in the wrong places could get you into serious trouble in the Islamic Republic. Then suddenly, I felt my notebook in my pocket and became nervous. If they went through it, they would find all they needed. I whispered to Hosseini that I should do something with it. He nodded his approval. I looked at the door and saw it was not guarded. I took the opportunity and ran out, down five flights of stairs, past the guards at the main office and into the street. Payam and Valaie were waiting for me outside. I indicated that they should come with me into a side-street.

'What's going on?' Payam asked frantically.

'I don't know. I have to go back up, but keep this.' I gave him my notebook and had to fight the temptation to jump into the car and leave.

On my way back up the five flights of stairs, I passed Rashidi. He darted a suspicious look at me. I nodded and continued upstairs. When I came back into the room Hosseini was still sitting where I had left him. He seemed to have digested the sinister colour of the place and looked nervous now. In a few minutes, two men appeared. One was small and dark with lively eyes and a sparse grey beard, the other was fairer, larger, with a broad face and a grim aspect. These were our interrogators. With a wave, they cleared a room of the two *chador*ed women manning a desk, and asked Hosseini to come in. I couldn't hear what was said, but it was a short conversation, and in a few minutes, Hosseini reappeared. The small, dark man came out after him, flashed me a smile and asked me in.

The large, fair man was the interrogator and he took his position behind a long desk, sprawling comfortably in a chair with wheels. The small, dark man was the translator. The larger man would ask a question in Farsi to his small, mean conduit. While he translated, his beady eyes glued to me, the larger man reclined in his chair, swivelled slightly and watched. The round-about way in which the questions reached me caused so much discomfort that I was inclined to think the larger man spoke perfect English and only introduced the other as part of a strategy to break me down. They told me to sit on a straight-backed chair placed against a pale, yellow wall.

The questions began immediately without any explanation of why I had been brought there in the first place.

'Where are your other two companions?' came the question in Farsi, then the anticipation, and finally the translated echo.

'One is the son of a family friend,' I said. 'The other works in his father's office.'

'What are their names?'

'Payam and Mr Valaie.'

'Their full names?'

'Payam Rahimi.'

'Rah?'

'Rahimi.'

'What is their connection to you?'

'His father is a family friend.'

'What's the father's name?'

'Muhammad Rahimi.'

'Rah?'

'Rahimi, like the son's name.'

'Are you staying at a hotel?'

'No, at a friend's flat.'

'Where?'

'Saman building, off Shiraz Avenue.'

'What number?'

'719C.'

'Whose flat is it?'

'Bahador,' I answered, swearing to myself that I would tell the truth, but try to withhold information where possible.

'Afkhami?' The larger interrogator snapped, relishing the surprise it created in me.

'Yes.'

'Bahador is here?'

'No. He's in London.'

'But you say you're staying in his flat?' the little man asked, his eyes widening.

'Yes, he let me stay there while I'm here.'

'Are you paying him money?'

'No. He's let me use it.'

'How do you know Mr Bahador?'

'From London.'

'Can you describe the exact circumstances of your first meeting?'

'Yes, we had lunch in London.'

'Who did you meet him through?'

'Through a mutual friend.'

'Can you say where you first heard of Mr Bahador?' I didn't know where this was leading, but the questions were coming so quickly I felt I could only rely on telling the truth, even though the truth was turning out to be more complicated than I first imagined.

'In Indonesia,' I answered, mystified by the strangeness of the word in this room.

'Do you know his job in Iran?'

'No. I don't think he has one.' Bahador was not connected

to any network, and as I didn't know much about his work in Iran, I hoped to get away with genuine ignorance.

'No?' the little man said, his voice brimming with sarcasm.

'As far as I know.'

'You have known him four or five years, Mr Aatish, he's letting you stay in his flat and you don't know what he does?'

'It's hard to say,' I mumbled aimlessly. 'I'm not sure he does anything.'

They looked at each other. The little one's beady eyes flashed and the big one leant back in his chair with a shrug, as if to say 'How can we help someone who won't help himself?'

'Then how can he live?' the little one asked, of his own accord.

'Perhaps he's well-off.'

'What?'

'Perhaps his family is well-off.'

They both looked away in disgust.

'You say Mr Bahador is not in the country so how did you get into his flat?'

'He sent me his keys with his driver to Isfahan.'

'Who was this driver?'

'Mr Sadeghi,' I answered, sad to drag his name into this.

'What's his number?'

'I'm sorry, I don't know it by heart. I have it at home.'

'He's based in Isfahan?'

'No, Tehran.'

'You said he picked you up in Isfahan.'

'Yes. He came from Tehran to Isfahan in order to pick me up.'

'Mr Aatish, you have a mobile phone in Iran.' This was not a question.

'Yes, I'm borrowing one.'

'What's the number?'

'I can't be sure, but I think it's . . .' As soon as I said it, I knew I'd made a mistake. I had given them a variation of my passport number, which began in a similar way, but I couldn't bring myself to correct it.

He wrote down the number and examined it closely. 'Where did you get this phone?'

'It's also Bahador's.'

'He gave you his phone?' the little man asked, always with his tone of incredulity.

'Yes.'

'How did he give you his phone?'

'Mr Sadeghi brought it to Isfahan.'

'Mr Sadeghi had his phone?'

'Yes.'

'What is Mr Sadeghi's phone number?'

'I told you, I don't know it by heart. I have it at home.'

'How much did you pay him?'

'I don't know – maybe sixty dollars?' I had spoken in a tone of exasperation and they eyed me as if to say, 'Watch it.'

'Mr Aatish, what is your purpose in Iran?'

'I'm writing a travel book. I've been travelling from Istanbul by land and hope to finish in India.'

'What is the book about?'

'It's a travel book based on my impressions,' I answered, hoping to find a middle route between Hosseini's suggestion and my actual purpose. 'I'm interested in religion and culture.' Religion had been an innocuous way of approaching more sensitive subjects in other countries and I hoped it would be the same in Iran.

'Did you have an interpreter in Iran?'

'No, I didn't,' I answered, thinking of all the interpreters I nearly had.

'You didn't need an interpreter?'

'No, I didn't.'

'Why? Do you speak Farsi?' The little man's face gleamed.

'No, but I'm just travelling through, recording my impressions, talking to people where I can. I haven't been doing interviews.'

'Mr Aatish,' the little man began, with an assertiveness that suggested someone who took pleasure in language and the sound of his own voice, 'we hear that you have been asking about religion, the changes in religion, and politics somehow.' I nearly smiled: it was a glorious, subtle formulation, encapsulating perfectly the closeness of religion and politics in Islam and the Islamic Republic, just in case I was confused.

'I've been asking only about religion, not politics,' I answered, with failing conviction.

'You were seen attending the Friday sermon given by Mr Rafsanjani.' This was not true, but it was nearly true. I had asked Payam's friend to take me to the Friday sermon at Tehran University. If the interrogators knew this, they would have overheard it on the telephone, and if they had been tapping my phone, they knew a great deal more.

At this stage, I made a mental shift from thinking of this as a short interrogation to just the first stage of a much longer detention.

'No, I did not attend the Friday prayers.'

'You were seen there.'

'That's impossible,' I said, with as much conviction as I could muster. 'I wasn't there.'

'Have you been visiting any seminaries in cities like Mashhad and Qom?' Now, a further wave of doubt came over me. Had they spoken to Reza?

'No.'

'But wouldn't you like to?' the little man asked patronisingly. 'They're very interesting for your work.'

'Yes, I would,' I answered, seeing no point in lying. 'I was hoping to go to Mashhad tomorrow night. But I've been to other places too.'

'Where?'

'I've been to Shiraz, Yazd, Isfahan . . .'

'From Tehran?'

'No, I flew to Shiraz and worked my way up.'

The big man got up and walked out of the room for a moment. The little interrogator's tone became suddenly friendly. 'Which city did you like the most?'

'Yazd,' I smiled.

'Why Yazd?' he asked, now sly again.

'I liked the desert nearby, the colour of the buildings, the Friday mosque.'

The other man walked back into the room. He spoke to the little one, who nodded. 'Mr Aatish, don't you need someone to arrange your travel for you, buy your tickets?'

Now I was sure they knew something about Reza. 'No, I do it myself.'

'All of it?'

'Yes – why not? For instance, I bought my ticket in Dubai for Shiraz. The hotel in Shiraz organised the car to Yazd.'

'How much did you pay him?' he asked, always relying on the relentlessness of his questions to wear down his subject.

'Oh, I don't know! Same as the other one – forty or fifty dollars?'

They looked between themselves, mean and dissatisfied.

'Mr Aatish,' the little man said, with his special sarcastic voice, making me feel as though I was in a Dickensian orphanage, 'you do know that you must always tell us the truth?'

'I am telling the truth,' I cried.

'I hope so,' said the little man, putting down his pen and rifling through some papers. Then, looking up, he added, 'For your sake.'

I became subdued and a new cycle of questioning began.

'Mr Aatish, how long have you been travelling for?'

'Since November, so six, seven months.'

'How did you have the money to travel?'

'It was my own money.'

'Yes, but who gave it you? A newspaper, an organisation or are you also "well-off"?'

'Yes, my family gave it to me,' I lied.

'Your father?'

'My mother, actually.'

'Where are your parents from?'

'My mother's Indian and my father's Pakistani.'

'What does he do?'

'He's a businessman.'

'What kind of business?'

'Telecommunications.'

'And your mother?'

'She's a writer.'

'In India?'

'Yes.'

A kind of fatigue set in. The interrogators looked thoroughly unhappy.

'Mr Aatish, why are you doing this trip in Iran?'

'I'm exploring the lands of my father's religion,' I said, surprising myself with how pompous I sounded.

'You are Muslim?'

'Yes!' I answered hopefully.

'Sunni or Shia?'

'Sunni,' I replied, realising too late that this wouldn't help me in the least.

'Mr Aatish, you know you have a tourist visa. You're not meant to be writing a book and asking questions. When you're a tourist, you just see the sights and then go home. Do you know what you've been doing in Iran is illegal?'

'No, I didn't. I was just talking to the people I met on the way.'

They looked at me sadly. I had no idea how much more they had up their sleeve. They told me to go out for a while and Hosseini was called back.

Hosseini was in for a few minutes, then came out, shaken. Poor man, I thought, he was too old to go through this. He made out that nothing was wrong. 'They're letting me go,' he said quietly. 'They want to ask you a few more questions. It's nothing. Should I wait downstairs?'

'Yes, please,' I said, hoping that it really would be 'nothing'.

They called me back into the room with the frosted-glass windows. Sitting behind the desk, from which the women in black had shuffled off like birds, now nearly two hours ago, they watched me as I sat down on the straight-backed chair against the wall.

'Mr Aatish,' the little man sighed, 'we hope you have thought about your answers and are now willing to tell us the truth. Do you have something new for us?'

'No,' I said, with fresh conviction. 'I'm doing a travel book. I've been travelling from Istanbul to India and I spoke to people on the way. That's all.'

'Mr Aatish, do you know Ms Violet?'

Of course! That was what this was about. Violet, the agency journalist who had introduced me to Jasib.

'Yes,' I said, slightly broken.

'How do you know her?'

'She was introduced to me by the Rahimis.'

'By whom?'

'My Iranian family friends.'

'They introduced you to her?'

'Yes.'

'What is your relationship with her?'

'I've only met her a few times.'

'When?'

'For dinner and for lunch.'

'When was the last time you saw her?'

'A few days ago.'

'When?'

'Two or three days ago.'

'What was the exact time?'

'I'm not sure, about noon.'

'It was only a few days ago. Try to remember.'

'Noon on Friday?'

'And what was the occasion?'

'We met some friends of hers.'

'Who?'

'Humeyra and her husband.'

'Their full names?'

'I don't know.'

'What do they do?'

'They're artists.'

It had been a very strange lunch full of expat Iranians who had recently moved back to Iran. Everyone spoke French and English and the lunch had become very drunken. Madonna played. A homosexual in a printed shirt danced close to a small, voluptuous woman. There was something childishly defiant about Madonna in Tehran, especially late in the afternoon. The gay man said, 'I hate this fucking revolution. Why us? It's not fair. Why not Turkey? We just picked the wrong number.' He enjoyed provoking me. 'We're waiting for the Americans,' he hissed, 'waiting for bombs!'

'And the time before that?' the interrogator asked.

'I met her for lunch.'

'Did you meet anyone with her?'

Now I could see what all this had built up to.

'Yes. We met a friend of hers who she thought could be a guide for me in Tehran.'

'Jasib!' the big man exclaimed, as he had done with Bahador
at the start of the interrogation.

'Yes,' I replied.

He emitted a satisfied grunt. 'Mr Aatish, you've had no
problem in the other cities, why did you need a guide here?'

'No, I've had no problem,' I answered, pretending to misun-
derstand him.

'Yes, so why did you need a guide here?'

'The other places were small cities, more manageable. Tehran
is vast. I thought I'd need some help.'

They seemed content with this explanation.

'So he was your guide?'

'No, his English wasn't good enough. I met him once and
that was that.'

'Mr Aatish, when did you arrive in Tehran?'

'On the fifteenth.'

'So, two weeks ago?'

'Yes, about.'

'Two weeks in Tehran! What did you do for so long?'

'I met my family friend, saw the city, saw how people lived
here.'

'For two weeks! What did you see?'

'I saw your palaces, the Gulestan, Sadabad,' I said, reaching
in my mind for other tourist destinations. 'Your crown jewels,
the national museum, the museum of contemporary arts.'

'And what else?'

'The museum of ceramics?' I managed. 'Which used to be
the Egyptian embassy.'

I could see from their bored expressions that they already
had what they were looking for.

'Can we see your mobile phone?'

I handed it to them. It was the worst moment in the
interrogation because I knew, now that they were through with

me, they wanted to go after all the people who had helped me in Iran. I recalled Desiré not giving names under duress. 'I don't know all the numbers in it,' I said, trying to make up for the cowardice of handing them the phone. 'It had some from before.' Fortunately, none of the names had surnames and I could pretend I didn't know them.

'You have a number in here that says Bahador's flat,' the interrogator asked, 'but it's a mobile-phone number.'

I asked to look at it and saw that it was the number of my mobile phone. 'This is the number of my mobile phone.'

The bigger man examined his sheet and shook his head.

The little interrogator said, 'But this is different from the number you gave us.' He read the number back to me.

'No, that was a mistake,' I stammered. 'I told you I might make one. This is the number of the phone. You can try it if you like.' For a moment, everything seemed to hang in the balance. Then they returned to the phone list, writing down all the names and numbers.

When they came to the end, they looked up at me and a neutral silence fell over the room.

'You would like an extension?' the man said at last.

'Yes, I would have liked an extension. I would have liked to travel more.'

'Why is your visa issued in Damascus?'

'I was there when I needed it. I've been getting them as I go along.'

'Did you get your Pakistani visa here?'

'I had that from before. My father's Pakistani.'

'What will you say about Iran?'

'Very positive things. I liked it very much.' I wanted to add, 'Until now!' 'I hope you'll let me come back.'

'Did you take notes?' he asked, ignoring the question.

'Yes.'

'On paper or the computer?'

'On the computer,' I answered, with relief at having got rid of my notebook.

'How many pages on Iran?'

'I'm not sure, eight to ten.'

'What will you write about Iran?'

'Very good things, I've really enjoyed my time here and wish I could stay on.'

'And you have Mr Sadeghi's number at home?' they asked again, making me think they would come for both that and the notes.

'Yes.'

'And where do you go next?'

'Pakistan.'

'When?'

'Well, in the next day or so, I only have two days.'

'And then you finish travelling in India?'

'Yes.'

They handed me back the phone and said, 'Have a good trip.'

'I'll try.' I smiled, walking out of the room, half expecting to be cut down before I reached the door.

\*

That night as I drove to the airport I felt a childish excitement at leaving Iran. My last hours in the Islamic Republic, and the nature of my departure, gave me a sense of escape. It made me feel the country's impoverishments more acutely. I would never have believed I could look forward so much to the freedom of the Dubai Duty Free.

Earlier I had gone to the flat for the last time. It was quiet, as always, and the windows showed another spring storm building over the hills. I packed all my things and went to Payam's house. The storm broke later that afternoon. Reza called and I agreed to meet him for coffee. The sky was black when I crossed the busy main road in front of Payam's house and the wind made the new leaves on the trees cling to their branches.

The coffee shop was in an open-air arcade. Reza arrived, looking sombre. He said he would have our tickets refunded and was sad I was leaving. He asked me what flight I was on. I didn't tell him I was booked on the Emirates night flight to Dubai. I didn't want to trust anyone: I was still worried they would come after my notes.

The three-hour interrogation covered every aspect of my shortened trip to Iran. When I looked back on the transcript of my interrogation, drawn from memory as soon as I left the country, I was amazed by its thoroughness. The questions that seemed incessant, and cut with fear in the interrogation room, were now a helpful way to retain everything about my time in Iran. Every car I hired, every kilometre I covered, every person I encountered made its way on to the interrogators' notepad. They took my phone, wrote down every name and number in it, making me fear for those who had helped me and now could end up in more trouble than me for the generosity they had shown to a visitor. I had vowed to tell the truth, but seven months of travel from Turkey to Iran can sound incredible. In the closed-off world of Iran, these strange, doubtful threads seemed to excite the interrogators' worst suspicions. At times, even as the interrogation was going on, I was grateful for it, grateful that I did not leave Iran disarmed, unaware of the regime's constant presence in the lives of the people I liked so much.

Then came that formulation I could hardly believe: 'Mr Aatish, we hear that you have been asking about religion, the changes in religion, and politics somehow.' Politics somehow!

All the faith's inability to deliver in the modern sense was contained in that 'somehow'. What I had discovered in Iran, and had sensed in Syria, was how violent and self-wounding the faith could become when it was converted from being a negative idea, a political and historical grievance against the modern world, into a positive one.

I had wanted to see what Butt and Abdullah's vision of Islamic completeness looked like when it was implemented in a modern society. In Iran it had been, and its small, irrelevant rules were turned on the people to serve the faith's political vision. For the faith to remain in power in a complex society, it had to beat down the bright and rebellious members of that society with its simplicities. In the end the big unpurified world won anyway, but terrible hypocrisies took shape: short marriages were condoned to allow prostitution; lashes were bought from the municipality as if they were no more than gas bills; and little girls were sexually taunted because Islam forbade West Highland terriers.

We drove through a velvety, smoke-filled night and passed a great white arch that looked as if its base was caught in a wind, causing it to fan out on all sides like a frock. The driver said it was the Azadi Monument. '*Azadi*' – 'freedom'; one of the many words that Farsi had in common with Urdu.

Imam Khomeini airport at that hour was deserted. The imam would have liked it the way I saw it: its sparseness, white lights and purple seats, its porters in red waistcoats gliding across the sparkling floors, or dozing against a trolley, gave it a heavenly aspect. To me, it was menacing. It stood for all that I had learnt about the Islamic Republic in the last twelve hours: brutality wrapped in godliness.

The airport was not real; it was a showpiece. The real airport was down the road and handled most of the air traffic in and out of Tehran. It was there that the noise, grime, long queues and commotion of other airports collected. None of that was permitted in the tube-lit serenity of the imam's airport. It was a symbol, more shrine than airport. It was big and modern, ablaze with fluorescent light; every surface spoke of newness. It didn't matter that the world had to be kept out for it to look as it did. The ideal was achieved – the simplicity, the quiet, the decorum – and that was all. It didn't matter that the ideal served, the Islamic perfection, had played no part in its construction. It was like the Islamic Republic in miniature: a violent imposition of religious perfection on the modern world, driven to illogic.

I bristled when I presented my passport and visa to Immigration, with its rude notation in red, stating that I had two days to leave the country. But the young woman inspecting it was unfazed and put a red-domed exit stamp over the blue one that had allowed me entry into Shiraz twenty-five days before. As the announcement for the Emirates flight came, and a small group of passengers walked on to the jet-way, I noticed some young female Tehran–Dubai regulars. The scarves were already slipping.

# Continuities

It was July in Delhi, 2002, when I made up my mind to visit Pakistan for the first time. The rains had broken, and for a short spell the air was hot and gassy; earthworms were flooded out of their holes and the fruit from *neem* trees, the same fat berries of my childhood, lay mashed in the wet earth. I was twenty-one.

All summer Indian and Pakistani troops had brooded on the border in huge numbers, and though foreign diplomats had been evacuated, and news bulletins flashed with talk of nuclear conflict, the joy and lethargy of the rainy season felt too deep that year to be interrupted by the sound of war. I'd wanted to go many times since the abortive phone conversation with my father, but was prevented by being at college in America and by worsening relations between India and Pakistan. This time, seeing a lull in hostilities, I decided I'd catch the cycle at its trough in case the next one was deeper still.

Getting to Pakistan from India in those months posed so many practical problems that meeting my father for the first time became more of a logistical challenge than an emotional one. There were no flights, trains or buses between the two countries, and it looked as though I would have to fly to Dubai, and from there to Lahore. This seemed complicated and expensive so I went to see the acting Pakistani high commissioner in Delhi to ask his advice. The High Commission, a blue-domed mausoleum of a building, enveloped in afternoon gloom, was deserted, like some embassy of a former ally after a revolution. I found the acting high commissioner surprisingly receptive to my problem. 'Why don't you drive?' he suggested.

'Isn't the border closed?'

'Only to Indian and Pakistani nationals. You have a British passport. I can give you a visa and you can cross by land at Wagah.'

By land! I thought. That moody frontier! It seemed impossible. I grew up thinking of the physical border as a land fault, a crevasse in the earth spitting fire. I would cross that border in a car?

'No, not in a car,' the acting high commissioner said. 'On foot.' Apparently, I could drive up to the border, but then would have to walk across it and someone else would have to meet me on the other side. With that, the high commissioner had a little blue and purple rectangle stuck in my passport that read: 'Islamic Republic of Pakistan, 28 days, Multiple Entry'.

'Do say hello to your abbu for me. I know him,' he said slyly, handing back my passport. 'They have a very nice farm near Lahore.'

My mother was not in Delhi at the time, but offered her full support for the trip. She called a friend of hers in Pakistan, also a friend of my father, to ask if I could stay with her. The friend said she would be happy to have me and would send her son to the border to pick me up.

I thought my mother must have suffered at my going, both out of concern for my well-being and for her own makeshift peace with that time. 'Just remember, my darling,' she said, 'you'll find him charming, interesting, very funny, but he'll always let you down.'

That morning, my flat in Delhi was dark and quiet, except for the dull hum of the air-conditioner. The marks of the morning were apparent. A crack of light came from the kitchen where Sati, the servant, moved around before anyone else; a Thermos of coffee had been left for me on the dining-table; newspapers lay unopened on the floor.

Sati came out of the kitchen when he heard my footsteps. I had been at university for many months and he still beamed at seeing me after so long. He handed me a blue polythene bag with my breakfast in it.

'Is Keval up?' I asked.

'Yes, he's in the car.'

Downstairs, it was a beautiful, clear dawn. The rain had come and gone, and though the night faded from one pale patch in the sky, no direct light had crept in yet. The brightening of the day could not be separated from the adjusting of the eyes.

Keval sat in the car, smoking a cigarette. When he saw me come out, he brought the car up, with no more fuss than if he were taking me to school.

'*Chalo* Pakistan,' I said, as if we were refugees in 1947.

'*Chalo* Pakistan!' he chortled.

We drove through the Delhi of roundabouts, long avenues and white colonial bungalows. Long stretches of dark, empty road, with off-duty traffic-lights, gave way to a headlight parade of trucks. Keval would accelerate until he was just inches behind one, and its bright, painted colours were visible, then he'd sidle over to the right to see if it was safe to overtake. Sometimes he'd overtake with oncoming headlights close in the distance, slipping between yellow lights and coloured trucks. We passed factories and warehouses, agriculture marooned in every corner of free space, until we were only among fields. I remember falling asleep just after we drove through the city's red stone gates.

When I woke up, a heavy pink sun was blanching fast. Salmon, gold and saffron light seeped into the hot haze, lifting from green, waterlogged fields. The town we drove into was Ludhiana. It was a town of cloth mills, and the evidence of this was everywhere. The industry invaded the inner streets. Rough mountains of fabric were heaped precariously outside every shop so that only wholesale purchases seemed possible. Trucks, with sack-cloth posteriors, bursting with cotton, clogged the town's narrow arteries. The bypass was under repair so highway traffic, impatient from recently moving at a steady pace, now inched behind the cotton trucks. Bicycles, two- and three-wheeler scooters completed the chaos, driving one little wheel into any opening. But for the porous fortification of open drains, the only indication of municipality, the street caved in on itself. Ludhiana itself was a town inside out, in which factories and highways sprung up in its centre and the people lived outside.

It was the first large Punjabi town we passed through. In my own complicated situation, Punjab was a way through the confusions of nationality and religion. My father was from Punjab across the border, but so was my mother's Sikh family. There was Punjab in India and Punjab in Pakistan. It was like a network of cultural familiarity that stretched over the two enemy countries. It was made up of language, song, poetry, clan affiliation, and a funereal obsession with certain tragic romances. Decades after Partition, it clung on, like the rods in a crumbling building, bent, mangled, but somehow, still fierce. More than India, it was Punjab that was divided to make Pakistan, and the pain of it was felt acutely on both sides.

There was a time when my entire journey from the moment we left Delhi would have been through Punjab. But what was left of the state in India after Partition was further divided into three smaller states. So, of the state that once stretched from Delhi to Kabul, only a patch remained in India, carrying the name Punjab. And when my father first saw Indian Punjab, all those years ago, he said, with characteristic delicacy to my mother, 'We got Punjab, you got the foreskin.'

There had been a substantial monsoon, and in this river country, every little stream and canal ran unsteadily, like an over-full glass, to drop-off points in the fields. The villages we drove past were single-storey brick constructions containing a surprising number of auto mechanics and chemists. The rains did the job of the municipality, producing a large patch of wet black mud, which served as a town square. Vegetable sellers, tea stalls and outdoor eating places fought for space. The idleness of cows and buffaloes seemed to rub off on the people, who lazed on rope beds.

Stout yellow and white milestones now read 'Jalandhar'. A functioning bypass swept away the town, and a cement bridge took us across a wide, muddy river. The Beas. One of the five rivers of Punjab, two of which remained in India, and from which the state derived its purely Persian name: *punj*, five, and *ab*, water; five waters.

Then, abruptly, in this landscape of fields, tractors, canals and red-brick houses, a road sign read: 'Lahore 43km.'

'Forty-three kilometres!' Keval cried. 'I could drive there in less than an hour!' Until now there had been no indication of the closeness of the border, and I hadn't expected to see any before Amritsar.

Keval was still shaking his head, his crooked protruding teeth frozen in a grimace, when the road took on a new aspect. It was no longer the busy run-down highway leading to Amritsar, but a leafy dual-carriageway with little traffic. Its construction and maintenance bore the unmistakable mark of military efficiency. The first signs of an army presence were soon visible: cadets and young recruits peered inquisitively out of the back of their camouflaged trucks; the Border Security Force's bases appeared, and some of the army vehicles turned into them. Their high walls, with bright bougainvillaea hanging over them, suggested army schools and peacetime routines. The occasional armoured car appeared, but there was nothing threatening in its heavy tread. The entire place possessed an old-fashioned cantonment atmosphere of good food and officers' evenings.

The only unnatural element was the fields: the massive, unending expanse of agriculture, which threatened to engulf the neat academies and bases that had been set up so incongruously on its stretch. These fields, heavy with rice and water, so removed from everything, seemed strange things to defend. Keval and I pushed on along this unexpected road, eaten up by fertile land, until we came at last to the moody frontier.

It appeared like a roadblock, at best a scenic stop, to interrupt the land's flat expanse. Hawkers and agents fell upon the car, selling soft drinks and postcards of the border-closing ceremony. It was a difficult moment for Keval and me. I felt bad at having to leave him behind. I also felt a degree of fear because I couldn't see into Pakistan and wasn't sure if my mother's friend's son would have come to pick me up. Keval registered my nervousness and said, 'No reason to worry. I'll wait for you for an hour until I know you've crossed.'

Shooing off hawkers, he led the way past the car park and refreshment stalls and through a small black gate. Here, an attendant asked for our passports. Keval gave me a tight hug and sent me off.

Through the gate, I could see the lavish excesses of the governments' imagination. A pink amphitheatre had been constructed where spectators at the daily border-closing ceremony could sit. It consisted of an exchange of huffs and salutes performed in symmetry by the Indian and Pakistani sides. Then two gates, painted to look like iron flags, were slammed shut before a hooting crowd. It was a choreographed piece of officialdom, a military extravaganza for the bureaucrat. Two concrete arches stood at equidistance from the open gates. In their shade, two men from the respective sides sat with ledgers in their laps. Someone had gone to a lot of trouble to finesse these symmetries in concrete.

I was ushered into a cool, dark office on the Indian side where a man inspected my passport. Then a coolie in a blue shirt and white pyjamas pushed my bag through an X-ray that wasn't switched on. I picked it up at the other end and was directed out of the office on to a bleak stretch of road leading up to the arches. The great trees of the sub-continent lined the road: dark green mango, frangipani, pale eucalyptus, dour, drooping *ashok* and the patriarchal and sacred *peepal*. Among them, appearing intermittently, were rusty billboards advertising Pepsi. Following the coolie, I saw the fields again. A great black two-faced fence, with a stooped back and tense barbed wire, ran for miles through them. On the other side, past the barbed wire, the fields continued. The morose screech of a koel broke the quiet.

When we reached the Indian arch, I saw in the ledger that the last person to cross had been a Nigerian some weeks before.

The coolie walked a few yards further, past the short shadow cast by the arch, to where another coolie in identical white pyjamas, but with a green shirt, took my bag from him. The exchange was made with so little ceremony that its meaning was nearly lost on me. The coolies' faces, tired and lined in the same way, next to the detail of their ragged shirts in different colours, seemed to mock the place. After the pomp before, that was all: I was in Pakistan.

The gate on the other side was of rust-coloured brick, with cream crenellations and turrets. In gold Urdu letters a sign read: 'Gate of Freedom.' Above it, the green – the darkest of all greens, a black forest green – and white of the Pakistani flag raced in the wind.

In the old-fashioned colonial offices on the other side, the reception was warm. They read the name in my passport and asked, unprompted, 'This is the People's Party Salmaan Taseer?'

'Yes,' I answered.

'You're not carrying alcohol, I hope?'

'No.'

I knew that my father was well-known in Pakistan for his political role, and later his businesses, but not the extent of it. Sitting in those shaded offices, heat and heavy trees outside, I knew that I had set in motion one of the biggest decisions of my life.

Then an unsettling exchange occurred. One of the men, effusive and warm at first, asked in Urdu, 'So, what brings you back this time?'

Urdu and Hindi were hardly different so I replied easily, 'Not much, boss. Just my friend's birthday.'

The hospitality evaporated and they stared at me in silence.

One of the men repeated the word I used for 'birthday', and suggested another. Then, he said, 'Oh, you've come from *India*?' The differences between the two languages were very slight and, growing up in Delhi, my language was heavily influenced by Urdu, but I had used the one word that only someone who grew up in India could have used.

And so it was that I took my first steps into Pakistan aware of my unique patrimony, knowing at once familiarity and unfamiliarity.

# Renaissance Now

Karachi, Pakistan, four years later. My arrival in Pakistan was sudden and unplanned. Two weeks ahead of schedule, I was on an Emirates flight, covering the short distance from Dubai to Karachi. We flew like a small plane, close to the land, sometimes over bright blue water, sometimes over desert, before dropping toward the Indus's saline mouth and the hard yellow land of Sind.

I chose Karachi, rather than Lahore, because I wasn't ready yet to see my father. I was also thinking of his letter and wanted to travel in his country before making my way north to him.

It was my first time in Karachi. The highway that brought me into town didn't bring me far enough for me to have a feel of the city. I expected a noisier, more congested city, more like Bombay or Tehran, but the city we entered was spread out, with empty residential streets. Long, unshaded main roads connected little markets and offices to colonies of golden-brown, California-style bungalows, with green, reflective-glass windows. There was in the hot breeze, the listless neighbourhoods, the bungalows, with large balconies, and the bleak, grid-like streets, here and there with the cowering shadow of a palm on them, seeming to rise to a distant point, and then dropping, a hint of the sea. There was also, in the high walls of houses, armed guards standing outside, white cars with tinted windows, through which it was possible to make out the silhouettes of body-guards, a hint of crime.

There was some talk of my staying at my father's guesthouse in Karachi, but my elder half-brother, whom I hardly knew, insisted I stay with him. He lived in one of Karachi's newer bungalows. It was a small, well-proportioned house, sparse and functional, with a large balcony. Most of the day it was quiet, except for the hum of an air-conditioner. Large Indian blinds kept the sun's blaze out and gave the little house a permanent feeling of afternoon. My brother ran it like a bachelor's home, with a single servant who brought up beers, lime water and meals on TV trays. I had a basic room, with a narrow bed, next to my brother's, which, after all these years of being an only child, gave me a taste of living with siblings.

I felt unexplained tenderness for my brother. My father and he had always had a complicated relationship, often related to my father's disapproval of the women he dated. I sensed damage in my brother, the kind that can sometimes occur in children whose parents have been too powerful or too successful. After years of being my father's heir, of being told who to marry and who not to marry, groomed at the best schools and universities in Europe, he was about to find himself, at the age of thirty-five, beginning life alone in a country where connections and influence were everything. He had known about me for many years before that first trip to Pakistan, and perhaps because of our troubled relationships with our father, we shared a special connection.

After Iran, and my sudden arrival in Pakistan, I was happy to rest for a few days. I felt the delayed strain of my night flight from Iran, of connections made and hours lost. I wanted to put off travelling, calling my father, and even thinking too much about Pakistan. But on that first evening, I had a fore-taste, among educated Pakistanis, of a great double-edged tension. As India came up again and again, in big and small ways, sometimes through caste references, sometimes through Bollywood, I was reminded, as I had been unexpectedly four years before at the border, that I was a stranger in Pakistan.

The evening I arrived, my brother was holding a business meeting. It was for his own pet project, a half-hour comedy show that dealt with the week's news called *The Cutting Edge*. Those present were the two hosts, an attractive single mother in her thirties and a paunchy, older man who was the star of the show. There was also a young, pretty girl, with an American accent, whom everyone called 'Princess', and a dark, effeminate man, who was just sitting in. The targets for the satire beyond what was in the news were Bush and Islamic fundamentalism; the General was liked and spared.

That day there had been a news item about a study by an American think tank that placed Pakistan at nine in the top ten failed nations of the world. The study was based on a number of indexes ranging from 'chronic and sustained human flight', to 'criminalisation and delegitimisation of the state', to 'progressive deterioration of public services' and 'rise of factionalised élite'. The year before, according to the same report, Pakistan had been at number thirty-four. The group now worked out how to tear apart the report on the show.

'We want to be number one,' the dark, effeminate man cooed. 'I hate competition.'

Another asked where India was in the list.

The effeminate man rolled his eyes and his gapped teeth closed over his lower lip. 'Why can't we just accept that they are a better, greater country?' Everyone looked at me and laughed.

'Is it my imagination,' my brother said, 'or are there just many more ugly people in India?'

'Yes!' the effeminate man hissed. A short discussion began about how ugly Indians were, especially in the south. I listened for a while, then mentioned that some of India's best-looking models and actors come from the south.

'Well turned-out,' the effeminate man said archly. 'Not beautiful.' Then suddenly, he thought I'd taken offence, and said how much he loved India and that he was there recently. 'But I really gave it to them for running after the Americans,' he added, lifting his limp wrists to his chest and making the sound of a dog panting. He was referring to the nuclear deal that America and India were working out.

The next news item was about a threat from fundamentalist groups, saying they planned to host parties for young, liberal people in order to bomb them.

'They're hitting us where it hurts,' the attractive presenter said.

'We've been to these parties,' my brother nodded. 'This is serious.'

They decided it was so serious they wouldn't satirise it. At most they would say, 'Islamabad, you needn't worry, but Karachi and Lahore, beware.'

The next news item said that ten Americans had been killed in Afghanistan. 'I know this is politically incorrect,' my brother said, 'but *yesssss!*'

There was some stray laughter, then the group set to work on how to satirise the American 'occupations' of Iraq and Afghanistan. The middle-aged presenter said they had to keep up a sustained campaign against George Bush. A song was devised. It was a spoof of 'This Land'. 'This land is my land, this land is *not* your land . . . from Iraq to Guantánamo Bay,' or somesuch variation.

My brother said that the programme was creating a sensation. He was very pleased that many of the jokes were too sophisticated for the censors to catch, jokes such as the attractive host yelling, 'It's coming, it's coming, it's coming, I'm coming!' and faking an orgasm on television.

'But you really have to do it properly,' someone said. 'Can you go through with it?'

The female presenter smiled uneasily and nodded, like a great actress agreeing to do all that was necessary for a part.

Many of the show's jokes were too sophisticated for me to catch, some mismatch of what the show's creators had picked up at university in Britain and America. My brother hoped the programme would be shown in other places. Apparently, networks in India had expressed interest. He asked me what I thought. I told him it wouldn't work. It would be difficult to air a show that so many people wouldn't understand.

'Yes, but what about your small niche audience?' my brother asked.

'It's not as influential as it is here.'

When everyone had gone, the servant brought up a few beers and I sat for a while with my brother. In Karachi, there had recently been bombs. There were often bombs in Karachi, but this was more serious. A suicide-bomber had come into a prayer meeting of a Sunni political group on the Prophet's birthday and, along with himself, blew up the group's leadership and nearly sixty other people. The tensions the bombing brought to the surface revealed divisions and sub-divisions of denomination, language and sect that were hard even for Pakistanis to follow. There was not just the Sunni–Shia divide, but identities within identities, and corresponding political parties. And then, of course, there was the perpetual tension between the old inhabitants of Sind and the *Muhajjir*, the Muslim immigrants from India, who came in 1947 to realise the dream of a homeland for Indian Muslims.

'It's a different religion,' my brother said of Shiism, 'make no mistake. It's linked to a state, like Israel, and Iran can draw the loyalty of Shias worldwide, over and above the loyalty to the country their passport says they're from. They say they have seventy thousand Shias in Pakistan, armed and ready to strike US interests, which include Pakistan. If they don't have seventy thousand, they at least have a thousand! And that will cause chaos in Pakistan.'

The post-9/11 climate affected him more than I thought. It came out as excitement at Pakistan having become an international story, and instead of encouraging reflection into the reasons for the country's new fame, it brought out a kind of exhibitionism.

'There's a feeling of total civilisational defeat,' he said.

'What civilisation do you have in mind?'

'European, non-European, Christian, non-Christian, Caucasian, non-Caucasian,' my brother answered.

'It's interesting that you don't think of your civilisation as Indian,' I said, now feeling directly, as I had with my father, that the 'Civilisation of Faith' stood between me and someone I felt culturally close to.

'Yes, that is very interesting. There has been a complete rejection of the sub-continent.'

'But do you consider it your own, a part of your history?'

'No, we don't own it,' he answered. 'I'll tell you. No matter how much education a Pakistani gets, his mindset is fixed at the age of ten or eleven. If you write in your exams that the devious – you have to write devious,' he said, noticing my surprise at his use of the word, '– that the devious Hindu did this and did that, then you pass.' Not religious himself, but perhaps questioning his own convictions, my brother continued, 'At a certain time in Europe, learning and education were in the hands of the religious orders. Perhaps here, too, some kind of renaissance could begin with education in the hands of the religious orders.'

A renaissance! The revival of the great Islamic past in Pakistan. It was the country's present darkness, what my brother said earlier, 'the feeling of total civilisational defeat', the contents of the American think tank's report, that made him dream of

renaissance. In his excitement, he forgot what constituted the
kind of renaissance he was thinking of. He forgot the industry
of those European monks all those centuries ago, translating
books from Arabic into the European languages. I'd been to
enough *madrassa*s in my life, in enough places, to know that the
majority not only ignored books outside the Islamic past, they
ignored the Islamic thinkers too; they taught only one Book.
Pakistan, the country founded for the faith, never part of the
tradition of high Islam, always, culturally, an adjunct of Persia
and Arabia, the country that today supplied the oil-rich sections
of that world with its menial labour, was alone left to believe
in a great Islamic future. And with that belief came always the
unsaid horror of India.

*

Karachi was a British city and hardly older than a hundred and
fifty years. Until the 1960s, it was one of the cleanest, pleas-
antest cities in the sub-continent to live in, a city whose older
inhabitants remembered the streets being washed in the morn-
ings. But immigration, and the transfer of the capital from
Karachi to Islamabad, initiated its decline, leaving it today riddled
with armed crime, sectarian strife, its old British streets in ruins.
In the most crowded sections, cluttered with mean, bright little
billboards, chemists, 'footwear' shops, electrical appliances and
mangled nests of wires, there were the remains of the city's
finest buildings.

Behind one pale yellow façade, exquisite with sleeping
columns, little raking cornices, blackened dentil ornaments and
balustrades, the actual building had fallen away. Through the
mask-like façade's semi-circular windows, it was possible today
to see the white open Karachi sky. In the street of elegant
buildings, domes and clock towers were barely hanging on, and

in many the second storey was sealed with splintering sheets of plywood. Scattered across the old British city were Karachi's squat administrative buildings and hotels, many with 1970s patterned concrete screens in front of them so that they looked as if they had no distinct levels or windows.

The Sind Club was in this part of the city, and women were not allowed into its billiards room and bar, not for Islamic reasons but for old-fashioned colonial ones. Uniformed bearers glided through the high-ceilinged room, bright where light escaped from low shades over green felt tables. They brought members the Scotch and soda that the club kept for them under lock and key. There were hunting trophies on the walls, a smell of kebabs in the air, and from the lights in the garden, I could see waterfalls of red bougainvillaea. I'd gone there with my brother a few evenings after I arrived. We sat outside with some businessmen at a round table under a portico of sturdy arches.

'I saw you the other day at the airport,' one stout man in a silky shirt said to another sitting next to him.

'I wasn't there,' the other, taller, more sober, replied.

'You were boarding a first-class flight to Dubai.'

'No.'

'You were complaining about your air miles and saying you had nine hundred million in your account.' The man who had initiated the conversation, seeing the confusion on the other's face, guffawed, 'It's a joke, man!' Then he became confidential and they began to discuss a deal. I heard him say, 'You approached me about it when I was drunk, but if you're serious you can have it for thirteen million.'

On certain nights of the week, the club went a little further and organised a dance called Casablanca. In a darkened room, a disco light threw red, green and pink patterns on the walls. Waiters in white, with red fezes, moved quickly through the room, serving girls in little black dresses and paunchy men in fussy shirts. Through a glass partition close to the ceiling, it was possible to see a library of sorts, not a great library, but like something you'd find in a school, deepening my sense of being at a middle-school dance. A Bollywood hit song played several times over, filling the dance-floor each time.

A cousin I had recently met yelled over the music, 'She assaulted him three times. One time she tore his shirt and twisted his Bulgari cufflinks. Her family are *chooda*s!' She was talking about her brother and his wife, but what interested me was her use of '*chooda*', which was used like the word 'nigger', to mean low-caste. But in Islam there was no caste. My cousin, who used the world freely, as did my brothers, grew up with it. It had resonance all over Pakistan, but many people used it without knowing where it came from or that it denoted caste. It was part of an unacknowledged carryover from India. It was like the song that brought everyone to the dance-floor.

But these commonalities, these memories of plural India, were not always easy for Pakistanis to take on. They were a hazy reminder of what had been lost. Pakistan's assertion of Islamic identity was not the theocracy of Iran. It was through purifying its population of non-Muslims, conducting the transfers of people, of which my maternal great-grandmother had been a part, that the new state realised its aims. But India, on the other side, was still as it had been, still plural, not symmetrically Hindu and with as many, if not more, Muslims than Pakistan. And there was no escaping the strangeness of that.

The Bombay film industry was a powerful reminder of composite India. It was full of Muslim stars and the Hindustani language it kept alive was replete with Urdu words. Though the films were officially banned in Pakistan, 'unofficially', my brother's dark, effeminate friend explained, 'Hindi films are released on

Fridays in India and the same night – the same night! – via piracy, they release in Karachi!' It meant that Pakistanis had a view of India every day in their homes. The reverse was not true. Pakistan's once significant film industry had sunk. The cause of its demise was like a roll call of the country's tragedies: the loss of half its audience when East Pakistan broke away to become Bangladesh, Bhutto's economic nationalisation in the 1970s and Zia's Islamic censorship in the 1980s.

'We used to have fifteen hundred cinemas,' my brother's friend moaned, 'and now we have some two hundred.'

He was worried about the tighter hold of religion in Pakistan. 'In Punjab and Sind,' he said, 'our Sufi culture will save us, but I worry about the North West Frontier Province and Balochistan. They could flood us. Otherwise, we are deeply immersed in our Sufi culture. And also our diversity will save us.'

'Are you religious?'

'It depends by whose definition.'

'By your own?'

'Well, I say my prayers and pray to Allah that I win the lottery. People say that that's gambling, but I say, 'Hey, thank Allah.' Then as if remembering what he had said earlier, he added, 'I think it's because they're LMC and there's a lot of guilt.' 'LMC' meant lower-middle class and it was a term rich Pakistanis used often to mean a rising section of the country that was also more religious. The remark was at once flippant, an aspect of his bitter wit, and significant. 'Guilt,' he went on, 'is the reason people are turning to religion. Many rich people made their money by illegal means and now they feel guilty.'

Corruption in Pakistan was something one always heard about, but I had never thought of it before as something for the religious imagination to seize on. Later, I would meet many admirable young people who made these kinds of connections.

'Your mother is a Sikh,' the effeminate man continued, 'but do you know that sixty per cent of the *Guru Granth Sahib* was written by Baba Farid?'

Farid was a twelfth-century Sufi teacher and his writings are included in the Sikh holy book, but the figure was an exaggeration. 'The tolerance!' the effeminate man hissed. 'The tolerance! That period should have had a renaissance, and it's all because of the white man, all because of him.'

The white man doesn't mean well for us. Nearly six decades after the 'white man' left, this weak refrain was all that could be found by way of self-examination. But it was not enough to blame the white man. It didn't explain why the white man's world should have posed such an affront to Muslim India and not to non-Muslim India. With my special feeling for undivided India, I would have liked nothing more than for the period he described to have a 'renaissance' – how strange it was to hear the word twice in such a short time from different people – but how could it when even men like my brother dreamed of Islamic renaissances in *madrassas*?

The party came to an end. Men in blue and brown safari suits, seeming like chaperones, appeared and oversaw the winding up. The girls in black dresses and their short, paunchy men, the country's 'factionalised élite', staggered out. The waiters in white became scarcer, then appeared with dishcloths, and were bald under the fezes they now carried in their hands. A small sadness, as at the end of a children's birthday party, prevailed. And finally, just before everyone was gone, bent, old women in white cotton *salwar kameez*, their faces tired at this late hour, came out with plastic dustpans and little brooms to sweep up the broken glasses and cigarette butts, the remains of Casablanca.

*

Soon after arriving in Karachi, I called my stepmother. She was warm and welcoming, as always, and said that, despite the heat, Sind's interior was very romantic. It was where I was intending to travel before I made my way up to Lahore. After we talked of the small regional towns and the important shrines I would visit, she said, 'Call Abba.'

'I will.' Then I squirmed.

'No, call him,' she stressed.

I thought up a few conversation points that would see us through the first few minutes of stilted conversation and called him. He was quiet but not unfriendly. I told him about Iran and my planned travels in Pakistan.

When I received my father's letter the year before, I knew nothing of Pakistan and even less about Islam. I wanted now, through travelling in Pakistan, to answer the second challenge his letter had posed, even though the two seemed in important ways to coalesce: of understanding 'the Pakistani ethos'. In the month in which I would travel, moving from south to north, I wanted to understand my unfamiliarity in Pakistan. I felt that this would help me understand the differences that had come up between my father and myself. My upbringing in India, together with seven months of travel in the Islamic world, formed a kind of Venn diagram, a problem in set theory, in which Pakistan, carved out of India in 1947 for the faith, was a common set between India and Islam.

My father listened to my travel plans, but there were no questions or comments. Before he hung up, he said, 'Call if you need anything.' And that was all.

Four years after our first meeting – and one, since the letter, spent in silence – I felt the thinness of our relationship.

# Nerve Blindness

That summer of 2002, I crossed the border and my mother's friend's son met me on the other side. I could make him out, standing by his car, in tight jeans and a close-fitting shirt. He had gelled hair and reflective sunglasses.

We drove away from the border in his air-conditioned car. The country that opened up, of mud chimneys, canals full of bathing children and small, congested neighbourhoods, with bright-coloured Urdu writing on the walls, might have been a Muslim neighbourhood in India. It seemed so familiar that one expected the diversity of the Indian scene to reveal itself. And when it didn't, it was unsettling. It really was an India for Muslims only.

The other feature of the landscape that troubled the eye was the absence of women. On the other side of the border, women had been riding bicycles – some in Punjab, with long plaits, had been on scooters and mopeds – but here, in crowded places, I could see thousands of men, many dressed like the officials at the border in *salwar kameez*, the same macho ease about them, but few women. When women did appear, they were either with other women, moving purposefully, as if with little time to spare, or with their men on an outing. There were no women waiting at bus stops, on their way to work, or canoodling with men in parks, or leisurely enjoying the weather. Their presence, slight as it was, seemed to be a matter of permission.

As the car entered the sections of Lahore built since Partition, I saw a strong resemblance to Delhi: dusty greenery, lazy flyovers passing from one quiet residential neighbourhood to another, the diffused sense of the city.

I was to stay with Nuscie, a friend of both my mother and my father. She lived in a large, whitewashed house off a main road. It was run the way houses in regional towns in India ran, with many servants, food at all times, long afternoons and family coming and going. Nuscie turned out to be a warm, hospitable woman with a keen sense of intrigue. She had fair skin, bright green eyes, and the lines on her face, seemed to come as much from laughter and mischief as age. And like her greying hair, they emphasised her once considerable beauty. She had met my mother through my father and they remained friends despite my parents' separation. She had always wanted me to meet him, and took me in knowing that he would be furious with her for helping me to do exactly that.

'Would you like me to call him first?' Nuscie asked, sipping tea, her eyes dancing with excitement.

'No, no, no, Nuscie, you mustn't. It's very important that an element of surprise works in my favour or he'll have time to back out.'

'Yes, of course, that's what I was thinking.'

I had cast aside earlier notions of just turning up at my father's house and introducing myself. It was totally impractical: there would be too many servants, guests and family to achieve the result I had fantasised about. In all likelihood, even if I was let into a room in which my father was, it would be full of people where my only line of introduction would be a stammered 'I'm Aatish Taseer.' I also found fault with my plan to meet my father on my own terms, anonymously, at a dinner party. I imagined we would spend many minutes talking, before he discovered I was his son. Absurd though they seemed, now that I was really in Lahore, these were some of the bizarre, cinematic ways that, as a child, I imagined our first meeting to be like.

Finally, against my imagination and with the dread of failure still in me, I realised I would have to telephone my father again. The thought of it aroused the worst feelings of disappointment in me. I had a superstitious fear that the bad luck from the time before would work against me. But I could see no way round it. No sooner had I decided on this course of action than, again, the foreignness of the place descended on me. Here I was, having travelled for fourteen hours to arrive at a near-stranger's house to make one telephone call that could end in anti-climax.

Once I resolved to do it, instinct told me to get on with it, as quickly, and with as little interference, as possible.

I excused myself and asked permission to go to my room.

'Yes, of course. You must be tired. Have a rest. Tonight we can go to the old city for dinner. There's a lovely little place there.'

I was not in the least bit tired; I was terrified. With meat patties and tea as the only weight holding down my body, I left the room. No sooner had I let the door close behind me than my eyes raced in search of a telephone, as if it were the antidote to my desperation. I went over the lines I had prepared, not caring any longer for their meaning but only that I was able to say them without my voice wavering. 'I can understand . . . why you may not . . .' I mouthed, as I saw the bright red instrument. I had written the number on a small chit, and held it now, tightly pressed between two fingers. I found the phone in a quiet corner between the drawing room and the kitchen. I was too restless to sit so I stood, leaning against the doorway, yawning with nerves. I dialled the number, and again, as I had years ago in my housemistress' apartment, hoped that there would be no answer.

The number this time, procured from Nuscie, was for a mobile phone. I took advantage of the personal access the technology afforded and began to talk mechanically as soon as I heard a voice.

'Hello, Salmaan. This is Aatish Taseer. I am in Lahore now and would like to see you.'

There was a brief silence and my father, as if his response had been years in the making, said, 'What would be the objective?'

I was grateful for the sting it caused. It gave me the indignation I needed. As long as I didn't give in to rudeness and insensitivity, I would retain the higher ground. It didn't feel like a tender reunion with my long-lost father but a contest, a Saturn and Jupiter fight to the finish.

'I can understand,' I started slowly, 'why you may not,' no waver, 'want to see me, but it is important to me that I see you, if only for a short time.'

He said nothing.

'Will this be possible?' I asked, in a still steadier voice.

'I'll have to think about it,' my father said. 'There are many things to consider.' He hung up.

I had failed to secure a meeting with my father. The anti-climax I was warned of had come and it felt worse than I imagined. I thought of my mother's words, 'Just remember, he'll always let you down,' and felt a kind of dread at having to face the other people in the house.

But that night my half-sister intervened. I bumped into her at a 'GT' – short in Lahore for a get-together – to which Nuscie's son had taken me. We spotted each other among a handful of attractive young people, dancing close together in a small, dimly lit, drawing room. I had met her once before in London. It was in 2000 after she sent me an email, having discovered that I was at college with a friend of hers. We met a few months later and liked each other very much. But my father was enraged when he found out. And as my sister was moving back to Pakistan to work for him, she couldn't afford to be on his bad side. We hadn't spoken since.

But seeing me now, unexpectedly in Lahore, she was full of warmth and affection. She said we would see each other over the next few days, even if we had to meet secretly. I told her of my conversation with our father; she said she would help, but couldn't tell how he would react.

Then, two days after my arrival, my sister called to say that my father had agreed to meet me. She would pick me up the next morning and take me to him.

\*

I met my father, for the first time in my memory, at his low, red-brick house in the cantonment area of Lahore. It had a large lawn, and a Land Cruiser brooded outside the front door. My sister led the way in, but disappeared almost immediately, with a smile and a supportive wave. I stopped at a large pencil portrait of my father as a young man. It gave me my first real sense of being in his house. It seemed to have hung there for years and it emphasised my absence from his life. To see the old yellowing portrait, which had been made at roughly the same time as my pictures of him had been taken, was to know that he had lived and that I had been elsewhere.

A moment later a servant showed me into his library. It was a room with floor-to-ceiling books and windows overlooking a swimming-pool. On a slim, marble table there were family pictures in polished silver frames. The physical resemblance of the people in them to me was another reminder of my absence. It was as if a kink in time and space had air-brushed me out. I didn't feel emotional or even nervous; I was overwhelmed by the unreality of the moment. Tea and sandwiches laid out on a tray seemed to mock me.

My father walked in a few minutes later with his young wife. Her hair was blow-dried and she had diamonds in her ears. He was in blue, wearing soft boots with tan insides. I noticed them because my mother would tell me he had weak ankles and bought expensive boots. Though I couldn't have known it at the time, I must have sought to bridge the time when she and I had known him with the time now. It was why I asked his wife if she would leave us alone. It was perhaps also why the pictures and the portrait had unsettled me.

My father's physical appearance riveted me. The man who walked in was a fatter, balder version of the man from my browning silver frame. I had seen him last when I was not even eighteen months old and had no image of him except from those old pictures. I noticed the light, greenish-amber eyes that my mother had described to me, the lines around the mouth that were like mine, and the way he dropped into his chair, uncaring of where his hands and legs fell. I would have liked to know what he smelt of.

I must have been in some state of shock because I can hardly remember a word that was said. I know that I wanted very quickly to provide him with good reasons for why he hadn't been in my life and offered his political career, which he took up readily. I also made a point of saying that now that he was no longer in politics, perhaps it would be easier for us to meet, even if we couldn't have a conventional father–son relationship. This, too, he accepted. And then we spoke of generalities: my journey, the differences between India and Pakistan, how similar the two countries were. I felt the conversation was stilted, but I didn't realise how much more open it would seem when compared with our later conversations. My father asked after my mother and said he had no hard feelings towards her. It was almost the only time in our relationship that he acknowledged I had known him in the past. It helped me to ground myself in the present situation.

Then, as we got up, he asked if I had any questions for him. I had many, but felt that since the meeting had gone well and he seemed open to seeing me again, there would be time later. But when his life in Lahore, the life I had not been part of, closed around him again, he was less willing.

# The Mango King

'I feel I've made a mistake in my attitude to Pakistan,' I said to the publisher. 'I arrived treating it as just another country. I was still thinking of Turkey, Syria and Iran when I got here. But I feel now that I'm more invested in Pakistan than I thought. I need to see more of it.'

He frowned and his eyebrows collected tightly above his eyes. He was a heavy man in a white *salwar kameez*, with short greying hair and moustache. His face was large and pinkish and his eyes intense. He published a major Pakistani newspaper. My mother had put us in touch, and though he wasn't sure what I was writing about, he seemed to understand my urgency. He did for me what I would have liked my father to have done: he insisted on my connection to Pakistan, the land, deeper than the border that divided India and Pakistan. He made no outward attempt to do this, but by arousing my interest in the cultural bonds that still existed between the two countries, in speaking to me of my paternal grandfather, an Urdu poet, in the pre-Partition years, and, most importantly, by communicating his own feeling for my situation, the publisher gave me the other side of the romance of an undivided India on which my maternal grandfather and my mother had raised me. Here was Pakistan, a whole country of unexplored connections. But where to begin?

Karachi, though it was the closest thing to a representative Pakistani city, was not like Istanbul was to Turkey or Tehran to Iran, not a city where a fifth or a sixth of the population lived. No one knew the exact figure, but a rough estimate put it at 16 million in a country of about 160 million. Pakistan, unlike any other country I had been in so far, was largely rural. People had said to me, 'You don't know the soul of Pakistan till you know feudal Pakistan.' And charged by the desire to see this feudal life, I asked the publisher if he could help.

We sat in his grand old Karachi house. He lay on a very high bed, smoking, dictating itineraries and making phone calls to people who might help me. The most famous twentieth-century Indian and Pakistani artists covered the high walls of his room; boxes and precarious stacks of books lay on the floor. The house had long dark corridors and whole wings seemed to be closed off. After a few hours of messages left, phone calls returned, lists made, lectures on safety and extreme heat, the publisher looked up at me, scribbling as he spoke. 'Can you leave tonight?'

'Tonight?'

His fierce, pinkish face, the face of a man used to getting things done, fixed on mine; something twitched. He seemed to show disappointment and anger that I had wasted his time and betrayed his romantic vision of travelling in the country of the Indus, of Mohenjodaro, of Sufi shrines and the oldest Indian civilisation.

'Yes,' I stammered. 'I can leave tonight.'

'Good.'

It was early evening when I went back to my brother's to pack my bags. I was to leave late that night with the Mango King for his lands in interior Sind.

*

I had dozed off on my brother's beanbag when the Mango King called to say he was outside. I looked at my watch and saw it was well past midnight. I picked up my bag and went downstairs. A warm breeze was blowing and the street, lit with flickering tube light, was quiet. A white car, with heavily tinted windows, stood outside. As I approached, one of its back doors opened, but no one stepped out. Instead, cold, air-conditioned air infused with a faint smell of cigarettes drifted out. I put my head into the car and saw a young man in the back seat, with a black moustache, fair skin and a handsome, slightly puffy, face. He peered at me through a dense haze of smoke and gestured to me to get in.

The chauffeur drove off as soon as I shut the door. I turned now to the Mango King, who lit another cigarette. The air was so smoky, so cold and unbreathable, and the black windows wound up so deliberately, that my first exchanges with him were a series of polite half-smiles, confused looks, gentle prodding, anything to steer the conversation in the direction of why we were driving in these conditions. The Mango King, if he registered my objections, showed no sign of it. He smoked continuously, slowly and deeply, looking out at the deserted streets. I could tell from his eyes and the thickness in his voice that he had been drinking.

'In the city I am a different person,' he said abruptly, 'and, you'll see, in the village I am a different person. One has to adjust. It gets pretty nasty,' he added suddenly. 'People steal water. Typical *vadhera*.' A *vadhera*, or landlord, was what the Mango King had become after his father died; his family were among the largest producers of mangoes in the country. 'But things won't change.'

'Why?'

'Not for another fifty years. There will still be feudalism.' I nodded and saw that he was drinking from a hip flask.

'Do you know why Sindi society is a failure?' the Mango King asked, in his abrupt way.

'No.'

'There's no middle class. There's us and there's them. We had a middle class, but they took off when what happened?' I thought it was a rhetorical question and didn't answer, but the Mango King's gaze held me, expecting a reply.

'Partition,' I answered obediently.

'Exactly. But, you know, life goes on, one day to the next. My father trained me to be a farmer.' The Mango King spoke in broken sentences, disconnected in thought and language. After a long silence, he said, 'Do you know why religion was invented?'

'Why?' I asked, wondering if some vague précis of my purpose had been passed on to him.

'A man can deal with everything but death.'

The Mango King lit up again, but this time my eyes focused on a new discomfort: an AK-47 was placed between him and me, and the ribs of its magazine, its short barrel and bulbous sight shone in the yellow streetlight. The Mango King was silent now, still drinking and smoking. The car's cold, fetid air made me feel ill. The gun's silhouette came in and out of shadow as we left Karachi. I kept catching it in the corner of my eye, and as there was a lull in the conversation, I thought I'd ask why the AK-47, particularly, was so popular.

'Three things you have to be able to trust,' the Mango King answered. 'Your lads, your woman and your weapon. It'll never jam on you. Anyone can fire it and it'll never jam.'

I don't know when I fell asleep, but I woke up once to see the Mango King still smoking. The next time, he was asleep, his head bobbing from side to side, the gun still visible at his feet, matt black with occasional yellow lustre.

I fell into a deeper sleep and woke next when I felt a touch on my hand. It was dawn, and we drove down a deserted country road, amid acres and acres of flat, empty fields.

'The estate begins here,' he said. The car swung left. 'This, on both sides, is my estate.' I looked around and saw that there were only shrubs and small trees on the land, thirsty even in the half-light. 'This is the land I don't grow.'

'Why?'

'No water.'

'How big is it?'

'Six thousand acres.' By the sub-continent's standards, this was a large holding.

Then after some silence, he straightened his posture and, with pregnant solemnity, said, 'This is my territory.'

We passed several acres of dense, low crop, then just before the house, like some last battalion of a great regiment or a vanishing tribe of horses, seeming almost to smile at their own dignity in the desolate fields around them, were the mango trees. The Mango King stared in dull-eyed wonder at the dark green, almost black canopies, heavy with fruit and dropping low in a curtsy against an immense saffron sky.

As we came closer, the trees that seemed to have a single, pointed canopy, concealing their short trunks, were in fact distinct clusters of long, curled leaves, as though warped by the heat. Their contours contained a bewitching interplay of pigment and shadow. The fruit was small and mostly unripe, but the end of each was yellow as though some tropical poison gathered its reserves before overwhelming the whole.

When we got out of the car, I saw that the Mango King was tall and well-built. His cream *salwar kameez* partially concealed a new paunch, and like the puffiness of his face, it was unattractive on a man of his looks.

A few men were stooped in greeting. The Mango King waved at them, then stumbled through a doorway. We entered a walled garden of palms, droopy *ashoka* trees and buoyant rubber plants. A cement walkway, like a Pac-man trail, led to the house. The

Mango King's fluttering cream figure reeled, tottered, straightened, and lurched down the narrow path, as his servants and I followed. The walkway finished in front of a low white bungalow. Darkness and a musty stench from thick, beige carpeting hit us as we entered. I couldn't make out much of the house in the dim morning light. At the far end, there was a square arrangement of low sofas.

The Mango King collapsed into one, and stared vacantly at me, as if only now seeing me. I wondered what he thought I wanted with him. Among pictures of the family, and one of the Mango King in a yellow tie, there were many books: a pictorial biography of Hitler, *National Geographic*s, Frederick Forsyth, *Jane's Aircraft Almanacs*, *Animals in Camera* and dozens on travel. I felt from the books, and from the framed posters of impressionist paintings, a longing for other places; it was like a longing for clemency, in colour, temperature and degree.

'Did your father read a lot?' I asked, scanning the shelves.

'Yes,' the Mango King replied. 'He was the sort of man you could talk to about anything and he would always have the right answer.' The description suggested a nightmare person, but the Mango King hadn't intended it to sound that way. 'I used to read,' he added, 'but I don't get the chance any more.' He showed me a book he'd recently bought. It was a guide to being a gentleman. 'It says that a gentleman never adjusts his crotch in public.' The Mango King chuckled and then we fell into silence. He sat there, looking neither at me nor at his men, but ahead, into the gloom, like a man who had just lost all his money. A servant brought him some water and a new AK-47, this time with a drum magazine. He leant it against the leg of his chair and, turning to me, said that this one was Chinese; more than a hundred countries produced them now. He asked me if I'd like to fire one.

'Yes,' I said, surprising myself.

'She wreaks havoc when she opens her mouth,' he smiled mirthlessly. He was prone to theatrical utterances and to clichés like 'Different strokes for different folks' or 'You can take the boy out of the country, but you can't take the country out of the boy,' which he said as if they'd never been said before. The idea of firing the gun was forgotten for now.

My own fatigue deepened just as the Mango King had a second wind. He ordered wine and asked if I'd like some dinner. The wine was unusual in the sub-continent, whisky and soda would have been more standard, but this, like the cigars and brandy that came afterwards, and the guide to being a gentleman, seemed like a recent feudal affectation.

I laughed at the suggestion of dinner, as it was already dawn; he stared at me.

'No, thank you,' I replied, more soberly.

'Yum-yum,' he said, looking at the feast that was now being laid out before us. There were several kinds of meat, rice, lentils, bread and more wine.

The Mango King rolled up his sleeves to eat and I saw that there were cigarette burns branded into his arm. The cutlery was Christofle, scattered stylishly among the ovenproof crockery and dinner trays.

Two minutes later he asked again. I declined once more and said that I'd like to go to bed. He gestured to a man to show me to my room, and just as I was leaving, he enquired one last time if I wouldn't have any dinner.

*

When I awoke a few hours later, I was lying under a wooden fan, with an inbuilt light, and a small chandelier. Next to my bed there was a copy of *Time* magazine and a guide to nightlife in Thailand. The little room, despite the air-conditioning, was suffocating. From the edges of tightly drawn curtains, a white blaze broke through. It was about ten o'clock and the house was quiet. I stepped into the drawing room and felt a wave of compressed heat. The room could not have been more badly designed for the fierce temperature beyond its darkened, sliding doors. It was low, like a garage, heavy with carpeting and velvety sofas, and without ventilation. I stepped out on to a white tiled courtyard and soon retreated. It was dangerous heat, the worst I'd ever experienced, sharp, unshaded, asphyxiating. It could make you sick if you went unprotected into it. Yet to be back in the room, in the bad, stale air, was hardly better. Outside, buffaloes lay in the shade of trees; little villages of straw, with brambly fences, dotted the Mango King's lands; and slim, black women, in bright colours, with white bangles all the way up their arms, walked along the edges of mud paths.

After tea, breakfast and a shower, I came into the main room of the house to find that the Mango King was up and inspecting weapons. 'You can't get this on licence,' he said cheerfully, as the man brought out an Uzi. The Mango King was freshly bathed, his eyes alert, his manner sprightly in a way I wouldn't have thought possible the night before. The deadened glaze had gone from his eyes and his mind made connections easily. He seemed to read my face and sense that I might be a little surprised at the gun parade before lunch. 'A lot of people in Karachi don't like farmers,' he said. 'They say they're feudal, but my feeling is that there are good and bad people in every field.' Still fixing magazines, looking through sights, handing back guns, he said, 'Can you imagine? Even I was kidnapped.'

I thought he was being deliberately provocative now and, concealing my surprise, I asked casually, 'How old were you?'

'I was twelve and when I came back I was thirteen. It was from 1984 to 1985, for six months. I was chained for the last two. My father wouldn't pay the ransom. When they called he started abusing them so they only called once. After that, they dealt with my uncle.' The kidnappers had picked him up outside his school in Hyderabad.

The Mango King did not alter his short, offhand style. His point was not to emphasise the violence in his life but to make clear that he had paid his dues.

It was difficult to take anything away from the story. The Mango King drank heavily; he had suspicious cigarette burns on his arms; he played with guns; his father, who knew the right answer to everything, sounded as if he had been difficult; and yet what might have seemed like cause for alarm was presented instead as emblematic of the feudal life. The violence he had experienced, and perhaps inflicted, became like a rite of passage.

'Was it traumatic?'

'Yes,' the Mango King replied, 'but you get used to anything.'

His reply reminded me of a story my father once told me of being in prison in Pakistan. His jailers had put him in a metal cage in heat similar to the kind outside. Then they threw a leather blanket over the top and sprinkled it with water so that the humidity made the air even less breathable. They wanted my father to sign an admission of guilt, which they didn't bring him until several hours into the process of breaking him down. When finally they did bring it, he wouldn't sign. His explanation was that they tortured him for too long: if they'd brought it sooner, he might have signed, but once he realised he could bear the unbearable, new resolve hardened in him.

Like the Mango King's, it was difficult to draw a message of courage from my father's story. At most, and this in part was why my father told it, it could give an idea of what was needed to enter politics in Pakistan. But that kind of mettle could not be asked of everyone. It couldn't be made a requirement of office, like promising to tell the truth. Most people would bend and enter a state of corruption, which wasn't really corruption given the duress. In the end, the story could only be seen in its context, a vignette in Pakistan's Hobbesian political life. The extreme shows of defiance – not signing the admission or not paying the ransom – could also come to seem like bravado rather than courage when the people who endured them saw them as training rather than injustice.

That evening the Mango King suggested I go with him to Mirpur Khas, a nearby town, to meet a lawyer who was working on a case he was fighting. The sun at last was loosening its grip on the day and the land, stunned and silent for many hours, came to life with the screeching of birds and the movement of animals. The evening brought with it colour that, after the white blaze, made it seem as if the sun was sinking behind a mountain of prisms.

Driving out of the Mango King's gate, I noticed something I hadn't seen earlier: under the name of the estate, it said, 'Veni Vidi Vici'.

'We used to send mangoes to the Queen of England,' the Mango King said proudly.

'You should start again.'

'No,' he smiled, 'but we send them to Musharraf.'

In the car, the Mango King and his tall, thin lieutenant discussed feudal revenge. The lieutenant was a *muhajjir* or immigrant from India. His family came to Pakistan after Partition from Jodhpur in Rajasthan. The feudal life needed men like the lieutenant. He was dark and bald, with the aspect of a grand vizier, and after the Mango King's father died, he served the son as a loyal adviser. They talked about how another feudal had killed the Mango King's friend in an argument over 350 acres. The Mango King said that the other landlords still teased the dead man's son for having been unable to exact revenge. 'What can he do?' The Mango King laughed. 'His father's killer is hardly in the country, and when he is, he's guarded heavily. There's a Sindi saying: "Love and revenge never get old."'

'Don't the police ever get involved?'

'Not in these things. The people come to me with their problems and family matters. If you're the landlord, you're politician and policeman too. The landowner's word is law.' Then, thinking about it for a moment, he said, 'In the end, it's not even about land. It's about who gets to be head honcho.' I thought he put it well: land at last was stabilising; this was about arbitrary power and the Mango King was also vulnerable.

The Mango King's lieutenant had been back to Jodhpur just once, in 1990, and from the moment he heard I was Indian, he could speak of nothing else. He craned his long neck forward and asked if I saw much difference between India and Pakistan.

'Not much,' I said, meaning to be polite. 'There's more feudalism here.'

'But between human beings, on a human level?'

'No, not really.'

'But there is!' He smiled.

'What?'

'In Pakistan, the clothes people wear are much better. There's far less poverty. India makes its own things, its own cars, but then you don't get Land Cruisers. In India, you get Indian needles. In Pakistan, we get Japanese needles!'

In India you now got Japanese needles too. The lieutenant had visited before economic liberalisation, but that was not the point. What struck me was how this man, who would never come close to owning a Land Cruiser, could talk of such things as core human differences. The poverty around him was as bad as anything I had ever seen, yet he spoke of expensive cars. It was as if the mere fact of difference was what he needed. It hardly mattered what the differences meant: that was taken care of by the inbuilt rejection of India. In the confusion about what Pakistan was meant to be, whether it was a secular state for Indian Muslims, a religious state, a military dictatorship, a fiefdom, that rejection could become more powerful an idea than the assertion of Pakistan.

'What other differences did you see?' he asked.

'It's hard to say as there's so much change within India. There are more differences between the north and the south than there are between north India and Pakistan.'

The lieutenant was not to be put down. He wanted to get something off his chest. 'The other difference,' he began, 'was that while men here wear flat colours, the men there are fond of floral prints, ladies' clothes.' Hindus weaker, more feminine, and Muslims stronger, manlier: this was the dull little heart of what the lieutenant wanted to say and a great satisfaction came over his face as he spoke. This was the way he reconnected with the glories of the Islamic past, of the time when the 'Civilisation of Faith' remained and the martial Muslims ruled the 'devious Hindu'.

The heat that seemed inescapable earlier had lifted magically and the din of insects made its way into the car. The land around us was completely dark, but for the occasional tube-light over a small structure somewhere in the fields.

'Were you scared when they kidnapped you?' I asked the Mango King, hoping to hear the rest of the story.

'The first fifteen minutes were scary, but then it was all right.'

After many minutes of silence, the Mango King began again, with a new softness in his voice, 'They said, "Now, OK, say your last prayers," but fortunately,' he chuckled, 'they did not kill me.' After four months he had tried to steal a kidnapper's gun and use it on two of them, but just as he picked it up, the third returned and wrested it from his hands. That was when they chained him as punishment. It was painful to think of the Mango King, so hard now, in so vulnerable a position.

I thought he wanted to say more, but his lieutenant interrupted: 'Tell me,' he said, 'why do you wear a *kara*?' He was referring to the steel bangle on my wrist.

'Because my grandmother is a Sikh and wanted me to wear it.'

'Your mother's Sikh and you're Muslim.'

'No,' I said, wishing to annoy him, 'my mother's Sikh and my father's Muslim.'

'Yes, yes, so you're Muslim.'

'I'm nothing.'

The lieutenant seemed to ask the question in the most basic sense. He could tell I wasn't a practising Muslim, but he wanted to know if I was Muslim somehow, in the way that my father was Muslim. My experience with my father had shown that this vague sense contained passions I didn't share so I thought it better to dissent early rather than have to explain myself later.

'Come on, you're Muslim. If you're father's Pakistani, you're Muslim.'

'If you say so, but don't you have to believe certain things to be a Muslim? If I don't believe, can I still be Muslim?'

He looked at me with fatigue. It was almost as if he wanted to say yes. It was as though, once acquired, this identity based on a testament of faith could not be peeled away, like caste in India. And really, I felt that if I could know the sanctity of his feeling of difference in relation to non-Muslim India, and the symbolic history that went with it, I would be as Muslim as he was.

'It's his decision,' the Mango King laughed.

The lieutenant fell into a moody silence. 'It's hotter in India than it is in Pakistan, isn't it?' he started again.

The Mango King groaned with irritation.

'No, it's the same!' I said. 'You see too many differences.'

Perhaps sensing that he had created bad feeling with a guest, he said, 'Sikhs have a very sweet way of speaking.'

'Their way of speaking is the same as ours!' the Mango King snapped, and the lieutenant retreated with a sad, stung expression.

Pakistan's economic advantage, the manliness of Muslim men, Land Cruisers and Japanese needles, even an imagined better climate: these were the small, daily manifestations that nourished a greater rejection of India, making the idea of Pakistan robust and the lieutenant's migration worthwhile. The Mango King didn't need the lieutenant's sense of the other. He was where his family had always been, sure of himself and, if anything, he felt the lack of the Hindu middle class that once completed his society. It reminded me of a story of a Pakistani aunt of mine: as a child, she had seen the waves of Muslim migration from India and said, 'Oh, look, the Pakistanis are coming!' The Mango King, unlike his lieutenant, hadn't migrated in search of a great Muslim homeland and found himself, still after six decades, an immigrant.

On the way into town, the Mango King explained the legal dispute. It was a complicated scenario in which the laws of the country, British law, with Islamic accents, came into conflict with the feudal agreements in his family. The Mango King's aunts inherited a small parcel of the land, which they wanted the Mango King to inherit, but as his cousins – with whom he'd had gun battles – would contest this, a spurious sale of sorts was organised, by which the land would come indirectly to the Mango King. The cousins were contesting the sale and the Mango King was looking for a way out.

The section of town we entered in moonlight had old-fashioned whitewashed buildings and tube-lit streets. Outside the lawyer's office there was an open drain from which a vast *peepal* tree grew at an angle, its prehensile roots threatening the foundation of both street and building. In the soft, pale light, the *peepal*'s long-stalked flat leaves, with their pointed apexes, were like little bits of silver foil, flittering noisily in the slightest wind. Under the tree, a man sold hot food from a cauldron of boiling oil and behind him colourful posters advertised a wrestling match. A bright red fire truck, with white Urdu writing on it, blocked the entrance to the lawyer's office.

The man inside the pistachio green room was like a caricature of a small-town lawyer. He was a squat, smiling man, with dimples, clefts and greasy hennaed hair. His eyes vanished when he smiled and light brown moles dotted his face and neck. His office contained a black briefcase, a glass-topped desk, green metal filing-cabinets and shelves stacked with volumes of *Pakistani Legal Decisions*.

He had been briefed about the case and, after offering us tea and soft drinks, he began immediately: 'You have two options, either of speaking the truth or . . . I've heard, sir,' he said, a smarmy smile lighting his face, 'that it is hard for you to tell a lie.'

The Mango King looked sternly at him. 'No, there's no such problem.'

'Another situation is that we tell the truth,' the lawyer said, shaking his head mournfully, as though drawing some pleasure from the foreplay of an illegal act.

'Please leave truth and lies aside,' the Mango King said. 'Let's just do what favours us.'

The lawyer, bowing from the waist, grinned. 'Are both women educated?'

'Yes, a little.'

'English-speaking?'

'Yes.'

The lawyer nodded sadly, feigning gloom.

'What difference does it make?' the Mango King barked.

'Because we could say the transaction was a fake,' the lawyer sputtered rapidly. 'The ladies did not understand what they were doing. We could make the plea that they didn't know what was in the documents when they signed them.'

'But then, wouldn't I, myself, end up looking like a fraud?'

'No, no,' the lawyer assured him, regaining his composure, 'you weren't present. We can say the ladies never sold the land. They received no monies.'

'But then you're making me a liar.'

'Just wait,' the lawyer replied, a tantalising smile coming to his lips. 'This is our ladies' plea. The court will accept it. We'll make this plea, but we'll have to tell lies.'

'Leave lies aside,' the Mango King snapped. 'Let's do what will help us.'

'See? The ladies will support us in this. We'll say the ladies knew nothing of this, that they were misguided,' he added, with relish. 'We'll have to interview the ladies beforehand and prepare them. I think this is better. There's more truth in it.'

'Leave truth—'

'No, no. One lie leads to another. Even smart people get caught out.'

'But they'll lie too.'

'Yes, but they have only one lie to tell.'

The Mango King looked as lost as I was. 'Does the judge accept bribes?' he asked. 'Can't we just bribe him?'

'He does in some cases and not in others,' the lawyer replied, as if delivering an official statement. 'But the other party can bribe him, too, so it doesn't matter.'

'Yes, but it shouldn't be that they just bribe him and close the whole matter. Anyway, so you think this is better?'

'Yes, because the women can speak the truth.'

'Leave the truth!' the Mango King roared. 'I want to do what will help us win.'

The lawyer, still smiling, winced. But I could see now that he was only interested in the truth because it made a simpler story for the old ladies to retell. 'Yes, yes,' he said. 'This will be easier to prove.'

'All right.' The Mango King nodded.

The lieutenant, who watched the rapid exchanges with keen interest, now said, 'Leave it. The case will keep going. You'll become old.'

'Can't we give them a little *danda* too?' the Mango King said, using the word for 'stick' to mean a beating.

The lawyer smiled serenely.

'The case will go to appeals,' the lieutenant said, 'It'll take ten years just there.'

'And if in twenty,' the Mango King asked, 'the court rules in their favour, how will they take possession of the land?'

'The police will come on order of the court,' the lawyer replied, defending the system of which he was a part.

'And if I resist?' the Mango King asked, seeming to threaten the lawyer.

'There will be cases against you, criminal cases.'

'Can the property be put in my mother's name?' the Mango King asked, then mentioned she was a German national, which created other problems.

'Why don't you get married?' the lawyer suggested.

'I have to find the right girl,' the Mango King laughed. 'Then I'll get married.'

We stood up to leave and the lawyer rose too, bowing and smiling.

Outside, the Mango King lit a cigarette. Turning to me, he said bitterly, 'Bloody feudal family disputes.' He seemed a little depressed and lonely.

In the car on the way back his lieutenant tried to convince him to get married. He said it would increase his strength.

'If we lose in the court, how soon can they take control of the land?' the Mango King asked, thinking aloud.

'We'll take it to a higher court,' the lieutenant comforted him.

'And if we lose there?'

'They can take control of the land, but then we'll bring it back to the lowest court on some excuse. Whole lifetimes go by and these things remain unresolved. You know you've done nothing illegitimate. And as long as you have done nothing illegitimate, Allah will protect you.'

What he could mean by 'legitimate' in this legal desert eluded me, but he seemed to summon up some higher notion of legitimacy and justice. The temporal example he gave a moment later was as ambiguous as the circumstances he'd begun with. 'Look,' he said, 'I'll give you an example. Nawaz Sharif tried to get rid of Musharraf in Pakistan and now Nawaz Sharif is in the black water.' But even as the lieutenant spoke, the general seemed to be heading towards 'black water' of his own, just one set of illegitimate circumstances replacing another.

'They've done a lot to subdue me,' the Mango King said.

'You just get married quickly,' the lieutenant said, trying to arrest the gloom that grew in the Mango King, 'and then you'll have a wife and an heir and at least they won't be able to say "he's all on his own." Your strength will improve greatly.' Strength was the right word: it was all that could make sense of the landscape around the Mango King. In the absence of a credible state, crude power, loose and available, was all there was to seize on to. 'Find a good relationship and get married. Aren't I right?' the lieutenant asked me.

'Yes,' I said.

'People are scared of my house,' the Mango King replied. 'Girls run away from it.'

'Why?'

'You know my pool in Karachi, right?'

'Yes,' I said, half expecting him to say it was having its water changed.

'Well, I had a party,' he said, 'and a guy drowned in it. And my cousins said that I paid money to the police and to the guy's family. Can you imagine? You have a party and a guy dies in your pool. It's terrible. And they say it's because I'm feudal. I think the guy was on drugs or something.'

\*

That night I sat with the Mango King on his veranda drinking whisky-sodas and talking. Though occasionally I felt his pain, I didn't understand his world; I didn't think it was a world that could be made understandable to someone who wasn't obliged to work by its arbitrary laws; its brutalities were its own. The Mango King said that things wouldn't change and that feudalism would go on. He also spoke of the importance of the Hindu middle class who left in 1947 and in doing so identified the key component in the change that came to feudal India but not to Pakistan: the middle class.

It was India's middle class, its growth and energy, more than anything else that set the two countries apart. The power of the middle class in India dismantled the old feudal structures. In Sind, the cost of realising the purity of the Indian Muslim state was the necessary departure of Sind's Hindu middle class. The *muhajjir* population that arrived in its place had not been able to replace its social function; the bonds that had held together the diverse society of Muslims and Hindus had not arisen among the co-religionists. And, without its middle class, Sind was not merely unchanged from 1947, not merely feudal: it was lawless, divided acrimoniously within itself; town and country were divorced from each other; 'the factionalised élite' that the think tank's report described had been created; and even men like the Mango King knew insecurity. The society had been dismembered.

The lieutenant, who had been sitting quietly on the edge of the veranda, now whispered slyly to me that he was a Rajput. This was another reference to the Hindu caste system, in this case high-caste, going deeper than Islam in Pakistan. But the lieutenant didn't know he spoke of caste. When I suggested to him that Islam, with its strong ideas of equality, forbade notions of caste, he became defensive and said that this was a matter of good and bad families. The Mango King thought it was tribe, but it was really caste.

'If you can have Rajputs, then you can have *chooda*s,' I said, using the derogatory word for 'low caste' that my cousin had used on the night of Casablanca.

'Of course you can have *chooda*s,' the lieutenant replied.

'Would you let your daughter marry one?'

'Never.'

'Even if he was Muslim?'

'Even if he was Muslim.'

On the one hand, there was the rejection of India that made Pakistan possible, and on the other, India was overwhelmingly at play in the deepest affiliations of Pakistanis, sometimes without their knowing it. It made Pakistan a country in which everything just existed because it did, eroded haphazardly by inevitable change. The country's roots, like some fearsome plumbing network, could never be examined to explain why something was the way it was, why the lieutenant, perhaps centuries after conversion, could still think of himself as a Rajput. And though I, with deep connections on both sides, could see the commonalities, they were not something to be celebrated: we spoke instead of difference. It was a country where you could imagine that, one day, no one would know where anything had come from.

Before I went to bed, the Mango King came to the end of the story of his kidnapping.

'Were you afraid they would harm you?' I asked him.

'Twice,' he said. 'Once when I tried to escape and the second time after my father had abused them and I heard them saying, "Should we bury his body or throw it in the river?" "I'm still alive," I was saying to myself, and that was pretty scary.'

Finally, after six months, the kidnappers gave him a bus ticket and released him in the Sindi town of Sukkur from where he made his way back to his father's house in Hyderabad. His hair had grown longer and when he got home, the watchman didn't recognise him. The Mango King said no ransom was ever paid.

When he was released they danced in the village. He went to get a passport photo taken, and the man in the shop had baked a cake for him. These were the details that remained with him after two decades. The whisky worked on the Mango King, at once deadening his eyes and bringing up unprocessed emotion. He'd gone to get a passport picture because he was going to Germany to see his mother for the first time in fourteen years. His separation from her was another secret in the life of the Mango King, but I had a feeling it was related to the father who always had the right answer for everything.

The next morning I left the Mango King's lands for Hyderabad. He was still asleep when I walked out, and even at that early hour, the small, musty house was filling with heat.

## Contact Paper

The answers to the questions I had wanted to ask my father at our first meeting were a way for me to string the world together. I wanted, with whatever shred of common memory I could find, to close the gap between the world that ended in 1982, when my father left my mother, and the world as it was now that my father and I had met. I was ready to shuttle between two families in two countries, but it helped to know that they had begun as one life, just as it helped to know that the two countries were once the same country. Like slipping a sheet of clear contact paper over another, both with partial images on them, to make a complete one, I sought to stabilise the new world I had gained with the one I had always known.

Even as our relationship grew, my father seemed resistant to my efforts to bridge the two worlds. Between my first and second visits, a few weeks apart, when he invited me to stay in his house, the initial openness between us had narrowed. I asked him a question about a time when he had known my mother and he reminded me bluntly, 'I asked you when we first met whether you had any questions for me.'

On one occasion he mentioned the plane Murtaza Bhutto hijacked and the comment he made to the BBC. I had heard about the event from my mother. To hear of it now from my father filled me with a kind of child's wonder. It was like hearing about what your parents had been doing just before you were born. In an effort to bring together the two versions of the same story, I asked him where my mother and I were when it happened. My father's face soured. 'I don't know what anyone else was doing at the time. I can tell you what I was doing. I was getting away from the police, who wanted to put me in jail.'

Despite the gaps and silences, our relationship grew over the next four years, during which I became a regular visitor to Lahore. The more I went, the less I saw of the country or even the city. My father's house became my world in Pakistan. On my first visit I had met three siblings: my elder sister from my father's first marriage and a younger brother and sister from his present marriage; over the next few months, I met three more. They, and my father's young, beautiful wife, were full of goodwill and affection for me. Having grown up as an only child, I was so overwhelmed by suddenly having brothers and sisters that getting to know them took up much of my time in Lahore. I managed to sneak into some of the small, exquisite mosques in the old city, saw the important monuments, the museum and that fine stretch of red-brick British buildings, which were like a lesson in civic planning, but that was all. I went with my sister to many more GTs. I met fashion designers, Lahore beauties, and spent more than a few orange dawns eating hot meat in the old city. In summer, we'd end up in my father's mango-shaped swimming-pool as the mullah's cry broke over the dark trees in his lawn. In those twice-yearly visits to Lahore, I felt at home and yet not, as if I was in a place I had been before but couldn't recall.

After university in America, I worked as a reporter for *Time* magazine, first in New York and then in London. During that time, my father and his family paid me a surprise visit in New York, and later I saw them regularly in London. Benazir Bhutto's self-imposed exile during the Musharraf years and my father's own electoral failures had distanced him from political life. Though politics was still his passion, he was now a far more successful businessman than he had ever been a politician. Still, some of the old embarrassment at having an Indian son lingered, and he was much more at ease with seeing me abroad than he was in Pakistan.

His embarrassment in Pakistan surfaced in small, telling ways. He prevented my siblings throwing a party they had planned for me; he rarely spoke to me at social occasions and never introduced me to anyone. I interpreted this as a hint that he didn't want to see me any more, but his family assured me that it was just his way and he enjoyed my visits. Sitting on worn sofas in his TV room, children and servants coming in and out, a drinks trolley in one corner, with an ice bucket on it, I felt that a kind of closeness had arisen between us. My father would often engage me in some long conversation about the great Punjabi Urdu poets of Lahore. His father was part of this milieu but died when my father was a child. Though it was never expressed, there was irony in our shared experience of absent fathers. He also let it be known that I was his only child who was like him – interested in books, politics and history – and though this also contained irony, it gave me great joy to have a kind of male approval I had never known. One last irony was that during a family holiday in Italy in 2005, a few weeks before the London bombings, before my article and my father's letter, and before the pain of the new silence between us, we were closer than ever before.

# Sind 360: The Open Wound

I t was a great relief to be on the road and independent of the Mango King's uncertain hours. It was from him that I gained an idea of Sind's composite society, complete with Hindus and Muslims. That completeness ended with the 1947 transfers of population. I looked now for what had taken its place. My father had spoken of the 'Pakistani ethos' in his letter, and with this in mind, I set out for the desert city of Hyderabad. My travelling was to be different from anything I had done so far. I wanted to avoid focusing on any one group but to see an array of life, a panorama, in a typical Sindi town. And for this I was meeting Laxman, one of the publisher's most trusted managers, on the outskirts of Hyderabad. My brother had arranged a driver, a dark, moustached man with mascaraed eyes.

The road to Hyderabad through the bleached, shrub-covered country was full of unexpected bursts of colour and activity. There were black flags with gold borders, their masts covered with coloured bulbs, commemorating the Shia mourning; tiny pink and orange figures of women working in sugar-cane fields; and green pools of water with children bathing in them. The shade of mango trees attracted old people in white and animals escaping the heat, including a hennaed donkey, with an impossible burden. The road was crowded with camels pulling carts, cattle crossing from one side to the other, and small, painted mosques, with grey loudspeakers, huddled close to the road.

We covered the distance at an irregular pace, stopping or slowing for varied traffic. At one point, we hit a little goat that the driver calculated would make way for him. I thought we'd killed it, but it picked itself up and, indignantly, with hardly any change in its pace, made its way across the road to join the herd. We passed a gold-domed and yellow-tiled Shia mosque, whose opulence among the surrounding thatched houses suggested Iranian contributions.

Laxman was waiting for us near a canal on the outskirts of Hyderabad. He was a stocky man, with thick, greasy hair and shiny black skin. He had a bristly moustache over a set of pearly, capped teeth. He greeted me in a furtive, hurried manner, and within minutes was organising me, making phone calls and giving the driver orders. He suggested we go first to a shrine just outside Hyderabad, where Sind's Muslims and few remaining Hindus prayed together. Sind's countryside was covered with the Sufi shrines of saints who were often honoured by Muslims and Hindus alike. They were part of a local form of Islam that served a once diverse society. It was this kind of worship that gave me the protective string on my wrist that the men in Mecca had minded so much.

An armed guard, who provided security to the newspaper's people when they travelled in the countryside, accompanied us. Laxman said the road was often struck at night by dacoits. Their ploy was to throw a stone or a bale of straw into the middle of the road, and to surround the car as soon as it slowed down. He said a man from the newspaper had been robbed recently. The dacoits had thrown a briefcase in front of the car. I didn't think that this was a particularly obstructive object so I asked him about it.

'He got greedy.' Laxman chuckled. 'He thought there was money inside it so he stopped.'

In the open land outside Hyderabad, a still, hot afternoon came to an end, solitude and isolation giving way to a more social hour. Children came out to play, truckers stopped for tea, and a wrestling match began in a clearing at the side of the road. Dozens of people gathered round a sandy ring, children watched from the branches of trees, and loudspeakers energised the crowd. The wrestlers, bare-chested and in tied-up *salwar*s, prowled around the edges of the ring, awaiting their fights. They were of varied ages and physiques, some young with slim, hard bodies, and others with heavy shoulders and barrel stomachs. It was clear from the dark brown welts on some of the younger men's backs that they were Shia and had flagellated themselves during the period of mourning.

The wrestlers had thick ropes tied round their waists. When their match was called, they approached each other as if about to give one another a low embrace. Then they grabbed their opponent's rope and began to pull. Sometimes one wrestler would do a kind of dance round the other, hoping to tire him out before leaping on him with all his weight and pushing him to the ground. At others, the heavier wrestler would engage the lighter one as soon as possible, entwining his more powerful legs round his opponent, causing him to lose his balance.

We drove past men on rope beds drinking tea, and boys playing in the hollow of a haystack, until the white shrine appeared among flat fields, dotted with large trees.

'It's proof of the Sufi time in Sind when Muslims and Hindus prayed together,' the driver said, as we approached. 'I think there's even a mention of it in the Indian movies.'

The story of the white shrine, with its turrets and little crenellations, was typical of what made the religious commingling of

Sufi India possible. An oppressive, fanatical king ill-treated his people, Hindu and Muslim alike, until the saint Oderolal, a white-bearded miracle man, arrived out of the water, preaching love and oneness, and used his powers to end the cruel king's abuse. He came to be loved by both Muslims and Hindus and, honouring his memory and message of unity, they prayed next to each other, though not actually together. 'Here the *azan* is about to be called,' a white-bearded man, in sunglasses and a red cap, explained, 'and there you can see Hindus are praying. That is the miracle.'

'Is it still like that today?'

'Like brothers. There is a lot of love.' He pointed me in the direction of a tree, which the saint had put down in the dry earth. 'That's the miracle,' the man said gaily. 'It needs no water. Look!' The leaves at the top are green.' The tree was in bad shape and I wasn't too surprised that it grew from a little patch of dry earth. Most of Sind was dry and only a few days before I'd seen a much bigger tree growing out of a building and a drain. The bearded fakir yanked down my head and said, 'Aatish, may you become cool,' then demanded money.

Laxman let out an evangelical cry and said, 'Ask! This is the time. Ask, if you ever meant to ask! Open your heart and ask!' The call to prayer sounded and a few Muslims on the other side of the white courtyard congregated. 'This was once the world!' Laxman said dramatically.

It was easy to see how the true relevance of a shrine like this would have grown from the society's former diversity. Unlike the idea on which the state was founded, here, the commonality of culture, language and local faith trumped doctrinal differences. One could imagine how it would have made the heart leap to put aside religious differences, Hindu caste notions or the Muslim horror of idols and images, in favour of a larger cultural unity.

In the white courtyard, under the shade of a *neem* tree, a

group of farmers and their families discussed something in low, serious tones. Laxman and I went up to them and sat down to listen. They spoke in Sindi and Laxman translated. They seemed upset. One man was saying, 'Conditions are so bad, these days, we don't know how we can continue.' Having just been with a landlord, I was keen to hear what else they would say, but Laxman was in a hurry: it was evening and he was worried about dacoits. After some persuasion, I managed to get the farmer's problem out of him. Three young men from the community, sitting solemnly together on one side, had struck a deal with the landlord in the hope of improving their lot. They had his land from him at a fixed price, with an eye to cultivating it and keeping whatever profit they made from the crop. But that year everyone's crops had failed. The three enter-prising farmers found that not only had they made no profit, they hadn't even made enough to pay the landlord his rent. They approached him and begged him to excuse part of their debt. The landlord agreed and said he would excuse them 40,000 rupees (some CAN$1,000), leaving them still to pay 50,000 (CAN$1,250). They managed to collect this amount, pooling together all that they had and borrowing the rest. But when they appeared at the landlord's with the money, he denied any recollection of their first meeting and demanded the entire sum.

Sitting in the shrine's courtyard, as they might always have done, the community elders, with leathery faces and white stubble, considered the dilemma. Children climbed over colour-fully dressed mothers and the three young farmers listened in gloomy silence. They had just reached some kind of solution when Laxman insisted we leave immediately, promising to explain the meeting's conclusion to me later.

In the car, he murmured something in his alarmist fashion about dacoits. It was hard to sense the danger in the sociable, rural scene, but Laxman was convinced that just after we had left the shrine a group of men had taken a picture of the car on a camera phone, with the intention of marking us for robbery. I hadn't seen them, but the driver said he had and accelerated down the country road. We passed police posts on the way, which I pointed out to Laxman, but he said it made no difference: the police were in collaboration with the dacoits. The driver agreed and said we were running just as much from the police as from the dacoits. Then, looking at our bodyguard, he added tenderly, 'Don't worry, we don't think you're police.'

'It's always an inside job,' Laxman explained. 'First, the dacoits gave the police ten per cent, then the police started demanding more, twenty, thirty, forty. Finally it was *phipty-phipty*. Then the police said, "Why let them do it when we can do it ourselves?" So now the off-duty policemen are the dacoits.'

When we were safely on the main road to Hyderabad, Laxman relaxed and I was able to extract from him the meeting's conclusion. I understood now why I had missed it the first few times: its innocence was like a failing of logic. The elders had decided, since the landlord could not remember excusing the debt, to approach two of the landlord's friends who were present at the time the debt was excused. Surely they would remind the man of his promise. If not, the community would pay off the young men's debt. In any event, it was clear that they were ruined.

Did they really not know that the landlord lied when he said he didn't remember excusing their debt? Had it not occurred to them that the landlord's friends would lie too? Or that they would be beaten for trying to get round the landlord in this way? I tried to put the scenes of disappointment or, worse, open flailing out of mind. It was an affecting final image of feudal life before the city.

*

Hyderabad was older than Karachi. Stray images from litho-graphs of a great fort and the Indus ran through my mind as we entered it. The Indus still unseen! Almost a lost river for Indians as only a shred of it remained in India. There was something especially evocative for me in thinking of my longer journey as ending near the Indus.

The traffic into Hyderabad showed signs of a city whose organisation had broken. Hundreds of small industries gath-ered close to the road. Trucks, carrying anything from cattle to black electrical meters, clogged the main road.

'Why electrical meters?' I asked Laxman.

'They've been confiscated because they've been tampered with,' Laxman replied. Lost in his own thoughts, he suddenly said, 'Because of the problem in Karachi, I don't know if it'll be all right for me to take you into a Sunni shrine or *madrassa*. Even though they say,' he added nervously, 'that the MQM did it.'

The 'problem in Karachi' was the bombing that had occurred a few weeks before my arrival. Hyderabad was once a Muslim town, with a highly successful Hindu merchant community. It was a perfect example of the society, complete with its Hindu middle class, whose loss the Mango King had mourned. After 1947, much of that middle class left and made good in places as far away as West Africa. *Muhajjirs* took their place, and a great urban tension existed between Sindi and *muhajjir*. The MQM Laxman spoke of was the *muhajjir* party.

I tried to unpack the varied currents in Laxman's comment. 'Why would it be a problem for me to go to Sunni *madrassa*?' I asked.

Laxman, with an evasiveness that I was beginning to recog-nise in him, said, 'Well, don't tell them you come from Iran.'

'I don't. I was just travelling through Iran.'

'Oh, that's fine,' he said quickly, seeming to adjust his judge-ment of me.

The communal landscape was hard to make sense of. Difference of denomination, region and political affiliation were on everyone's mind.

Laxman had booked a room for me at the Indus Hotel. It was a modern place, on a bleak stretch of road, full of fake flowers and scenic pictures of places cooler than Hyderabad. He told me he would give me some time to 'get fresh', but almost as soon as we arrived, he was keen to get going. He wanted me to meet his bureau chief at the newspaper's offices. He even followed me upstairs, extolling the man's merits and usefulness to me. My room was reached by a transparent lift that was out of order, and overlooked the driveway and main road. The hotel's designers must not have envisaged it breaking down because the only staircase provided was a grubby service entrance.

The room had a large white plywood bed, with a satiny bedcover and thin, dirt-encrusted carpeting. As we entered, Laxman asked, unprompted, if I'd like some beer.

'No, thanks,' I said, finding the question strange, given the hour and that alcohol was illegal in Pakistan.

But he seemed to be trying to tell me something else. A moment later, he came out with it. 'There's no problem for me,' he said. 'I am a minority. I am allowed a permit.'

'What minority?' I asked, then felt like an idiot. Of course I knew that Laxman was Hindu, but outwardly the similarity between India and Pakistan was so great that my awareness of being in Pakistan had faded momentarily. I had stopped thinking of him as a Hindu in a state for Indian Muslims; I had forgotten about the transfers of population. But he, a member of a tiny minority, a remainder of the city's once great diversity, never forgot he was that rarest of rare things: a Pakistani Hindu. It made him want to know where everyone else stood and I saw now that the offer of beer had, perhaps, been a way to find out whether I was Muslim and, if so, how Muslim.

'What's happening underground will definitely burst,' he said mysteriously, as he loitered in the doorway.

'What's underground?' I asked, unpacking my bags, and truly confused by all this intrigue.

'Hatred,' he replied.

'Between whom?'

He looked at me, a suspicious eye-darting look, at once worried about who was listening and whether I was playing with him. 'Sindi and *muhajjir*.'

The road on which the Indus Hotel stood was called Cool Street. It formed, I discovered from Laxman as he bundled me out of my room, an enemy line between the Urdu-speaking *muhajjir* section of town and the Sindi-speaking Sindi section. On the way to the newspaper's offices, it was possible to see from the systematic organisation of the streets, and the occasional fine row of whitewashed buildings, with Hindu names and motifs, that Hyderabad was once an attractive town. And the black wires, starved animals, paper and polythene that grew over the scene only made its past harmony more apparent.

The newspaper's offices were in an old building, up a darkened flight of stone steps. Its wood and glass partitions, old furniture, typewriters and yellowing files seemed to have been unchanged for decades. The bureau chief was at his desk, a tall, elderly man, with thick glasses, deep lines on his face and neatly combed grey hair.

He was full of gloom. Minutes after we met, he launched into talk of religious and regional divisions, corruption, water shortages, feudalism and crime. 'The MQM is trying to start a problem between Sunni and Shia to have in-fighting while they keep their vote bank.' The religious parties, which came up under General Zia, have come of age, and are instilling in the minds of youth that death is imminent, and that they must fight the enemies of Islam. Crime is rampant: you can't go ten kilometres outside Hyderabad without someone throwing a stone in front of your car and taking your money at gunpoint. The Indus, which used to roar like a lion through Sind, is running dry.

'The Indus dry?' I said, hoping to stop the torrent.

'Yes,' he replied. 'There's dust flowing in it now.'

He was in a panic because some nights ago he had had to hold back the paper's printing to include the speech of the MQM leader. 'The district news must be finished up by ten,' he cried, 'because the page is laid out. But the story of the leader's speech was filed at a quarter to one in the morning and a paper like ours had to wait for it. We don't even wait for the president, but we had to wait for this story because they have Kalashnikovs in their hands so we are helpless. Just imagine one thing. Their leader had only a 50cc Honda and a small house, but he's living in London now. You know how costly that is, and with secretaries? Where is the money coming from? That is the question nobody in Pakistan dares to ask.'

I didn't know the answer.

'This is the worst time I've seen!' he cried. 'We've lived through difficult times, but this is the worst.'

'Why?' I asked, thinking of the Zia years.

'Because there's no faith in anyone. Someone becomes your friend and the next minute they stab you in the back. There are suicides because people are so short of money. The frustration is terrible.'

I spoke to him for nearly an hour, told him something of my travels so far, and he offered to help me meet some people over the next few days. I didn't have a fixed plan. I was happy to be in other hands; happy to be shown what people thought I should see. We arranged to meet the following morning at the newspaper offices.

When Laxman and I walked down the dark flight of stairs, a sandstorm had begun on the once beautiful street. It cleared the crowds and traffic of a few hours before and brown swirls of smoke and dust now pounced on little scraps of paper, and raced down the empty street. A purplish-brown haze made it seem later than it was. We drove over a truss bridge. Below, there was a vast bed of white sand, reeds and a ribbon of green water. Laxman, looking down at it, shook his head. 'There were times when they would warn the residents on the shore to leave their houses because a flood was coming,' he said. 'And now, look, in the same river children are playing.'

His words didn't sink in immediately. Then, with the special horror reserved for something close to death, I turned again to look through the lattice of iron beams at the remains of one of the world's great rivers. 'That's the Indus?'

Laxman nodded. I told the driver to pull over. The car took a left and stopped near a large *peepal* tree, under which a man sold balloons and green-bottled soft drinks lay about on plastic tables. Steep black steps led down to the Indus. From just the height and gradient of the bank I could imagine what the river had once been. Halfway down the stairs, the strip of greenish water was lost in the white dunes and reeds. I walked for some minutes across the riverbed, over sinking sand, before I came upon it again. It was possible at this dusk hour to see the clear outline of the moon and this, along with the darkened sky and the wind blowing the green water in the opposite direction from the one in which it flowed so frailly, gave the scene a final, twilight aspect. A line of roaring traffic went by on the bridge many metres above. A small blue boat bobbed in the narrow strip of water, spanning half its breadth, and the river seemed, at once and ever, like a scene of beginnings and of endings.

Laxman crept up behind me. 'It's an amazing thing. We are standing in the Indus, not in a boat or anything, but in the Indus. People pray to this river. The Sindhu river! But where is the water? It's just sand.'

Laxman, the Hindu, thought of the river with the special, religious regard much of the sub-continent gave its rivers. In Sind, the story was that Punjab was stealing the water. Some wanted Punjab to be divided again, not because that would make a large state easier to govern, but so that it would not dominate the other states. There was an irony to these regional differences coming up on account of the Indus because it was the closest thing Pakistan had to a national river. It was almost like a symbol of national unity, a coronary artery flowing through the middle of the country, for which the scattered rivers of Punjab came together to feed its once great expanse. Sindi nationalist parties had taken up the issue and the splintering, faction within faction, difference within difference, that I had seen since I arrived in Pakistan, and was hardly able to follow, was spreading through the political arena.

And here there was a deeper irony. It was thought that the faith, as the basis of Pakistan, would trump all other identities. It didn't matter what kind of Muslim you were, what language you spoke or even if you lived at the other end of India. As long as you were Muslim, Islam would bridge the differences. It reminded me of the faith Abdullah, in Istanbul, placed in all the Muslims of the world he hadn't met. 'You mentioned the conflict between Islamic countries,' he had said, 'but I'm trying to say that to be a Muslim is a very different experience from any other, no matter where you are. To be Muslim is to be above history.' But history did matter, not just the faith's encased and symbolic history, but history as realised in language and culture. It was a distortion of faith that all this didn't matter, and in Pakistan people seemed to fall back on regional, linguistic and denominational differences.

Laxman, now determined to exercise his minority privileges, insisted I join him for a beer. On the way to his house, we drove through a gated urban colony, with run-down buildings, open drains and walls covered with slogans. '"Sunnis, when will you awake?"' Laxman read, in a fearful whisper, as if the words leapt off the walls at him. It was a reference to the bombing in Karachi and, Laxman thought, a call to arms. As we left the quiet, concrete colony, domestic scenes overhead and hatred on the walls, Laxman hissed, 'See? See? It's boiling. If something doesn't happen, it'll rip.'

*

That night at Laxman's house, the bureau chief called, wanting to know my father's name. That made me nervous. My father was well-known in Pakistan and I would have preferred to travel with a degree of anonymity; I had done well so far. Laxman gave it to him, then put down the phone and gave me his hunted-minority look. His room was filled with fake flowers, dusty stuffed toys, calendars and pink curtains. His bed was of a black and gold laminate, and a fake vine of maple leaves in autumnal colours drooped over one corner. A drinks trolley, still in its plastic covering of years, came in.

'What is it, Laxman? Why did he want to know?'

'Nothing, Aatish. God is great.' I noticed as we fled the men who'd marked our car that he had said, 'God is great.' It seemed he always did when trouble lay ahead.

'Laxman?'

'No, it's just that this is the time that the ISI [Pakistani Intelligence] come round to his office. He's their man. He does their drafting and translation.'

'What? Why didn't you tell me?'

'It was only when he called that it came into my mind. But, don't worry, Aatish, God is great.'

'Please, let's leave God out of this for a minute. I really don't want to be stuck in an interrogation room again.' I told him about Iran.

'Is it possible they have informed him?' he asked, taking pleasure, I thought, in the world turning out to be just as shadowy as he imagined it.

'I don't know. Listen, I hate this sort of thing. I needn't have met him. Why didn't you warn me?'

Two doubts circulated in my head: the first was that perhaps Laxman wasn't trustworthy, the second was how the bureau chief could have informed Pakistan's intelligence services about me when I was a guest of his boss, the publisher. I felt I was being brought in line with the level of suspicion that people in Hyderabad felt for one another.

'I'll tell you what, then,' Laxman said. 'Don't stay in the hotel tonight. We won't meet him tomorrow. We'll leave for Sehwan Sharif [a shrine] and come back in a day or so when things have calmed down.'

'No, Laxman. That's not how I want to work. Either it's safe for me or it's not.'

'It's safe. God is great.'

I said I was calling the publisher, half expecting Laxman to admit he was being alarmist, but he said, 'Good idea.' I tried a few numbers, then finally had the man on the phone. He listened to what I had to say and then, with a protective growl, said, 'Give me Laxman.'

I handed over the receiver. They spoke for a few minutes and hung up. Laxman tittered with excitement at the scene unfolding.

A few minutes later the publisher called back. 'Remember that you're a British national, that you have done nothing wrong and have nothing to worry about. I have spoken to him [the bureau chief] and have told him in a chilling, but indirect, way that you are my friend and he'd better take care of you.'

'I can't face another interrogation.'

'It's a minor inconvenience!' the publisher bellowed.

'Should I see him tomorrow?'

'Yes, yes. It's fine.'

Laxman was in a state of high excitement. 'See?' he said. 'See how disloyal these people are who only want money despite how well *saab* keeps them? Us minorities are much more loyal.'

I liked the bureau chief and could only think that in his way he had warned me. I thought he spoke from the heart when he said, 'The frustration is terrible.' And it was the most basic frustration of how to survive and earn an honest living, free of coercion and fear. In calling the publisher I'd put a counterweight to the fear the intelligence men would have exerted on the bureau chief, the fear of losing his job, and the smaller man had come into line. It was so easy to slip into the interplay of corruption and power that made the society work and I, who felt quite righteous when I arrived, was less full of high sentence when I left.

*

The next morning in the Indus Hotel's breakfast room, a boy on television sang in a shrill voice about the rule of God and never uttering a lie. He was in his early teens and wore a red tunic and a black turban. He smiled as he sang, his hands opening and closing to the beat of his own moral tunes. There was something grotesquely compelling about him. I drank a cup of unusually good coffee and waited for Laxman.

We were such an unlikely pairing, Laxman and I: a Pakistani Hindu showing an Indian, with Pakistani origins, Pakistan. It was as if the publisher, with his feeling for undivided India, was having a joke. But it was not an insignificant joke. I think that because Laxman was my guide, I felt closer to Sind's multi-religious past and, also, to its decay. I found it interesting that Laxman's distrust of others was not along religious lines but cultural ones. He was suspicious, as were Sindi Muslims, of the non-Sindi; he had close relationships with Sindi Muslims. (And I think even his problem with the bureau chief boiled down to him being Punjabi.) In his like-mindedness to his Muslim counterparts, Laxman was like a living relic of what had been Sind's composite culture.

He appeared a few minutes later in high spirits; he was taking me to a wedding. I tried to resist, citing the meeting with the bureau chief, but Laxman was insistent and said we'd meet him after the wedding.

I'm not sure how I was able to tell any longer – and maybe it was only because I'd left an air-conditioned room – but when I stepped out on to Cool Street that morning, I was sure it was the hottest day so far. It was barely nine and white vapour sucked the colour out of the day.

The heat in this treeless desert city was made worse by the kind of work people did, work which involved vats of boiling oil and colourfully painted blowtorches. Men came out of their industrial cubby-holes to water the searing streets. No sooner had the water touched the grey-white surface, robbed for a moment of wobbling mirages, than it vanished and the hypnotic heat returned. The earth at the roadside was so dry that the water skittered over the surface like mercury, and it was a few moments before the tension around the dust-covered drops broke. Skeletons of buses lay bent and mangled in unclaimed plots of destroyed earth and the backs of old trucks, propped up on stocky, wooden beams, were used for storage.

The drive to the wedding took us past the full destruction that had come to Hyderabad. In front of a pink sandstone colonial mansion, once the lord mayor's residence, there was a blue and green sign that read 'Govt. Khadija Girls H/S School'. The building's stained-glass windows were broken, their old shutters fell from their frames like dead skin, and many were boarded up. The balcony railings were rusted over, the sunken pillars cracked, and even the decorative urn on the left side of the building had fallen over and smashed in two.

In another area, the buildings once belonged to Hindu merchants. One had an especially fine façade, on which the Hindu name of Hassaram Vishindas 1924 still remained. It stood on a hairpin bend and had what was once a semi-circular balcony. A wall of unplastered bricks now rose from the balcony's balustrade and the space was divided into little rooms.

'Is anyone living there?'

'No. Now they're just *muhajjirs*,' Laxman said.

'Maybe, but are they living there?'

'Yes, and they have their shops below.'

Further on, whole streets of pale town-houses were deserted, entire neighbourhoods abandoned. It was amazing to see how, even after six decades, the city's once effortless harmony had not been regained. As if mourning the wholeness of its society, the breaking up of its diverse, interlocking components, the city retreated into ghettos. The *muhajjir*s, who had left behind diversities of their own, felt the worth they knew in other societies – a usefulness formed over centuries – extinguished in the one they came to. The disappointment would have been immense: to have begun with the idea of the religious homeland and to have ended with the divisions between the old and new Muslims deepening into walls, political parties and militias. My mother's family were the equivalent of *muhajjir*s in India – they had come as refugees from the Pakistani side, just as the people here had come from the Indian side – but in India there was no equivalent grouping: the concept didn't exist.

The *muhajjir*s in Hyderabad were holed up, as if in a communal sulk, in the fort I remembered from the lithographs. They lived in a warren of tight, winding streets among the ramparts where Laxman was too scared to go. The fort's red-brick walls were falling away, its crenellations crumbling, and the windows of people's homes had been broken into its walls. Outside, in the heat, a market had sprung up next to an open cesspool, with a giant slab of concrete lying in it. A polio victim sat in a wooden cart under a blue tarpaulin. Gearboxes, grey car seats, lubricants and the greasy coils of suspension springs baked in the sun near him.

Next to a particularly beautiful yellow house, with gables and a balcony of high pointed arches, the wedding preparations were under way. A rectangular section of the street, crowded with donkey carts, sacks of cement and yellow phone booths, had been tented off. No one had arrived yet, but a woman of the house welcomed us in a state of high excitement. 'The big function is tonight,' she said. 'There'll be dancing and singing, you watch. Yes, yes, the whole society will come! We won't sleep, it'll go on all night! We don't even have to tell people, they will come on their own.'

With this, she rushed off. I was introduced to a bearded old man in blue, with a skullcap and a prayer mark so high on his head that I wondered how he was able to touch it to the floor. It turned out that he was the father of the groom. He knew Laxman as the man from the newspaper and must have thought I was a journalist because he began to grumble to me about the government: 'Ask me why they have forbidden us to serve food at our weddings.'

'Have they?'

'Yes.'

'Why?'

'Just like that.'

'No reason?'

'No reason.'

'They must have said something.'

'No, and they've also banned the loudspeaker at the mosque, even when there's a visitor from out of town.'

'They've banned singing and dancing too,' Laxman said.

'No,' the man interrupted, 'that's allowed, but we can only serve one dish at the wedding.'

'They want to discourage all this extra spending,' Laxman said.

Though Pakistanis denied it, in places like Iran where laws of this kind existed, the practical justification was only a cover for a deeper Islamic desire to rid the marriage ceremony of all things that were cultural and not strictly Islamic. I couldn't see why else, in this lawless region where the state could not be relied on to bring basic governance, it would bother to make sure that ordinary people followed hospitality guidelines for weddings.

Laxman went off looking for food, and the old man turned to me with a gleam in his eyes. 'I shouldn't say this,' he said, with a crooked smile, 'but my son works at the paper. His position there is not permanent. Do you think you could help him become permanent? He's been there seven or eight years and his position is still temporary.'

'I'll try,' I said, not wanting to disappoint the man on his son's wedding day.

We were still talking when the son arrived. He was dark and heavy, with a thick, black beard and a prayer mark that was just a dot. I saw these marks with a feeling of dread now, as if everywhere one looked people were catching a terrible new disease. All the trainers in my brother's gym had them. In seven months in the Muslim world, I had seen the prayer callous, with its rough, thick texture only once, in Syria, and now in Pakistan every other man had one. He was speaking on his mobile phone and continued to do so as he told us that we were to make our way to a mosque across the street for the wedding.

A small gathering of men left the tented area and walked to the white marble mosque. It was crowded, with a pungent smell and fluorescent and tinted glass lights. There were other worshippers too, some with red, hennaed beards. Laxman tried to make me wear a plastic skullcap for those who didn't have their own, but when I saw him in his red shirt and white plastic cap, looking so foolish, I couldn't bring myself to do it. I sat down next to the old man, and as we watched the bustle at the front of the mosque, he said, 'There was a time when the priest came to the house. Our weddings used to last seven days, but today many of the traditions are dying out. There's only one day for the wedding and we have to come to the mosque for the ceremony. When I was little, weddings took place with great festivity. They're forgetting how to get married!'

The old man put it well. This was the loss of history that was not just in books, but real and felt. The weddings he described were like weddings I knew in India; often the only difference between religions was the ceremony, which was the shortest part of the occasion. It was easy to imagine, as with the Sufi shrine, how weddings would have been an event for people of all faiths. There would have been a special feeling of goodwill at attending the wedding of someone from another faith, yet of the same culture. There was no cultural familiarity for me now: it was only a Muslim wedding. The dumbing-down of the wedding to its bare Islamic essentials was part of the rejection of India as a cultural entity, part of the rejection of the composite culture, which left only the bare bones of religion. The old man was religious, but he missed his culture. That culture, like the Sufi religion of Sind and the city of Hyderabad, had relied on its diversity. The sudden fact of homogeneity in a composite culture was a shock, like imagining London or New York stripped of their diversity. It affected values, and the assumption of homogeneity in my father's house – the jibes against Hindus, Jews, gays, blacks and Americans, the language untempered by just the awareness of others – was more alien to me than anything else.

In my confusion, I kept expecting a bejewelled bride in red to appear so I was little surprised when the father indicated that his son, after signing a few documents, had become married while sitting next to another man who was also getting married.

We walked back to the rectangular tent and the women beat kitchen utensils and sang songs about their brother's happiness. When they saw that the groom was lagging behind on his mobile phone they stopped, and started again a few minutes later. Many more people arrived and men who looked like blacksmiths, in greasy vests and beards, brought in great metal pots of steaming food.

The attorney general drove up in an air-conditioned car, opened his window and shook the groom's hand. Laxman ran up to him to introduce me as a journalist from London. He

smiled, gave me his card and then the tinted windows went up.
We had to go too; we were meant to meet the bureau chief. I
looked into the tent before leaving. Large, listless men, with hot
faces, were standing by a row of blue tables, putting away great
mouthfuls of rice and chicken.

When we arrived at the newspaper offices, the bureau chief
wanted me to meet someone who had just stepped out of the
office to prayer. I felt some tension from the night before pass
between us, then he said, 'I don't know if I should be telling
you this, but only twice in the twenty years that I've been
working here has *saab* called me. But he called yesterday and
he said, "What you do for him, you'll be doing for me." So,
you have asked for the moon and I will move heaven and
earth.'

I was embarrassed to see the dignified old man put in this
position, but Laxman's face gleamed with satisfaction. The
awkwardness in the room ended with the appearance of a tall,
fair man, with a thick, black moustache and a prayer mark.

The man, in his early forties, was a member of Sind's legisla-
tive assembly. He had made his way up in Pakistani politics
through channels that were now closed. He began his career
in the student unions in 1971, the year East Pakistan was lost.
'That time was good.' He smiled. 'Student life was very good.
We were getting a lot of talent, but then Zia banned the student
unions and their leaders. All the good politicians you see now,
who aren't scared of the army, came up during that time.' The
student unions, like the film industry, never recovered. They
were one of those fragile organisations that take decades to
build but only months to smother. And in 1979, the year Bhutto
was executed, the year before my parents met, the young politician who in all likelihood would have joined a large, secular
party, like the People's Party, joined a religious one instead.

Though his aspiration for Pakistan was the most basic, non-religious desire for good government, he felt that only Islam could bring true democracy.

'The army won't let it come,' he said. 'They listen to what America says. When they wanted to fight the Russians, the army brought the Taleban and General Zia and it was all *namaz* and *Allah Allah*. Then they wanted the Taleban out and they brought Musharraf who knows nothing about these things. The Islamic movement is strong, and if there were free and fair elections, we would sweep into power. But there are bogus elections and ballot stuffing. In 1947, *madrassa*s were only a few hundred and now there are twenty-five thousand. Isn't religion growing? Do you see the attendance at religious events?' In the past, religious parties had never swept the ballot boxes, but the politician was sure that the mood had changed.

'People are becoming more Islamic-minded. When Muslims are being killed in Waziristan, won't religion increase? Musharraf says, "Take Islamic culture out of textbooks," and people say, "Fine, we'll teach it at home." Religion is growing because they're trying to suppress it. They did away with the Taleban, which controlled the people very well, curbed crime, stopped opium, ended injustice, and it just made people turn more towards religion.'

'How do you want religion in Pakistan to be?'

'In everything.'

'Shariah?'

'Yes.'

'Saudi?'

'No, that's a kingdom.'

'Iran?'

'No, that's something else.'

'Then what?'

'Like in the time of the Prophet. An Islamic republic.'

'But there was no republic then.'

'Yes, but what is a republic, after all?'

'A European concept coming out of ancient Greece.'

'No. A republic,' he said, 'came from Islam.'

What he had in mind was not really a political entity but a vision of a just society. He quoted a story I had heard many time now about the caliph Omar. In the story, the caliph is questioned publicly over why he uses more cloth in his dress than his fellow Muslims. Despite his high office, he is not offended by the query and explains that he has more cloth because his son has given him his share. Muslims liked the story for its message of equality and political accountability. But beyond these simplicities, when the young politician's demands were boiled down to details, they bore a resemblance to a modern, Western-style republic, not a Taleban-style state.

'We want to improve education. We want full education – maths, chemistry, economics. We want to improve hospital facilities, services, utilities. We are not allowed to present these things in the Assembly. We present them and they block us.' But how could it happen in a deeper sense until men like the young politician stopped standing for the faith and stood instead for what they wanted? Wouldn't the Islamic lens always distort the real priorities? Wouldn't it be better to think of models in places where republics of this kind had been achieved, rather than the Prophet's example? The reason it couldn't work, this finding something in one place and recasting it in a palatable Islamic mould, was that the faith's distortions were too many. Even now, in the country founded for the faith, the young politician was ready to blame foreign powers for the inefficiencies of the local legislature.

'The Sind Assembly hasn't passed a single law in three years!' he cried. 'It's huge, with money and ministries, but the people have no relief. But ask us to find Osama bin Laden in Waziristan and we're doing it. That's why I think my government is in foreign hands. Because it is not a republic, it is not in our hands. One man, controlled by international powers, is controlling everything, a controlled and engineered democracy.

'I have a constituency,' he continued, 'I want to get it medicine, but I can't. There's a board, but they don't give us a vote on it. There's no elected representative on it! People are corrupt, and in this country they make corruption files only to blackmail people, not to bring them to justice. The rate of commission for any government development project is thirty per cent. I was given five million for development in my constituency, but out of that the government contractor wants thirty per cent. That's just the rate. My guy wants even more. He says, "Let's speak in terms of fifty."'

In the end, the young politician came back to religion. He quoted the great slogan of the religious parties, the final logic of the secular state for Indian Muslims: 'Pakistan ka matlab kya, la illa il allah. What is the meaning of Pakistan? There is no God but God.'

The politician struck me as sincere and I felt that the corruption he saw around him drove him to the purities of faith. He offered to take me to the Assembly and we exchanged details. When I told him my name, he smiled and said, 'Taseer. I'll remember it. It was the name of a great Pakistani leader.'

This mention of my father, like the one at the border when I first came to Pakistan, surprised me. I wouldn't have thought the young politician would know of him. The respect people in Pakistan had for my father complicated my assessment of him. I felt a certain pride when ordinary people spoke of his courage in the Zia years, and when young executives looked up to him for the business empire he created at the age of fifty in a country where it wasn't easy to rise on your own. But I didn't know how I could let their opinions influence my own difficult relationship with him. I think it's impossible to see your parents in any role other than the intense, personal one you need with them. My peace with my father couldn't include knowledge of his success in public life. What good was he to me as a charismatic politician and businessman if he wasn't willing to be my father?

In his letter, my father had mentioned the 'Pakistani ethos'. I had had it in mind all the time in Hyderabad, but how strange it was to think of that phrase now, in this desert city, where in the name of a Pakistani ethos the city's harmony, still engraved in its buildings, had been carved into ghettoes of faction. Pakistanis offered their natural differences, differences in culture and language, as an explanation for the battle lines that had come up, but this was hardly an explanation when next door in India deeper differences had been bridged. Not only that, but in Sind too, where once great variety had been absorbed, bitter division was to be found in what was now relative homogeneity. And Sind, for centuries so diverse, its culture and worship formed from that diversity, was for the first time in its history no longer a place of confluence.

As we walked down the stairs, Laxman scuttled up to me. 'Now, he's set.' He meant the bureau chief, whom we were dropping off at the Press Club. The bureau chief had mentioned earlier that one of the political parties had called for a strike and the streets now were emptier than usual. It was early afternoon and the heat that had been building since the morning surpassed all expectations. The stillness of the trees, the knife-like edges of Urdu slogans on the walls, the near-solidity of shadows brought a phantasmagoric aspect to the day. The greenery of trees seemed sometimes to be red, and the whole scene was stained like a photographic negative. The heat pressed against my head and it took all my strength to get out of the car and thank the bureau chief for his help.

I was leaving Hyderabad later that afternoon for a rally in another town. I had just said goodbye to the bureau chief and was turning away to get back into the car when, barely a few feet from me, there was a man wearing nothing but a fragment of cloth. It was his nakedness that made me look again, and when I did, I saw that sections of flesh had been torn from his legs, his arms and his chest. A blue polythene bag hung from his wrist. His frail, dark body trembled and shook and tears streamed down his small, bearded face. He wasn't with anyone, he didn't approach anyone, he just stood alone outside the Press Club, almost naked, covered with open wounds, looking up at the white sky with his glassy eyes, and weeping, not like a child but like a fully grown man, a deep broken groan from the depths of his wretched body.

It was as complete an impasse as I had ever found myself in. I had turned away from all kinds of horror in my life, but this man, the extent of his injuries, the climate he stood in and the cry coming from his mouth made it impossible to look away. Laxman and I ran up to him and yelled to the bureau chief, who turned and came back. The man could hardly speak, but he managed to tell the bureau chief that he had been burnt, and it was possible now to see that the wounds were broad swathes of burns. As the man tried to speak, a young man in a powder blue *salwar kameez* appeared. He said that a fire had broken out and the man had been burnt in it. He was taken to the civil hospital burns ward, but because he told the press he was not being treated properly, they had left him without treatment as punishment. 'For twenty days,' the young man said, 'he has been lying without treatment.'

'These stories happen every day, Aatish *saab*,' the bureau chief said. 'Best to leave it alone.'

'How was he burnt? In a factory or house?'

'In a garbage dump,' the man said.

285

'What was he doing there?'

'He's an addict.'

'In Hyderabad,' the bureau chief clarified, 'garbage is disposed of by burning.'

'Yes, but what was he doing in it?'

'He's an addict. He doesn't feel anything,' the chief said. 'He was lying in the garbage when they burnt it. Don't worry too much about these cases. They are a daily occurrence.'

Pakistan had among the highest number of heroin addicts in the world and this, too, like so much else in Pakistan, had happened since 1979.

'What's he going to do?'

'I'm treating him,' the man in blue said.

'Who are you?'

'Saeed.'

'Who's he?' I asked the bureau chief.

'A quack,' the bureau chief replied, 'In Pakistan, if you cannot afford a doctor, you go to a quack.'

The man had run away from the hospital when it refused to treat him and Saeed found him. He seemed now to be using the burnt man to some end of his own. He had brought him to the Press Club in the hope of calling attention to the story. He seemed half amused, a little exhilarated. He asked me my full name and then, trying to form some religious judgement about me, asked why I wore the Sikh bangle on my wrist. I ignored him.

It was a story full of ambiguity. Everyone seemed to have some incalculable motive; no one's account was clear; the press, the hospital, the authorities, the quack were all implicated, but then there was the bare, inadmissible fact, the fact big enough to stop anyone in their path, of a man, half burnt to death, standing in the street sobbing in fifty-degree heat. I could hardly believe – after a cycle in feudal Sind, after the violence of the

Mango King's world, after Dickensian lawyers, informant journalists and bloodthirsty slogans – that this was my last vision, the most voiceless creature in this degraded chain. When this reality was seen against the exalted expectations for the religious homeland, it was possible to imagine that this was the darkness, the almost religious darkness, so potent a myth in the Muslim imagination, of a time when no man was left uncorrupt, and from whose depths, surely, a messiah was at hand.

## The Idea Country

My father had written about India and Pakistan in his letter and now the publisher wanted me to write about continuities between the two. I felt I couldn't. He said I was in a unique position to see them. And perhaps I was. But after my panorama in Sind, I felt that what remained common were remains; the countries had gone their own ways. He became irritated. Educated Pakistanis didn't like to hear of the inroads the faith had made over the past fifty years. They pointed to the Sufi religion of Punjab and Sind, how so many people were as they had always been, hardworking, no veils, no beards. And they were right. But that Sufi faith, with its shrines and poetry and wide appeal, was not the religion that was gaining ground in Pakistan, but a more literal, streamlined faith. In many who didn't have veils and beards, it had made its trespasses. The secular state for Indian Muslims had been muddied over the decades; democracy with dictatorship; Bhutto's populism died with him; and after everything else had been allowed to fall away, the men who believed that Pakistan was created for faith would always have the force of logic on their side.

The 'Pakistani ethos' was hard to pin down, but I could tell that the rejection of India was an important part of it. So it was not because continuties did not exist that I didn't wish to write about them, but because their reassertion was not part of the Pakistani story. To write about them was to write about obscurity.

If Iran found Islamic expression in a modern context through the Islamic Republic, so did Pakistan, but the nature of the republic, and even the impulses behind it, were very different. At first, it hadn't been an Islamic republic at all, the 'Islamic' was added a decade later; it was a secular state for Indian Muslims. And, in the beginning, that was all: no Shariah, no clerics, no ban on alcohol; people remembered women on bicycles. It was as if a trust like Abdullah's – that the Muslims he had never met possessed a certain basic identity – had been the impulse behind gathering the sub-continent's various and disparate Muslims into a single state. That was Pakistan's first religious battle: the cleansing of the population.

Pakistan's founders were not clerics and fanatics, but poets and secularists. It was from the most sophisticated Muslims of that time that the case for the country was made. The poet Iqbal, the country's intellectual founder, was a contemporary of my grandfather. He actually wrote and performed my grandparents' marriage ceremony. And yet among these genteel people an idea was expressed whose full ugliness, and violence, only became clear in the cruder, more basic articulations that followed. For me, until I saw the faith's unspoken hold on my father's notions of history and politics, and the chauvinism it could produce, the idea would almost have been too strange to understand. Though it was disguised as an economic argument, a fear of being swamped by money-minded Hindus, it was really just a refinement of what Abdullah had said to me half a century later in Istanbul, also now free of its diversity: 'I think that Muslims have to be at the top, at the centre of the system. We have to determine all the things in the world, otherwise we won't be free ourselves . . . A Christian may live with us here, but not like a Muslim. He may live here, but we have to be dominant.'

Translated into political terms, he was saying that Muslims needed their own state. This had also been the demand for Pakistan. But despite its apparent political objective, the demand was less concrete than it seemed. Its impracticality, but also the frustration that arose from its failure, became clear when, in my last few days in Karachi, I met an Islamic ideologue.

'When you see him,' Salim, the reporter, said, 'you would never expect him to be such an Islamist, but he's a real hard-liner.' Salim was stocky and bearded, with tired eyes. He was a star reporter at the publisher's paper and obsessed with the war on terror. The ideologue, he said, supplied some of the country's fiercest religious groups with their philosophy. His description of an outwardly irreligious man, with political ideas that had all the force of religion, made me want to meet the ideologue.

We arranged lunch at the Usmaniye restaurant in the outer reaches of Karachi, deep within the city of cement and corrugated-iron. Once we left the broken streets on the outskirts of Karachi, the road signs and pavements continued for some distance, then fell away in parts. At traffic-lights, a couple of black eunuchs dressed in pink, with cloudy eyes and yellow teeth, begged for money. It was a big, treeless intersection full of open-backed trucks and scooters. The heat and the smoke made the outlines of the buildings tremble. On a grey cement wall, a colourful scrawl read, 'Crush Israel' and 'Down with Denmark'. A boy salvaged pens and plastic bags from a mountain of hardened garbage at the centre of which there was a half-full dumpster. The flags of local parties appeared in clusters, reds, greens and a worn-out Pakistani People's Party flag. It was Bhutto's party, my father's party, at times the great hope of Pakistani democracy, still popular, especially in Sind, and now awaiting another life.

We passed another mountain of waste and compressed poly-thene, from which shreds of pink and blue fluttered in the hot breeze. Below it I saw a still body of black water, disturbed now and then by a mysterious sputtering of bead-like bubbles. Where there might have been rocks at the edge, there were hillocks of filth and little clumps of bright grass.

The restaurant was cool and dimly lit, away from the roar of the street. The ideologue wore an olive green shirt. He was dark, clean-shaven and his eyes were sunken. He smoked many cigarettes.

He didn't want to talk about himself. 'Nothing is personal in all of this. I don't believe in personal opinion as far as reli-gion is concerned. Nothing I say has to do with who I am or my own experience.'

He had grown up in Karachi, born just before the first war with India in 1965. In 1971, he told me, 'Pakistan became two pieces. I have very little memory of that time,' he recalled, his thin lips pulling at the cigarette, 'but I was aware that we didn't cook three meals a day in our house. The good thing about our house, though, and many others was that we read a lot, two or three papers a day, literature, we discussed politics. I had read all of Premchand [the short-story writer] by the time I was ten. We might have been misguided, but the political motivation was there. At times it might have been wrong, but it was there, and this was without it being associated with any one political party. But now all that is gone.'

The ideologue spoke some English, and refined Urdu. His intense, studious manner and nicotine-stained fingertips reminded me of an old-fashioned Marxist intellectual. But there was something missing about him – humanity, perhaps. He seemed hard and hollow.

'Why is it gone?'

'The people became disillusioned. We always thought Pakistan was made to be realised. This sense was lost, and with it, we lost many other things.'

'What else?'

'A sense of destiny, collective self-confidence. Our political framework was dismembered. But with Muslims, geography is not very important. If even after 1971 our ruling élite had bounced back, we would have bounced back because we've never been fascinated with geography. We are fascinated with ideas. If even then an idea could have come . . .'

The ideologue grew up talking about the idea of Pakistan. 'Discussing Pakistan,' he said, 'was like discussing Islam. Pakistan was made in the name of Islam. It had to be a role model for the rest of the Islamic world. We identified characters who were responsible for its failure: Mujibur Rahman [the founder of Bangladesh], Bhutto, India, Mrs Gandhi. We thought one day we'd become one again. It was a very simplistic world-view. We were closely associated with the notion of Pakistan. It was more like a being than a country. It was all-living. It wasn't geography or politics. It was more than that. It was a collective consciousness. This was the idea of many.'

And now, put this way, I felt the ideologue's description wasn't of a real place but of a religious Utopia. This man who could be so clear and down-to-earth had an almost magical side to him.

'But this is such a country,' he said, with new softness in his voice, 'that has never let it be decided where it was headed. That's why you see the situation of today. Look at the India of 1946. It was fractured, but then one idea came and the whole sub-continent was united and held together by this idea. Even if we had decided to become a secular state or a nation state, we would be in a good position now. But we did not follow a liberal model or an Islamic one. Nor did we achieve material success or build a bond. We have a lot of diversity, rare diversity, of language, of culture, of religion. This could have been a great force, but it was turned into contradiction by our political élite.'

'Why was it so bad here?'

'Our ruling élite was such that it never thought of anything but its own vested interest. It never thought of Pakistan as a nation, only as a private limited company.' It was the first time in months that I had heard a Pakistani blame Pakistanis, not the foreign hand, for the country's failures. Hearing him speak, I felt as I had when I met the young politician in Hyderabad: the faith was getting all the good people.

'And the idea now?'

'It's still alive and kicking,' he said sadly.

'Of a state that embodies Islamic principles?'

'Absolutely.'

'Have you thought more about a model?'

'Islam doesn't depend on form,' he said. 'Form is not important. Essence is the main thing. If the essence is there, you can derive from it any kind of model.'

It was the most untrue thing I had heard. This dependence on sacred essence, and disregard of form, political models and institutions, had been the undoing of Pakistan, and Iran.

'Do you think that if Pakistan had been a successful secular country, you would be writing about political Islam today?'

'There is no such thing as political Islam. There is just Islam, which has a political component. That is a Western phrase designed to distort the totality of Islam.

'The problem with us,' he said, 'is that somewhere along the way we stopped being a country guided by an idea and just became a place where people lived.'

That remark stopped the ideologue's torrent; he seemed to

sense that he'd said a painful but amazing thing. So many places were just places where people lived, but Pakistan, which was made for an idea, and which had broken with history for that idea – which, if not for that idea, was just a handful of Indian Muslim states, with linguistic and cultural differences – depended on it for its survival.

'There are two kinds of history,' he said, of the connection to India, 'dead history and living. Dead history is something on a shelf or in a museum and living history is part of your consciousness, something in your blood that inspires you.'

'But why is the pre-Islamic history of Iran living?'

'There is a reason for this,' he replied. 'If all India became Muslim, we might have been able to identify with the Hindu past. We would have modified something. But since it didn't happen that way, we can't choose something that goes against our taste. You won't wear a T-shirt you don't like.'

'It's very unusual,' he continued, 'in the case of Europe, that the Christian world should have abandoned its roots and looked to Hellenistic civilisation. It ran away from the Christian golden period, when Constantine accepted Christianity and it spread through Europe. They abandoned it and ran towards Greece. It shows that they did not have a law, and that for the law, they had to run to Rome. They didn't have *shariat*. We have spirituality and we have a law.' The ideologue knew that those histories had flowed from each other, but couldn't accept an origin other than in faith. It was interesting that he didn't choose Jesus as a starting-point, but Constantine and Christianity's political triumph.

'Who's "we"?'

'The Muslims.'

'You say it as though you were Arab.'

'This doesn't arise in the case of Muslims – Arab, non-Arab. It's a civilisation of faith. We are Muslims.'

A 'Civilisation of Faith'. This was also the civilisation to which my father belonged. It was the thousand-year culture, of which Abdullah had spoken. It was what all Muslims had in common, believing or non-believing, moderate or extremist. For me, there was something miraculous in this transfiguration of one's culture and history, by either a profession of faith, or an inherited profession of faith. There was something miraculous in the idea that if Even, my Norwegian friend, converted to Islam that this would also become his history. The poet Iqbal's family, after all, were only recent converts to Islam. And how had I fallen through the cracks? What would it take to believe in a history like that? A profession of faith? My father had made none, but believed in the history. My mother gave me no religion, so how was it that my father and I had ended up being from two different nations having been once from the same country, and even, the same region? Perhaps it was like retaining certain moralities without believing in God, or religion. Perhaps it was kept in place by everyone around you believing.

It was time for me to make the final part of my journey north to see my father.

## Articles of Faith

I made my way to Lahore by train. My father hadn't called me once during my time in Pakistan and I feared an unfriendly reception.

In Karachi railway station, beyond a line of peach-coloured arches, listless railwaymen sat with their feet on desks in dark offices, with open doors and brown mesh windows. One picked at his feet as he spoke to his colleague. An old-fashioned red metal roof came down over the arches, protecting the platform from the late-afternoon blaze. Among the hurried movements of porters in orange, men sat on their haunches next to swollen plastic sacks and women, on the floor in groups, fanned themselves. A great brass bell, a blue phone booth, a Pizza Hut and a black-tiled water fountain were arranged in a line down the platform. Sunken polythene bags and candy wrappers hung in the few inches of grey water that lay between the tracks. The large families and skullcapped men waiting for a train under droning fans seemed like characters in a Partition scene.

Talk of the train began. The crowd on the platform compressed, then broke loose, all moving at once with the arrival of the Tezgam, an elegant pool-table-green train with beige and red stripes. My brother's driver, who waited quietly with me, now said, 'Wherever you look, there's public. People I've spoken to say the condition of India is better than Pakistan.'

I didn't answer, wishing to avoid the conversation of differences. What I did know was that discovering Pakistan, its closeness to India and the trap I felt it had fallen into where religion was concerned, filled me with an affection for the country that I hadn't expected.

'Yes, on our side, things have yet to be established,' the driver said. He spoke in Urdu, but said 'establish' in English.

We found the sleeper by the numbers written in white chalk on the side of the carriage; a crest said 'Islamabad Carriage Factory'. The cabin was air-conditioned with its own bathroom and the most spacious since Istanbul. The dark green seats were wide and springy, the walls were of plywood, and the windows darkened. A smart, painted sign with yellow letters and black outlines, reminiscent of another time, read: 'To seat 3 sleep 2'; I had it to myself. My brother's driver put the white box of Sind Club sandwiches that the publisher sent for me on the table. His large, mascaraed eyes scanned the carriage and he said, 'If there's been any error on my part, please pardon it.' Then he went off and stood on the platform until the train left.

The sign for the Inward Parcel Office, a mountain of packages, men sleeping on plastic sacks, and a policeman lying on a bench, drifted by as the Tezgam left Karachi. We passed heaps of burning garbage, smoke rising against cement walls, with black writing on them. I thought of the bureau chief's words, 'In Hyderabad, garbage is disposed of by burning.' The train climbed past the top of the city, and a final film reel played out through tinted windows: the coloured roofs of buses, the upper storeys of small apartment buildings, corrugated-iron roofs held down by bricks, mango-tree canopies, bougainvillaea from terraces, barbers' shops, the green and white domes of mosques modelled on Medina's, the span of a flyover, water tanks and green satiny flags, with gold trimmings, fluttering in the black smoke from burning garbage. A village of cloth and sticks appeared near the tracks amid the devastation of blue plastic bags. Thorny bushes reached out to touch the train. The cement city, with men sitting on rooftops, families of buffaloes in manure and the watermarked walls of warehouses, passed just before sunset.

At dusk, the eternal Sind scene: flat, dry land throwing up magnificent, double-storey cacti, with fleshy depressions and sparse giant thorns.

The next morning we were in Punjab. At Multan station, the carriage attendant looked into my cabin and smiled. I asked for some tea.

'Yes, yes,' he said. 'Everything is available. I'll send the boy.'

A few minutes later an old man in a green uniform arrived to take my order. 'Just tea?' he said, with surprise.

'What else is there?'

'Eggs, double *roti* and butter.'

'OK. Bring them all.'

He came back with bread, marmalade, teabags, real milk and sugar, and an omelette on a white napkin and a steel plate. One station later, a young man with long, greased-back hair and a silver wire in his ear came into my cabin with a red brush to sweep the place while I sat on my haunches. The station, though smaller than Karachi's, had the same colonial elements: sloping metal roofs with a carved skirting; a whitewashed platform, blackboards and blue and white signs that said 'Battery Room'; 'Unity – Discipline – Faith', the motto that Pakistan's founder gave the country hung on a wall. There was a pink marble mosque and people washing for prayer outside.

Soon afterwards, a boy with a pointed face and crooked teeth knocked on my door. He was looking for a plug point to charge his phone. I said I hadn't seen one, but that he was free to look. He went away, then came back and sat down. His name was Rizwan and he was an electrical-engineering student in Karachi. 'Where are you from?' he asked.

'Karachi.'

'But in reality where are you from?'

'London.'

'I could tell from your accent.'

'Is it apparent?'

'Slightly. Are you Muslim?'

'Yes,' I replied, not wishing to enter into a long explanation.

'Nationality is British?'

'Yes.'

'I can tell.' He smiled. 'If you have any need in Pindi, I'm there. For a hotel, car, whatever.'

'Thank you.'

He said he had two more years left before he got his BSc in electrical engineering.

'Then?'

'Middle East. There's a lot of demand there. Maybe UK too.'

'Aren't visas tough, these days?'

'Yes, very. Don't even ask how tough, but Allah will help and when it happens I won't even know how it happened.'

'Where in the Middle East?'

'Dubai and Saudi. Both have a lot of demand, but Dubai is like ours.'

Just then, the carriage attendant and a man in a white uniform, with shiny silver buttons, knocked on the door, came in and asked to see my ticket.

'Who's he?' he asked, seeing that my ticket was for one person.

'We were just talking.'

The man turned to Rizwan and said sternly, 'Please go back to your seat.'

'No, no, we were just—'

'Please go back to your seat! You're lucky it was just me. Another conductor would have fined you.'

Rizwan rose, I made one last plea on his behalf, but the conductor reminded me that I was lucky it was just him.

Outside, a few boys in *salwar kameez* played in a canal. Another defecated near the tracks while a friend kept him company, running to get him water when he needed it. Under a cloth roof held up by four poles, a few women lazed next to a buffalo in a patch of mud. In Punjab, the houses were firmer and the majority in red brick. White domes and rust red minarets rose out of the low townscapes. There were big-leafed papaya trees in the fields and a golden layer of ripening corn. There was also much more water: in the fields, in the tube wells and in the wide network of canals. At the stations, men used old-fashioned hand pumps outside signs that said 'Lamp Room'.

Being in Punjab made me think ahead to my arrival at my father's house. My doubts had faded; the travelling made me optimistic. I felt that it would appeal to my father's sense of adventure that I was showing up on his doorstep after eight months of journeying from Europe to Pakistan. I also thought that if we were to move forward from our recent problems, we might set a new tone in our relationship. Fighting with someone, whatever its other effects, was at least a sign of emotion and openness. I thought that it might help make our relationship more instinctive.

At sunset, not far from Lahore, Adil, a Kashmiri boy, knocked on my door. The train had stopped and he felt like a chat. He had pale skin, light brown hair, amber eyes and prominent, very pink gums. He was a marine-biology student in Karachi and there was something intense and restless about him, even about the way in which he'd barged into my cabin for a friendly chat. He was off to Kashmir for a memorial service to his uncle who died in the October earthquake, which happened a few weeks before my trip began.

Adil had a brother in Abu Dhabi, but he was reluctant to go abroad. 'You can say you're a Muslim abroad,' he said, 'but you can't say you're a Pakistani because immediately people will say, "He's a terrorist." You tell me, how can you go to a foreign country and not even be able to say what your nationality is?'

'Do you think Pakistan's reputation has become that bad?'

'It didn't become bad. It was broken.'

'Who broke it?'

'Indians. They really maligned us abroad.'

I started to become nervous as the conversation grew more sub-continental.

'Are you Muslim?' he asked.

'Yes.'

'Then why do you wear that string?'

'It's from a shrine in Sind,' I lied.

'OK, then why do you wear this bangle?'

'My grandmother gave it to me. She's a Sikh.'

'But you?'

'Muslim. My father's Muslim.'

'And your mother?'

'She was Sikh,' I lied further, 'but she became a Muslim.'

'What does your father do?'

'Business.'

'What kind?'

At last I got him off the topic by asking how Karachi was. He said it was great, and that it was fun to tease the girls there.

'How do you tease them?'

'We go up to them, a few friends and I, and we sing songs to them.'

'Like what?'

He laughed and began to sing: 'Come, come, my little queen, tonight I have the emperor's right on you. Who will free you from my grip? Tonight, you've been caught, caught, caught . . .'

He laughed again and stayed talking until the silver-buttoned conductor appeared to eject him and announce the train's destination.

\*

And so, with the ease and inevitability of a train pulling into a station, I found myself, one hot evening in Lahore, almost at the point where I had begun a journey to find my father four years before. But for the short flights in and out of Iran, I had travelled by land and it amazed me now that the journey which had begun in Europe, by train from Venice to Istanbul to Damascus, and by road through Arabia, had yielded the sub-continent, Lahore and, even more miraculously, my father. I had travelled eight months for this meeting, but the confluence of time, distance and expectation made it feel even longer.

I arrived to a house full of people. My younger sister was graduating from Lahore's American School and brothers, sisters, their spouses, uncles and grandparents had all flown down for the ceremony. My stepmother was involved in organising the graduation. There was to be a party at the house, and a few days later, it was my father's birthday. The level of activity was close to that of a wedding. Tents went up in the lawn as I drove in and a steady stream of tailors, caterers and hairdressers passed in and out of the house.

The mistake I made with my father was to be ready for anything other than indifference. That evening, standing on his doorstep after a year of silence, I thought we'd do something we'd never done before: have a meal together, a drink, a conversation about what had happened since we'd last met.

The trip had not left me unchanged. My relationship with Islam was no longer a negative space. I had learnt about the faith in the early part of my journey. Then, from my conversations with men like Abdullah, I discovered it wasn't faith in an obvious way that I needed to understand, but the political and historical demands it made and how it reshaped countries like Iran and Pakistan. This aspect of the religion, which could make my half-brother feel 'civilisational defeat' without being a believer, and which my father could possess without the faith, was not open to me. The way into that kind of faith was closed. It would once have been part of a whole system of belief, complete with ideas of politics, law and behaviour. In Pakistan and Iran, I had been shocked by the violence of reviving the faith in the form of Islamic republics and religious homelands. But all this seemed very far away now that I was at my father's doorstep. At that moment I thought only of our relationship. I couldn't see how these amorphous things, politics and history, could bring up real differences between two people. I had never lost a relationship over such differences and I couldn't believe that they might encumber my relationship with the father I had found after so many years.

And though I was more confident in some ways, arriving into the commotion at that low, red-brick house, I felt my courage fail me at an emotional level. Somehow I was a weaker man than I had been four years before when I walked boldly into his life. It was easier then for me to be the person I wished to be with him, to be able to say frankly that I'd like to talk to him alone. Now, even before I walked into my father's house, I felt myself fall into line with the rules of the place.

I found my father, as I had always known him, lying on his

bed surrounded by family. He didn't get up, but from the nod and smile in my direction, I could tell that there was no bad feeling. He was in high spirits. At one minute he was answering his phone or laughing as he read aloud a funny text message, at the next he was serious, discussing the price of his shares with his brother-in-law. My stepmother sat on the bed, speaking to friends, organisers, dealing with my sister's sartorial panics. My two younger brothers came in from a football match on the lawn. An older sister was arriving later that night with her husband, who worked at one of the American banks. It was a scene I had witnessed many times before and occasionally felt part of. It was a scene in which you could be present yet sink into your own thoughts without anyone noticing.

My stepmother, always very welcoming, managed between many chores to ask me about myself and if I needed anything while I was in Lahore. Over the next few days my father and I came to rely on her to defuse the awkwardness of speaking directly to one another. Our conversation became neutered. In the past, we spoke openly about history and politics, but this time, those topics were off limits. Though I could tell from my father's manner that he meant to make amends, it was as if an unspoken distance, a sense of my having joined another camp, had arisen between us. I found it strange that, over the next few days, he didn't ask me once about my trip through the Muslim world or my travels in Pakistan. It was as if he didn't want to know.

At last I felt I had to raise the subject and I walked into his room, three or four days after I arrived, with that purpose. He seemed pleased to see me, but after a while, when some of the family had dispersed and I told him what I wanted to talk to him about, his face darkened. 'It depends on what you're writing. If it's another filthy anti-Pakistan diatribe, I want no part in it.

I've read some of what you've written and I don't think much of it.'

He said that what angered him about the article I wrote after the London bombings was that I had posed as a Pakistani. He said that he and his father were known as defenders of Pakistan and had been patriots all their lives, that he could play no part in an attack on Pakistan and Islam.

He lay on his bed as he spoke, occasionally turning to me, but mostly text-messaging. He seemed bored yet irritated. He described the faith as a brotherhood, something he'd grown up in. He said that the other day he'd been in Udaipur where some numbers, '786', were written on a wall. He asked his guide what they meant and the man replied that they were a lucky charm. 'No,' my father had said, 'it's bismillah rahman e rahim [in the name of God, the compassionate and the merciful].'

'Oh, you're Muslim,' the guide replied, and shook his hand.

'So, yes, there is a brotherhood,' my father said. 'People are warm to you, they bring you in, show you friendship.'

I asked him what it meant to be a 'cultural Muslim'.

'You see it all around you,' he replied. 'Everyone I know is Muslim. You see *namaz* [prayers], and *roza*s [fasts], all the servants are Muslim, and with Islam, people believe deeply. It happens that I don't privately, but I wouldn't dream of criticising Islam. I am not a practising Muslim, but my wife is and it would hurt her feelings.' He compared it to drinking in front of your friends when you wouldn't dream of doing so in front of your grandmother. 'It's offensive.'

His description of the 'cultural Muslim' seemed hardly different from my earliest idea of it, nothing more than festivals, ritual and language, but my journey had made me feel it contained deeper elements that he was not raising. My first hint of this was my father stressing many times that I was not Pakistani and not Muslim. The way he said it, with relish, he seemed almost to suggest that I wasn't really his son either. He stressed my not being Muslim so strongly that I became curious about the question with which my journey had begun: how could he be Muslim, if he claimed not to believe? How were we at this strange impasse where he, who didn't believe in the faith's most basic law, its Book, was telling me as a Muslim that I wasn't Muslim when by every law of the faith I was, and certainly if he was? He spoke with such passion, attaching some deeper importance to the idea of being Muslim, that I felt he couldn't be speaking only of culture.

During those days I spent in my father's house, I wanted very much for us to do something together that would help us regain the closeness we had known before I had received that letter. But our conversations now, with all that remained unsaid, reminded me of the first few years when I had known my father. There was the same embarrassment, but it was touched now with lack of interest.

And then, amid a minefield of family occasions, the perfect opportunity seemed to arise. I received a call from Yusuf, a cousin of my father, and on his mother's side the grandson of Iqbal, the poet and intellectual founder of Pakistan. It was Yusuf's great-grandmother who had rescued my grandfather all those years ago when the plague killed off his family. My grandfather grew up in Yusuf's *haveli*, or mansion, in the old city and I had been in touch with him since I arrived to find out more about my grandfather. Like the publisher, Yusuf had a special feeling for my connection to Pakistan and arranged meetings for me with his ancient uncles, who drank Chivas Regal in the evenings and had known my grandfather. That night Yusuf was calling to say that the famous Pakistani singer, Farida Khanum, was practising in the *haveli* and would I like to come? I accepted his invitation immediately, then asked my father if he would like to come with me. Even for people who lived in Pakistan, the chance to hear Farida practise was rare.

His eyes brightened. 'Farida Khanum in the *haveli*?'

'Yes.'

Then, inexplicably, his mood changed and he declined. It was the way it always with us: we were forever on the verge of doing something that might deepen our relationship so that it might be relied on, but it never happened.

So, I went off that night to Yusuf's *haveli* on my own. It was in the heart of the old city, which, after the still heat of the day, had come alive. A great doorway and a red-brick drive rose out of the tightly packed streets, leading up to the house, full of courtyards, slim balconies, leaning trees and a collage of old city houses peering down at the scene below. I found Farida Khanum in a room reached by a narrow staircase. She sat on the floor, in a pistachio green sari, eating mangoes. She ate them with her hands and off the skin, her dark red lipstick smudged. She was large and old, with dyed black hair, her skin drooped, but her every gesture was touched with femininity and whimsy: the gentle theatrics of an ageing star. When, finally, she began to sing, all that melted away. Her voice was insistent, filled with regret and seduction. She seemed to notice that she'd moved a new, young admirer nearly to tears and decided to drive the knife deeper. Yusuf had told her when I came in that I was my grandfather's grandson and now, helped by him, she put one of my grandfather's poems to music. Awakening his ghost in this house where he'd lived, she gave me, couplet by couplet, the one thing of my grandfather's that all poets hope will remain of them.

As soon as she finished singing, Yusuf slipped away. He returned a few minutes later and said he wanted to give me something. He held a beautiful handmade watch with a grey face and a shabby black strap. He said that my English great-grandfather had presented the watch to the head of Yusuf's family when my grandparents had got married. The watch had come down to Yusuf, and though my father had insisted on having it, Yusuf wanted to give it to me because I'd been Dr Taseer's only grandchild ever to ask about him. He warned me that it would probably cause more problems for me at home, but that I should stand firm. I was thrilled to have the watch. I already felt a connection to my grandfather, in part because he was a poet but also because I had been named after his main work.

The next morning, my stepmother said, 'Please don't tell Abba. He'll be really angry. He really wanted that watch.' Her mother suggested I give it to him for his birthday, but I decided, recalling the affection with which it had been given to me the night before, that I would wait. By now, it was as if everyone in the house sensed the strain between my father and me.

In the breakfast room, newspapers strewn everywhere, I found my father sitting in his blue cotton nightsuit with his legs up on the sofa, sometimes flicking through TV channels, sometimes playing with his phone. He was always up early and I was hoping to catch him alone, but a few minutes later, my elder sister, my stepmother and her father, who was old and in a wheelchair, joined us. A conversation began about a circle of homeopathic doctors in New York to which my sister belonged. They had received a group email about Ahmadinejad's denial of the Holocaust.

'I never respond,' my sister said in a loud voice, 'but this time I said, "There'd better have been a Holocaust because the only people who've paid for it for the last fifty years have been Muslims."'

My father sniggered. 'All the Germans paid was the gas bill.' He felt that the number of people who had died in the Holocaust was wildly exaggerated. Even if the Germans were working day and night through the whole war they couldn't have killed as many people as it was claimed. 'The job was too big. I've seen Belsen by the way,' he sneered. 'I was expecting a big warehouse or something. It was hardly bigger than this room. There's no way they could have fitted in more than three hundred people a day. Then they brought them in a train, which had to go back and forth . . . I'm not denying the Holocaust, the Jews were definitely gassed, but not so many.'

He said that the people who trumped up the Holocaust were like those who said the Pakistanis killed a million people in Bangladesh in 1971. He was about to use the same argument he did for Bangladesh, about to ask where the graves were, when he must have remembered that the Nazis hadn't bothered with graves.

I had said nothing so far because I had the incredible suspicion that he was needling me. I say 'incredible' because if this was needling what possible 'us and them' theory could be behind it? What group was I part of that made it automatic for me to object to a derisive attitude towards a well-documented genocide? But he must have been right because the satisfaction with which my sister made her remark, and the pleasure my father seemed to derive from downplaying the Holocaust, disgusted me. It was not just disgust at their hatred for the Jews and Israel, but at the smallness of my father's world, the homogeneity of the place, in which people voiced ugly opinions without challenge: a safe area for casual hatred.

My father, returning to the subject of the Holocaust, made the point more than once that he was not denying the Holocaust, just objecting to the figures. At last I became curious as to what number he could have arrived at that made the Holocaust not such a bad thing after all.

'So, how many?' I asked.

His amber eyes shone with irritation. 'I don't know, but the eight million figure people quote is rubbish.'

'Six?'

'No, and by the way, there were Romanians and Gypsies too.'

So what? I wanted to say.

'Four and a half million Jews?'

He shrugged. 'When I hear people go on about the Holocaust,' he said, 'I just shake my head and keep silent because the whole might of the Judaeo-Christian lobby will come down on you.'

My sister said that she objected to anyone who doubted the Holocaust being labelled anti-Semitic. I had heard that before, but usually it was framed as an objection to anyone criticising the State of Israel, not the Holocaust, being labelled anti-Semitic. Knowingly or unknowingly, my sister distorted this little bit of college speak. But it was a revealing error: it prompted my curiosity about what lay behind this wrangling over numbers.

'What has made you adjust these numbers?'

'What I've seen,' he answered, 'and what I've read.'

I knew the historians who refuted the Holocaust. When I thought of my father, who read vast amounts of history, reading these discredited historians, I thought that he would have had to go against all his better instincts, abandon all the ways in which he formed his other historical opinions, to believe what those books said.

I heard the Muslim denial or downplaying of the Holocaust many times in my journey, especially during the cartoon riots in Syria. It was done because the Holocaust was thought to have played a part in the creation of Israel. Muslims felt Jews had occupied a Muslim country and that their cause was taken up by the West in part out of guilt that the Holocaust had taken place. The politics of faith then, produced a distortion that was both ugly and magical: the Holocaust never happened or was grossly exaggerated; it was a myth concocted by the enemies of Islam. The chain of Islamic logic ended with Muslims denying a well-documented genocide that they hadn't committed.

The deeper reason, I felt, that my father chose the Holocaust was that in the West its memory was sacred. Perhaps he thought he would provoke me, show me how it felt to desecrate something sacred. He made a mistake for two reasons: I wasn't Jewish or from the West, and the Holocaust was committed in the West by the West. For the West then, to hold up the Holocaust with near holy dread, forcing itself never to forget the evil of those years, in which it considered itself, not just the Germans, as complicit, was one of the most important treatments of history in modern times. It could not be reduced to the founding of Israel; it hadn't happened with a political end in mind; and it happened as much for the sake of the victimisers as for that of the victims. For me, on the outside, not from the West, to see the beauty of how another part of the world could move forward, could grow from such a terrible history, was a testament to history standing alone. You didn't have to be Jewish or European to accept the truth of it.

It was precisely the opposite of how the faith viewed history. Throughout my journey, this was the obstacle I had encountered: history fused with faith; the robbery of the great Islamic past, the pain and resentment that followed. It was what I, with my small idea of the faith, could not have acquired. It didn't need faith but, like faith, it had to be felt. And it was the reason why I had come to believe that there was more to being a 'cultural Muslim' than was apparent from the description.

'The real horror of the Holocaust,' I said, surprised at the tone in my voice, 'is not whether two, three or four million were killed, but that it was a mechanised, systematic extermination of a people. The state of Israel was many years in the making. It's possible to pry apart the causes for the creation of Israel from the fact of the Holocaust. You don't have to deny a Holocaust you didn't commit just because you hate Israel.'

Suddenly I looked round the room and felt bad. I thought,

I'm making such a nuisance of myself. My sister and step-mother looked worried about the direction the conversation was taking. My stepmother's father, his mouth open, was staring at me, wide-eyed.

My father nodded, then began on Israel and on the massacres in Sabra and Shatila, how women and children were killed, and what made that so different from the Holocaust. I didn't say any more. I had begun my journey asking why my father was Muslim and this was why: I felt sure that none of Islam's once powerful moral imperatives existed within him, but he was Muslim because he doubted the Holocaust, hated America and Israel, thought Hindus were weak and cowardly, and because the glories of the Islamic past excited him.

The faith decayed within him, ceased to be dynamic, ceased to provide moral guidance, became nothing but a deep, unreachable historical and political identity. This was all that still had the force of faith. It was significant because in the end this was the moderate Muslim, and it was too little moderation, and in the wrong areas. It didn't matter how someone prayed, how much they prayed, what dress they wore, whether they chose to drink or not, but it did matter that someone harboured feelings of hatred, for Jews, Americans or Hindus, that were founded in faith and only masked in political arguments.

Later he confessed that though he didn't believe Lahore drawing-room talk that 9/11 was a conspiracy, unanswered questions about the size of the hole in the Pentagon and Muhammad Atta's passport turning up at the crash site, produced doubt in him. 'I just don't know what to say when people bring up these things.' The 9/11 conspiracy theory was being added as the most recent article of faith for believer and non-believer alike.

I rose to leave the room. It was if a bank had burst. My father and I, for the first time, were beyond embarrassment.

I returned a few moments later to say goodbye to him, but

he had left for the day without a word. The now empty room produced a corresponding vacancy in me that was like despair. I wanted somehow to feel whole again; not reconciliation, that would be asking too much, just not this feeling of waste: my journey to find my father ending in an empty room in Lahore, with the clear light of a bright morning breaking in to land on the criss-crossing arcs of a freshly swabbed floor.

As the crow flies, the distance between my father and me had never been much, but the land had been marked by history for a unique division, of which I had inherited both broken pieces. My journey to seek out my father, and through him, his country, was a way for me to make my peace with that history. And it had not been without its rewards. My deep connection to the land that is Pakistan had been renewed. I felt lucky to have both countries; I felt that I'd been given what Partition had denied many. For me it meant the possibility of a different education, of embracing the three-tier history of India whole, perhaps an intellectual troika of Sanskrit, Urdu and English. These mismatches were the lot of people with garbled histories, but I preferred them to violent purities. The world is richer in its hybrids.

But then there was the futility of the empty room, rupture on rupture, for which I could find no consolation except that my father's existence, so ghostly all my life, had at last acquired a gram of material weight. And, if not for that, who knows what sterile obsessions might still have held me fast?

# Postscript: Distrust

A year later, in a Lahore shoe shop full of bulbs and mirrors and the smell of leather, the shopkeeper swivelled round to turn off a small television before he took my money. But I had seen something and so had a few bejewelled ladies standing next to me, so we asked him what had happened. His thick dyed moustache, clamped shut over his mouth and his expression grew dark. He muttered, 'Benazir Bhutto has expired.'

He was aware of what happens when a demagogue dies on the sub-continent. 'When a big tree falls, the earth is bound to shake,' Rajiv Gandhi had said, when violence broke out against the Sikhs after his mother, Indira Gandhi, was killed. And violence was my first thought when I stepped out of the shop's bright lights and mirrors on to a cold, smoky Liberty Market, swiftly waking up to the fact that Benazir Bhutto was dead.

That name – Benazir Bhutto – already filled with music, a name that was more like a chant, a carryover from the greatness of the father, a name perhaps bigger than the person to whom it belonged, now linked with death, which brought drama to ordinary names, had alarmed the shopkeeper. Benazir Bhutto is dead. It was too much. We were in a city of slogans and the Lahore shopkeeper, who would have heard that name turned to slogan on so many memorable occasions and so often in relation to long life, knew that he had said something he would only ever say once in a lifetime. It began the last rite in the life of a demagogue, that one moment when the indestructible icon of the people, the person who replaced institutions, who herself was an echo of her name, was human, cut down and sacrificed, before becoming immortal again, her spirit passed to the heir on the back of a sympathy vote.

Benazir Bhutto is dead! Long live Benazir Bhutto!

*

There was to have been an election.

The year had been full of events. In the summer, there was the siege and storming of the Red Mosque in Islamabad where more than a hundred people were killed. In the autumn, the country's major political leaders tried to return from exile to take charge of their parties. Nawaz Sharif, allowed by the Supreme Court to return, was deported on arrival. Benazir Bhutto, as part of a deal with the Americans, returned in October and narrowly escaped a bomb blast at her welcome rally. In November, the General put an end to his year-long battle with the Supreme Court and declared a state of emergency, rescinding press freedom, imprisoning his opposition and sacking over sixty judges. By the end of the month, he had removed his uniform and installed himself as a civilian president in preparation for the election. And all the time the bombs had continued, and parts of the country that were once holiday destinations were in the hands of extremists. The demand for more literal Islam, so long in the background and often absorbed electorally, had turned renegade and become the country's main battle. By the time December came round and the emergency was lifted, it was difficult to trust that anything as positive as a genuine election could occur in this climate of extremism and extra-legality.

Interwoven in these national dramas was a personal surprise for me. Watching Musharraf swear in his caretaker government on television in November, I noticed my father's brother-in-law in the audience. And in the next bulletin I saw, in the foreground, that my father, the lifelong PPP man and the once close ally of Benazir Bhutto, was being sworn in as a minister to the ex-general's new cabinet.

Though I congratulated him, his elevation ensured that when I arrived in Lahore a few weeks later to cover the elections, I wouldn't stay with him. His political aspirations had been the reason for our original distance. I felt that staying with him now that he was in an official position, and especially after the ill feeling that had arisen between us, would cause embarrassment. So I asked my uncle Yusuf, with the rambling house in the old city where my grandfather grew up, if I could stay with him. 'On the condition you don't write anything about your father or Pakistan,' he pleaded. I half agreed.

And when I arrived there was not much to write about. Lahore was full of Christmas and New Year parties and election posters – white bicycles on green backgrounds, promoting the pro-Musharraf alliance, lined the city's canals. But there was a general air of malaise and distrust. People talked of rigging and pre-decided elections. After a few days of watching the atmosphere in the old city, usually the nerve centre of election excitement, my uncle declared, 'Such a cold election I never saw. At least a few gunshots should have gone off.'

We sat on low beds in the courtyard of his house near the Royal Mosque. There was much about the *haveli* that I missed in my earlier visits: frangipani trees and the lamp-lit shadows of their long leaves; semi-circular transoms in green, red and orange glass, particularly beautiful in the evenings;

chocolate-coloured screens of varying size, bringing harmony to the mismatch of whitewashed buildings. I had recently begun to read and understand my grandfather's poetry, and it was a source of wonder to inherit and slowly decipher a book in a new script from a dead, unseen grandfather. Yusuf was keen that I try to make contact with my father, and at his behest I did, but after a few unsuccessful attempts, unreturned calls and messages, I gave up.

Shortly after I arrived, Yusuf left to spend New Year in India. The election was still 'cold' when he left. Looking back at the year of protest, and how it had been subdued – the emergency that was like an act of irritation on the General's part at having to deal with real constitutional constraints – it didn't seem as if the election would ever warm up or become more than an ornament in the General's make-believe democracy.

And yet Benazir Bhutto and Nawaz Sharif, whatever their sins, were not part of this world of cosmetic democracy. The sight of a giant billboard of Benazir at the edge of the old city, pictured in blue against a vast crowd holding red, black and green People's Party flags, was enough to renew my faith in a genuine fight, if not a genuine election. The reason in part was that Benazir's fight, the fight my father had been part of, was the truest fight Pakistan had known against its inner demons, military dictatorship and fundamentalism. And though it had not fulfilled its promise, Benazir still seemed to have so much fight in her.

Benazir, unlike the general, didn't have to say she was liberal; people knew she was liberal. She was also one other thing that no one in the race could stake claim to: she was the only national politician, with support in all four provinces, in a country threatened with dissolution. So I felt that, despite talk of deals with the Americans and with Musharraf himself, if Benazir was in

317

the race she would bring the 'noise and chaos' of democracy that her father had once written kept India in one piece.

But now, like her father, Benazir Bhutto was dead.

My thoughts went to my father. I knew he would be devastated. He'd fought General Zia alongside Benazir througout the eighties, been jailed for their shared cause, seen her triumphant return and electoral victory in 1988, been her party spokesman and travelled with her. And there was also the special pain he would feel of being estranged at death from someone he'd known and loved. But though my heart went out to him, the distrust that had grown between us in the past year made me feel that if I went to see him he would think I had come in bad faith.

I stood now, alone for a moment in the crowded market, naked bulbs coming on and evening traffic clogging the narrow street. I saw my brother's friend waiting for him to bring out the car and told him what I'd heard in the shop. He took in the information greedily, leant into the car as soon as it pulled up and told the others.

Before we had left the market, phone calls were coming in, telling us to get off the streets. We flicked through radio stations, hoping for more information, but the news had either been suppressed or the radio stations hadn't picked it up because they were leading with electoral stories. And what election could there be now? My brother wondered if there would still be a New Year's Eve ball. He wasn't being callous: he had paid a lot of money for the ticket and we were in an enclosed setting, with no perspective from TV or radio, trying to link the world as we'd just known it to the news that seemed to alter it so profoundly.

I called Nuscie, my mother's friend with whom I had stayed when I first came to Pakistan. She was sobbing and saying again and again, 'I just can't believe it. I can't believe they killed her.'

The news rebounding, forming webs, made real what was fantastical in the car's sealed environment. Then the mobile phones jammed, a sure sign of the city, so indifferent moments ago, becoming aware that Benazir Bhutto was dead.

The night was changing fast as we drove to my father's house. The street- and traffic-lights stopped working; there was a power cut of sorts; the traffic became more frantic and police barricades appeared.

When we reached my father's house, no one was sure whether or not I should go in to see him. 'This is the worst time,' my brother kept saying. My sister said she would go and see how he was taking the news before advising whether I should go in or not. In the meantime my mother called, also on the verge of tears. She had covered Pakistan for decades. In November 1988 she was in Lahore for Benazir's arrival. She wrote:

I arrived in Lahore on the night of Nawaz Sharif's last rally of the campaign. The night before it had been Benazir's turn and everyone was still talking about the unbelievable welcome she had received. The city waited till dawn to hear her speak. It took all night for her to drive in from Gujranwala because of the thousands who lined the route. They lay down in front of her Pajero [a Japanese Land Rover that has become a political status symbol since she started using one], they danced in the streets, and when she finally spoke many wept. 'Lahore,' she said, 'is a city of lights,' quoting Faiz Ahmed Faiz's famous poem. 'Lahore is a city of people whose hearts are alive. Lahore is Benazir Bhutto's city.'

'It's too awful,' my mother wept. 'I first saw her when I was with your father. We were in Islamabad and he said, "That's Benazir Bhutto." She was so young, so pretty. She had no business dying.'

Whatever her faults she didn't deserve to die like this.' My mother had witnessed the death of the great Indian demagogues, Indira Gandhi and her son, Rajiv. She understood demagoguery. She knew that in countries like ours, more so in Pakistan, where institutions are weak, where the state is threatened, these seemingly indestructible icons thrown up by the people bring a kind of solidity to the political landscape: they make it impossible to imagine the world without them.

I was still wavering when my father's brother-in-law entered the room. He had just been with my father and seemed to reflect the heaviness of his mood. 'Go in and see your father,' he said.

I began to say I wasn't sure that this was the right time.

'He's your father,' he said firmly. And then an old courage sprang up in me. I thought, I've met him in circumstances far more strained than these. How can I stand in the same house dithering over whether or not I should go in and see him?

I grabbed my little brother and walked into my father's house, past the pencil portrait of him, the courtyard, through the corridors that always smelt of food, and into the television room where we had parted on bad terms a year before. My father sat in his blue cotton nightsuit with his legs up on the sofa. He looked in my direction, a glimmer of surprise passing over his face, but didn't say a word. 'Abba,' I managed quietly. His gaze returned to the television, but he was haggard, his shock and grief written into the droop of his face and the dullness of his eyes. For forty minutes we sat in silence, our eyes following an Urdu/English news cycle of the bomb scene, riots spreading through the country, the PPP spokesman breaking the news, then breaking down. My father watched with two lenses: in one lens he was the lifelong PPP man, shaken to his core at seeing his leader cut down. He knew whose car she travelled in; he recognised all the people around her; as the one-time spokesman of the PPP, he had been in those situations so many times. In the other lens, he was a minister in Musharraf's caretaker government, fearful of what this could mean for it.

In that silence, I wondered why I was there. How despite our distances and unforeseen plans had the small works of Fate brought me to my father on the night Benazir Bhutto was killed? What was I to understand of the man – what was I to offer him? – on that cold and tense night, in a country that was noticeably more desolate, and by degrees, more violent?

When his shock subsided enough for him to speak, he said that the terrorists deliberately sought to rid the political landscape of its heroes. The men who wanted the faith to triumph knew that the country had to be destabilised, the robust society made bleaker. The ideologue in Karachi was right: the faith encouraged essence, and form was unimportant. But it also encouraged a dismantling of existing forms. Intellectual life, student unions, film industries and, eventually, judiciaries and constitutions were swept away; the cricket team began to focus on prayer; and, as the landscape became more desolate, the religious vision grew clearer, the anticipation of it more urgent. With every cycle, the conditions for faith were increased and the world was gradually undone till only the essence, of which the ideologue had spoken, remained.

I didn't need to be Pakistani to understand what my father meant, only perhaps the degree to which he meant it. The death of the demagogue would demoralise the population. But in a country with few national leaders, removing Benazir made the very idea of the federation less viable. 'And now you'll see the disintegration of the PPP,' my father said.

That disintegration was part of the Pakistani story. Just that year, Musharraf had hobbled the judiciary, and that institution, once one of the better ones in Pakistan, would not recover. My father now spoke of the country's biggest political party disintegrating.

But there was something else: no one believed the regime when they said the Taleban and al-Qaeda killed Benazir. The great majority of people believed some combination of the agencies, Musharraf and his allied party killed her. It was witnessing this distrust that made me understand what it meant to live in a state that had been discredited. And at a time when the regime claimed to be fighting the gravest threat to the state's existence!

My father's mind, with its double vision, fastened on a conundrum: on the one hand, elections couldn't be held in the present environment; on the other, the nation was in need of release, in need of legitimacy. Perhaps sensing his own mortality, he said, 'You can't have a caretaker government go on and on.'

Then images of the coffin flashed on the screen. Party workers handled it and beat their heads on it; the camera panned to a glass aperture on it its lid through which a white sheet was visible. My father's face turned to horror; he sucked his teeth and pressed his folded hands against the bridge of his nose. It was the same gesture Benazir had made when she stepped off the plane in Karachi a few months before, unspeakably moving, a gesture of fighting emotion in public.

'Like her brother,' my father said, 'shot in the neck.' He referred to Murtaza Bhutto, who was gunned down outside his house in 1996 when Benazir was prime minister.

'And in the same place as her father,' my brother-in-law added.

'What?' my father said, a flicker of his normal, energetic manner returning to him.

'Bhutto was executed in Rawalpindi,' my brother-in-law clarified. My father nodded and sank into silence.

Zulfikar Ali Bhutto had, in a way, also died from a wound to the neck. That had been the beginning of my father's political fight. The person we watched taken away in a simple coffin, now with no fight left in her, was his leader when that career came to fruition. It could be said that all my father's idealism – his jail time, the small success and the great disappointment, the years when he struggled for democracy in his country – were flanked by this father and daughter who both died of fatal wounds to the neck. And running parallel to these futile threads, with which my father could string his life together, were the generals, one whom he had fought and the other in whose cabinet he was now a minister.

For it to be possible for men to live with such disconnect, for my father to live so many lives, the past had to be swept away each time. The original break with history that Pakistan made to realise the impulses of the faith, and which gave it the rootlessness it knew today, had to be repeated. Like the year of events, which had ended in trauma, all that could be wished for was the distraction of the next event. But in these small interims when the past could be seen as a whole, when my father could cast painful bridges over history, I felt a great sympathy as I watched the man I had judged so harshly, for not facing his past when it came to me, muse on the pain of history in his country. And maybe this was all that the gods had wished me to see, the grimace on my father's face, and for us, both in our own ways strangers to history, to be together on the night that Benazir Bhutto was killed.

# *Acknowledgements*

The journey I made for this book was longer than the text suggests. It began in Venice and ended in Delhi. There were countries like Jordan, Yemen and Oman that I travelled in, but was unable to write about. In eight months of travel, many more people helped than I can remember here. In some cases, I've had to leave out people because of the nature of the regimes they live in. For the same reason, certain names in the text have been changed. There are a few people whose generosity stands out, but I must emphasise it can only be attributed to the best traditions of warmth and hospitality, and is not an endorsement of what I have written, for which I am solely responsible. In Turkey: Eyup Ozer; Ömer Koç; Cigdem Simavi; Ömer Karacan. In Syria: Chad Sherif-Pasha; Even Nord. In Saudi Arabia: Fady Jameel; Salman bin Laden; Hisham Attar; Kareem Idriss. In Iran: Jack Gelardi. In Pakistan: Salmaan and Aamna Taseer; Shaan Taseer; Nuscie Jamil; Hameed Haroon; Yusuf Salahuddin.

I would like also to thank Claire Paterson, Andrew Kidd, Andy Miller, Anya Serota, Chiki Sarkar, Nick Davies.

Ajit Gulabchand, for his belief in me, and his unfaltering support.

And Ella Windsor, whose love and friendship run silently through each of these pages.